Abstracts

of

Colonial Wills

of the

State of Georgia

1733-1777

With an Index
by
Willard E. Wight

Southern Historical Press, Inc.
Greenville, South Carolina

This volume was reproduced
from a personal copy located in
the Publishers private library

Please direct all correspondence and book orders to:
SOUTHERN HISTORICAL PRESS, Inc.
PO Box 1267
Greenville, SC   29602-1267

Originally printed: Atlanta, GA 1962
ISBN #978-1-63914-137-1
Printed in the United States of America

ADDENDA

NOTE: The will abstracted below has been located since publication of the 1962 edition of these abstracts and, consequently, does not appear in that edition. The corrections were suggested following publication of the 1962 edition.

Will of Hannah Stewart

Hannah Stewart, parish of St. John's, widow, To Loving Mother Hannah Stewart Negroe Wench Dauphny During her life and at her Death to Sister Rebekah Stewart for her and her heirs and assigns; To Brother Daniel Stewart Negroe Boy Abram; to Sister Rebekah Negroe Boy Cuffey; to neace Sarah Quarterman Daughter of Brother John Stewart Negroe boy Nero, riding Chair & Chair horse; Warring Apperrel Equally Divided among my three Sisters; to Brother James Stewart Negroe Boy Billy and one sixth of the remainder of my Estate Except two hundred pound South Carolina Currency which Bequeath to Elizabeth Wilson, Daughter of William Wilson to be paid to her at age twenty one or marriage but in case She Should Die before age or marriage then to Brother John Stewart. All residue of Estate Equally Divided among other Brothers and Sisters Namely, John Stewart, Daniel Stewart and Sisters Mary McClaughling, Elizabeth McLeer and Rebekah Stewart. Brothers John, Daniel and James Stewart exors. Wit: Richard Baker, William Graves, Henry Petty. D. 17 April 1770 P. 14 Jan. 1774 R. 17 Jan 1774 p.p. 378–380 WBA

NELL IRWIN PAYNE

Corrections

P.1: Amelia Alther — that is St. Gall; remove Gale and question mark.

P.21: Mary Bryan — date misprinted; she died in 1766, not 1776.

P.25: Joseph Butler — Montgomery instead of Maegomery (?).

P.31: Heriot Crooke — Bermuda or Col. Heron's Island, instead of Burbuda and Heru's.

P.32: Hariot Crooke, Jr. — should be Heriot.

P.40: Daniel Derisous — should be Derizoux.

P.61: John Giovanoli — should be Gionovoli.

P.66: Francis Harris — read "Dau: Elizabeth Harris, all tracts" instead of "Dau: Elizabeth Harresall, tracts."

P.97: Alexander Moon — Combahee instead of Combahoo.

P.117: Badasar Rieser — should be Balthasar.

LILLA M. HAWES

Abstracts
of
Colonial Wills
of the
State of Georgia
1733-1777

Published by the
ATLANTA TOWN COMMITTEE
of the
NATIONAL SOCIETY
COLONIAL DAMES OF AMERICA
in the
STATE OF GEORGIA
for the
DEPARTMENT OF ARCHIVES AND HISTORY
in the
OFFICE OF SECRETARY OF STATE
STATE OF GEORGIA

One of the most interesting and important departments of the work in the Society of Colonial Dames is its Historic Activities Committee which is that committee which encourages the investigation and preservation of all manner of old records, and the printing and disseminating of information obtained from them.

ACKNOWLEDGEMENTS

The Atlanta Town Committee of the National Society of the Colonial Dames of America in the State of Georgia, wishes to express appreciation to Secretary of State, Ben W. Fortson, Jr., and to his Director of the Department of Archives and History, State of Georgia, Mrs. Mary Givens Bryan, for assisting us in making this volume possible. Working with Mrs. Bryan, were James F. Garmon, of Pittsburgh, Pa., a former student at Emory University, Atlanta; State Archives staff members, Carroll Hart, Assistant Archivist, Mrs. Martha Murray Liipfert, Secretary, and Mrs. Philip W. Bryant, office of Surveyor General. To them we express our gratitude.

We also acknowledge the assistance given by Mr. John Bonner and Mrs. William Tate, Special Collections, University of Georgia Libraries, Athens, for research and making available official public documents in the University collections; Mrs. Lilla M. Hawes, Director, Georgia Historical Society, Hodgson Hall, Savannah, for her interest and assistance in the compilation of the Georgia Colonial Wills.

The colonial map was made available to us by Dr. Kenneth Coleman of the University of Georgia, author of *The American Revolution in Georgia,* 1763-1789, and the University of Georgia Press, who owns the copyright.

Our appreciation is expressed to members of the Atlanta Town Committee whose financial contributions made this publication possible.

HISTORIC ACTIVITIES COMMITTEE

Mrs. William E. Waters, Chairman

Mrs. Harold N. Cooledge

Mrs. Malcolm N. Fleming

Mrs. Charles D. Hurt

Mrs. Ivan Allen, Jr.

PRINTED IN U. S. A.
BY
LONGINO & PORTER, INC.
HAPEVILLE, GEORGIA
1962

INTRODUCTION

The abstracts of Georgia's Colonial Wills, 1733 - 1777, are offered here in print for the first time in one hundred and ninety-five years (1777-1962). The Colonial archives of Georgia, dating from the charter for "Founding the Colony of Georgia in America," obtained by James Edward Oglethorpe, English philanthropist, and twenty-one members of a Board of Trustees, from King George II, and signed June 9, 1732, is filled with romance and pathos. Interwoven into the picture of archives is one of progress, war, and neglect. Because so many colonial records were irretrievably lost, the student of colonial history continues to struggle under difficulties of not having access to a complete file of Colonial archives of the Colony of Georgia.

When Savannah, then the capital of Georgia, fell into the hands of the British in 1778, the Secretary of State, Captain John Milton, by order of Governor John Houstoun, conveyed the most important records of the Office of Secretary of State and the Executive Department to Charleston, South Carolina, to prevent their capture by the enemy. The removal was overland by waggons and teamsters. Prior to the fall of Charleston in 1780, Secretary of State Milton again removed the records, to Newbern, North Carolina, and left them in the care of the Governor of North Carolina. When North Carolina was invaded, and the Georgia records again in danger of capture, Captain John Milton secured leave of absence from his command and carried them to the Upper part of Virginia, and finally to Maryland. Here they remained until 1783, when the State arranged to have them returned to Savannah, the Capital, by the same mode of travel — two waggons and teamsters. Thus were saved through the Revolutionary War, papers and documents pertaining to the Office of Secretary of State, and only part of the records belonging to the Office of Governor (Executive Department).

The older records pertaining to the early colonial period, and the period of the Royal Governors, were left behind, many being lost, carried off, or destroyed.

Daniel Sturges, Surveyor General of Georgia, wrote Governor James Jackson, under date of August 20, 1799, on the subject of the deficiency of the records in his office. These consisted of land surveys and plats dealing with the colonial period, prior to 1775. He further stated the deficiency of records "is owing to their being taken off by a Mr. McKenzie, a British adherent, an officer in whose charge those papers were on the evacuation of Savannah by the British forces, to the Bahamas, from whence it is said the other books were carried, with other publick papers of the State, to England, and are lodged in the Tower of London. Book C (Surveys of land), as he is further informed was brought back by a refugee who wished to make his peace with the State." Sturges urged the Governor to recover other public documents lodged in the Tower of London. It had come to Governor James Jackson's attention as early as January 24, 1799, through William Sims, of Columbia County, Georgia, who made affidavit under date of February 6, 1799, "that on the first day of February, 1799, Mr. Charles Goodwin told him the deponant when the said Goodwin was in England last, he saw a great many papers deposited in the Tower belonging to the State of Georgia, and that those papers were carried from this State to the Bahama Islands, from thence to Scotland and from Scotland to London, which he, the said Goodwin, declared to be in the Tower . . ."

The interest in the records, and discovery of them in the Tower of London, seemed to come about from the "Galphin Claims." An Irishman, George Galphin, Indian Trader, had established during the period of Royal Government, his trading house at Silver Bluff, below Augusta, just across the Savannah River in South Carolina, where for many years he carried on successful trade operations from Charleston to St. Augustine and Mobile.

James Wright, last Royal Governor of Georgia, and John Stuart, Indian Superintendent, met with the Cherokee and Creek Chieftains, at Augusta in 1773. The Indians, who had become deeply in debt to the Indian Traders, those debts amounting to forty or fifty thousand pounds, agreed to give up their surplus hunting grounds — two great tracts of land, which the prosperous royal colony of Georgia needed to bring in new settlers. In turn, Governor Wright agreed to release the Indians from their debts to the Indian Traders. The British Government pledged itself to the Indian Traders to meet their obligations by paying them monies due them by the Indians. In due time, all seem to have secured settlements except George Galphin. As the

Revolution soon came, Galphin's claims were disallowed because the British held that he had supported the Revolutionists, but after the War, Georgia refused to pay on the ground that the debt was an obligation of the Federal Government.

Charles Goodwin, attorney and agent for the Heirs of the late George Galphin wrote Governor James Jackson, in reply to a letter from him, dated "Silver Bluff, February 1, 1799," about the Georgia papers he had seen in England. Goodwin states "Whenever the State of Georgia is disposed to do justice to the claim of the late George Galphin against the Ceded Lands, on the behalf of whose children I went to England, I shall then feel myself at liberty to give every information that you could require and that it were in my power to give — Till that Period Arrives it is my Duty to be silent."

Correspondence between Governor James Jackson, George Sibbald of Louisville; Mr. Thomas Fitzsimmons of Philadelphia, and Mr. Sitgreaves, Commissioners of the United States on British Treaties, brought about, despite the silence of the attorney for the Galphin Heirs, the delivering up of the public papers by the Court of St. James to Rufus King, the American Ambassador to England, on a requisition by his Excellency Governor James Jackson. Perhaps the records in the two trunks received in 1801 by Georgia were disappointing to the State Officials, appointed by the Governor to attend to the opening, arranging, and scheduling of the papers. The State Officials had hoped, perhaps, the trunks would contain some of the land grants and surveys, so greatly needed as background information to pass new laws regarding land.

On Saturday, November 14, 1801, William Hutchinson from the Senate Committee reported "that they have taken a cursory survey of the books and papers, late from Europe, and find them to consist partly of old Registers of Deeds, Wills, etc. and partly of old court files and other useless papers; and upon the whole are of opinion (with the exception of one or two books containing a record of Wills and deeds of Conveyance) that they are of no use to the State and therefore not worth the attention of the Legislature." (Senate Journal, 1801, p. 180).

Such causes as lack of vision, removal of the capital of Georgia four times, the Civil War, fire, theft, damage by water, neglect, mice and squirrels, have left with us a paucity of early archives. Yet, in spite of all the factors mentioned, it is amazing how much still remains, due to dedicated individuals, to give us the parital story of our early history.

Colonial Will Books A and AA and over three hundred loose wills in the Department of Archives, and **five** in the University of Georgia Libraries, Special Collections, Athens, contain not only pertinent genealogical information, but reflect the social customs and economic trends of the day. The charm and color gleaned from the frankness of these early people as expressed in their wills, give us an insight into the past so unique today.

Although the Galphin Claims dragged on until 1849 before final settlement, it was due to these claims, and the vision of Governor James Jackson with the co-operation of the British Government, that some colonial public records exist today in Georgia's State Archives. The wills abstracted in this publication once spent nearly twenty years in "The Tower of London," going by way of The Bahamas and Scotland, before being lodged in the Tower.

Book B of Georgia's Colonial Wills has never been found. Perhaps this, as well as other records belonging to the Colony of Georgia, will be found in due course of time, and be made available to scholarship. Valuable treasures in the way of archives, and great paintings, have been lost or buried in institutions for hundreds of years, and sometimes finally do come to light.

It is hoped that these abstracts will stimulate a series of publications of colonial public documents found in State Archives. Series of Inventories of Estates, Bonds and Bills of Sale, and Conveyances remain to be published in the future. These wills and other records tell so much about the lives of our first settlers; their problems and how they solved them; their successes and how they gloried in them. Their deeds have become the tap root of the great oak which is Georgia today.

For additional information about the people who left wills, the following published sources are recommended:

Candler, Allen D. *Colonial Records of Georgia* (25 Vols., Atlanta, 1904-1916). Vols. 20, 27-39 (unpublished), are available in typescript form or on microfilm in State Archives.

Coulter, E. Merton and Albert B. Saye, ed. *A List of the Early Settlers of Georgia.* The University of Georgia Press, Athens, 1949.

Historical Collections of the Joseph Habersham Chapter, Georgia Society, D.A.R., 1910. PP. 161-179 list 394 wills, with year made or probated. Not abstracted.

Mrs. Mary Givens Bryan
Director - Archivist
Department of Archives and History
State of Georgia

HISTORICAL

Savannah was the capital of Georgia, from its settlement in 1733 until 1786, with the exception of a few interruptions during the Revolutionary War period. Georgia was not entirely without British rule until 1782.

During the Proprietary Government, 1733 until surrender of the charter by the Trustees to the Crown, June 23, 1752, the Colony had the following **Chief Executives.** Their names and terms of office were:

1. James Edward Oglethorpe _____1733-1743

2. William Stephens _____1743-1751

3. Henry Parker _____1751-1754

Under the Royal Government, the following held titles as "Captain General and Commander in Chief in and over his Majesty's province of Georgia, and Ordinary of Same":

4. John Reynolds _____1754-1757

5. Henry Ellis _____1757-1760

6. James Wright _____1760-1771; 1773-1776

7. James Habersham _____1771-1772

James Wright also served as Restored Royal Governor from 1779 until 1782.

The Chief Executives of the Colony, therefore, acted as Ordinary (Probate Judge), or had the power to appoint a deputy "as recorder of wills".

Will Books A and AA cover English probates, Nov. 25, 1754-to July 30, 1772; American probates, August 22, 1776-April 16, 1777. **Colonial Loose Wills** cover the period, 1733-1777.

GEORGIA'S COLONIAL DISTRICTS, TOWNS, AND PARISHES

1732-1758 DISTRICTS and TOWNS	1758-1765 PARISH	1765-1777 PARISH	1777 COUNTY
District of Augusta	St. Paul	St. Paul	Richmond
District of Halifax	St. George	St. George	Burke
District of Abercorn	St. Matthew	St. Matthew	Effingham
District of Goshen	St. Matthew	St. Matthew	Effingham
District of Ebenezer	St. Matthew	St. Matthew	Effingham
District of Ogeechee (above Canouchee River)	St. Philip	St. Philip	Effingham
District of Ogeechee (below Canouchee River)	St. Philip	St. Philip	Chatham
Town of Hardwick	St. Philip	St. Philip	Chatham
Town of Savannah	Christ Church	Christ Church	Chatham
District of Savannah	Christ Church	Christ Church	Chatham
Sea Islands north of Great Ogeechee River	Christ Church	Christ Church	Chatham
Town of Sunbury	St. John	St. John	Liberty
District of Midway	St. John	St. John	Liberty
District of Newport	St. John	St. John	Liberty
St. Catherine's Island	St. John	St. John	Liberty
Bermuda Island	St. John	St. John	Liberty
Town of Darien	St. Andrew	St. Andrew	Liberty
District of Darien	St. Andrew	St. Andrew	Liberty
Sapelo Island	St. Andrew	St. Andrew	Liberty
Eastwood Island	St. Andrew	St. Andrew	Liberty
Sea Islands between Great Ogeechee & Altamaha Rivers	St. Andrew	St. Andrew	Liberty
Town of Frederica	St. James	St. James	Liberty
District of Frederica	St. James	St. James	Liberty
Great St. Simons Island	St. James	St. James	Liberty
Little St. Simons Island	St. James	St. James	Liberty
Sea Islands south of Altamaha River	St. James	St. James	Liberty
Between Altamaha and Turtle Rivers		St. David	Glynn
Between Turtle and Little Sittille Rivers		St. Patrick	Glynn
Between Little Sittille and Great Sittille Rivers		St. Thomas	Camden
Between Great Sittille and St. Mary's Rivers		St. Mary	Camden

Act of March 15, 1758

Act of March 25, 1765

Constitution of 1777

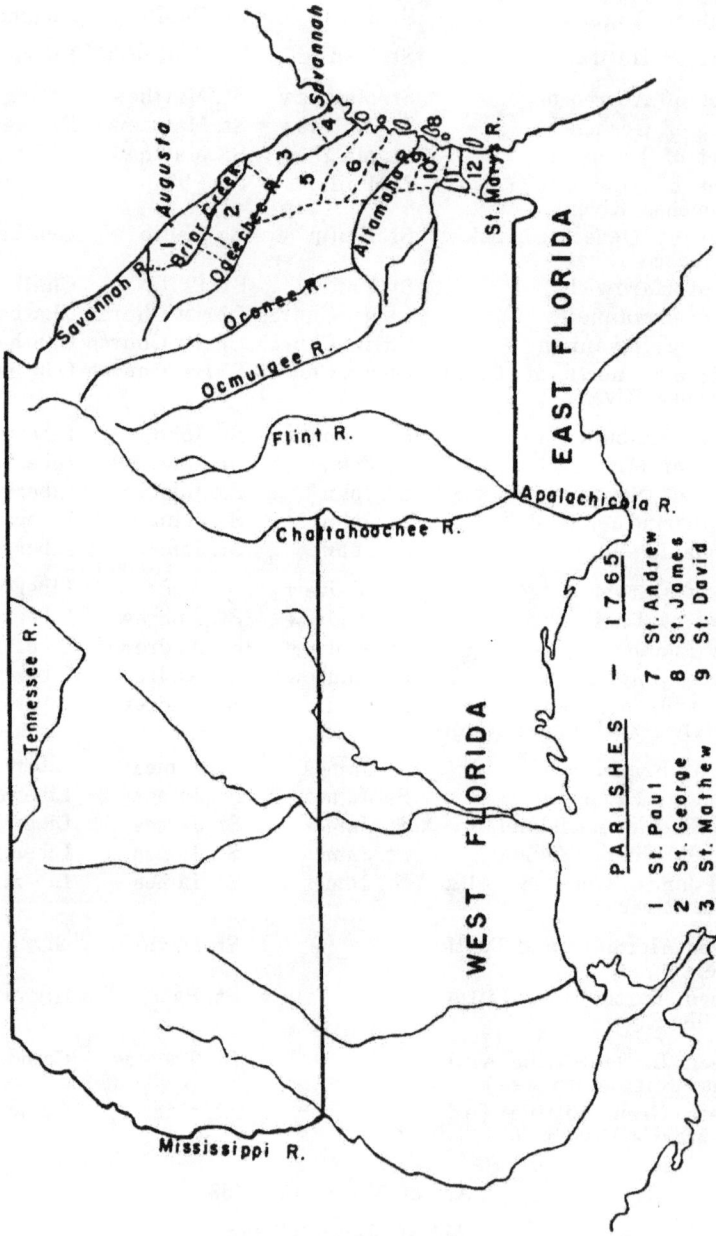

GEORGIA IN 1765

Savannah R.
Augusta
Brier Creek
Ogeechee R.
Savannah
Oconee R.
Ocmulgee R.
Altamaha R.
St. Mary's R.
Flint R.
Tennessee R.
Apalachicola R.
Chattahoochee R.
Mississippi R.

EAST FLORIDA
WEST FLORIDA

PARISHES — 1765

1 St. Paul
2 St. George
3 St. Mathew
4 Christ Church
5 St. Philip
6 St. John
7 St. Andrew
8 St. James
9 St. David
10 St. Patrick
11 St. Thomas
12 St. Mary

John Mackay's will, earliest found recorded in Georgia, July 25, 1733. From *Colonial Loose Will Collection*, State Archives.

KEY TO ABBREVIATIONS

D: Date will was written.

P: Date that will was proved.

R: Date that will was recorded.

n.d.: No date of will, proof, or recording.

Dau: Daughter.

Gent: Gentleman.

Esq: Esquire.

Exor: Executor.

Extrix: Executrix.

WBA: Will Book A.

WBAA: Will Book AA.

Explanatory note: The original Colonial spellings and phrases have been adhered to in order to preserve the uniqueness.

Robert Adams, St. Andrew's Parish, planter. Son: Robert, to receive four Negroes, named Isaac, Satyra, Emey, Quibus. Daus: Esther Adams, in South Carolina, six Negroes named Abram, Chloe, Betty, Delia, Joe, Dick; Rebecca Beard, two Negroes named Teena and July; Rachel Smith, of South Carolina, two Negroes named Katey and Phebe; Mary Brown, six negroes named Jacob, Minnerva, Mamello(2), and Guy(2). Exors: son-in-law, William Brown; son, Robert. Wit: Strong Ashmore, Nicholas Smith.

D: 19 Jan. 1775. P: 31 Jan. 1775. R: n.d. pp. 120-22 WBAA.

William Alexander, Hallifax, St. George's Parish, Gent. Wife: Marey, twenty-one pounds Sterling, a horse and saddle, a feather bed, and furniture. Brother: David, clothes, saddle and bridle, a silver watch. Remainder of estate to be sold to pay debts. What is left is to be divided among three children: Ann, Alirmer, Jean. Mentions: Thomas Irwin's son, Jared, a "mair," a cow, and a calf to him. Exors: Thomas Irwin; brother, David Alexander. Wit: John Wertsch, Martin Dasher.

D: 21 April 1760. P: 5 May 1760. R: 22 June 1761. pp. 56-57 WBA.

Amelia Alther, her mark, widow, St. Gale (Gall?)*, near Savannah. Brother: Martin Shirmeister of Kempton(?), all estate. If he is dead, then to his children or grandchildren. If no descendants, to exor. to be used as he sees fit. Exor: The Reverend John Joachim Zubley. Wit: Samuel Pryce, mariner.

D: 25 Dec. 1770. P: 14 Feb. 1771. R: 16 Feb. 1771. pp. 380-381 WBA.

Johannes Altherr, (English translation from German, sworn to as accurate by Adrian Mayer, 23 Dec. 1775), Savannah, boutcher. Wife: Amalia Altherrin, fifty pounds Sterling according to our marriage contract, two cows, return to her, her property that she brought to me. Son: Joseph, plantation of 117 acres, two cows, fifty pounds Sterling (instead of the two Negroes which I promised him). Rest of my estate, moveable and immovable, to be divided among all my children. Exors: Reverend

---

*St. Gale (Gall; St. Gallen) another name for Yamacraw (Savannah).

Master Bartholomew Zuberbuehler; son, Joseph. Wit: Joh: Joachim Zublius, Frederic Treictlen.

D: 5 April 1755. P: 19 Jan. 1756. R: n.d. p. 14 WBA.

Captain George Anderson, New York, mariner. Wife: Deborah of New York, all estate, after debts are paid, extrix. Mentions: David Montaigut, Esq., of Savannah, J.P.; Francis Knowles of Savannah, merchant; Hugh Inglis of Savannah, mariner; William Ewen, Esq.; ship, Georgia packet which Anderson commanded. Anderson died aboard ship on the way from Georgia to Great Britain. Wit: Charles Harrison; Thomas Grummell, his mark; John Joseware.

D: 9 April 1761. P: 3 Nov. 1775. R: n.d. pp. 194-196 WBAA.

James Anderson, parish of Christ Church, Carpenter. Wife: Mary, her choice of the feather beds and furniture, my bay horse called Rock, her choice of two Negroes. Sons: David, 300 acres in St. George's Parish on Rockey Creek, ten pounds Sterling; James, 300 acres in St. George's Parish on Rocky Creek, ten pounds Sterling; William, 300 acres in St. George's Parish on Rocky Creek, ten pounds Sterling. Daus: Mary, ten pounds Sterling; Tabitha, ten pounds Sterling; Cynthia, ten pounds Sterling; Ann, ten pounds Sterling; Elizabeth Matthews shall have use of what things she hath of mine in her possession for her natural life and then dispose of them as she pleases. Rest of estate to be divided between wife and seven children, named David, James, Mary, Tabitha, Cynthia, Ann, William. Wife to use any part of the estate to pay off the legacy when the children come of age or marry as long as she is a widow. If she marry, estate to be equally divided between her and the children. Son, William, is at the age of fifteen, to be bound out for the term of five years to any trade or occupation that he chooses at that time. Also desires that sons, David and James be all the assistance they can in maintaining the family until they are twenty-one. Meanwhile, they are to be employed by such persons as they think most proper to teach and instruct them in the trade of a carpenter and "hous Joiner." Exors. wife; sons, David and James. Wit: Peter Blythe, Thomas Barwick, Thomas Day.

D: 24 Aug. 1764. P: 6 Jan. 1769. R: 9 Jan. 1769. pp. 296-98 WBA.

William Anderson, St. John's Parish, planter. Brother: Robert, blockmaker in London "who served his time in Liverpool and born in Dumfries, Scotland, thirty pounds Sterling. Wife: Elizabeth, all real and personal estate. Exors: wife, William Peacock, John Cubbedge. Wit: Sarah Cubbedge, Benjamin Sheffield, John Gibbons.

D: 4 Jan. 1772. P: 7 Feb. 1772. R: 10 Feb. 1772. pp. 430-431 WBA.

James Andrew, St. John's Parish, planter. Wife: Esther, one-third of personal estate and the use of one-third of this tract of land I live on and while she remains my widow a seat in Midway meeting house on my right of subscription. Impower exors., if they think it best, to sell whole or part of my land in St. Andrew's Parish, and with this money purchase young slaves for my estate. Sons: John, Thomas, both under twenty years of age, remainder of my estate to be equally divided: lands mentioned: lot in town of Sunbury, lot at Newport Publick landing, Publick Road. Sons to receive their estate at age of twenty. If sons die without heirs, one third their estate to wife; one-third to John Winn, for the support of the Gospel in the District of Midway and Newport; one-third to nephews, Benjamin Andrew, John Godfrey, and nieces, Mary Bacon, Mary Baker. Mentions: William Baker; eldest son shall be kept at school until he has learned the Latin tongue, and then if further education is deemed useful, he shall continue school. Exors: brother, Benjamin; Richard Baker; Samuel Jones. Wit: Thomas Sillivant, John Swinney, Brice McCleland.

D: 19 July 1770. P: 27 Mar. 1771. R: 29 Mar. 1771. pp. 398-400 WBA.

Francis Arven, Savannah, merchant. Estate to be sold. Wife: Hannah, one-half the product of the sale. Other one-half to Grey Elliott, Esq., of Savannah to administer in trust for my daughter, Mary Arven, Spital fields, Middlesex County. Exors: Grey Elliott, Esq.; James Read, Esq. of Savannah. In case of absence of Elliott, Josiah Tatnell appointed in his stead. Wit: Noble Wimberly Jones, Ann Cater, William Stephens.

D: 23 Oct. 1769. P: 30 Oct. 1769. R: 4 Nov. 1769. pp. 329-331 WBA.

James Aycock, Chatham District. Wife: to enjoy during her widowhood the manner plantation (200 acres); Negro wench, Venice; feather bed, furniture, three cows and calves; bay horse, Derby, bought from Job Hinton, with her bridle and side saddle. Dau: Agnes Pace, one Negro girl, Silva. Eldest son: William, manner plantation (200 acres) which I lent to my beloved wife at the day of her marriage or death. Son: Richard, 200 acres adjoining the manner plantation on the lower estate. Perishable estate to be sold. Remainder of the estate not already bequeathed to be equally divided and not sold until eldest son, William reaches the age of twenty-one. To be equally divided by three honest freeholders appointed by the chairman of the court. Mentions: sons, William, Richard, James, John, Sherod. Exors: Thomas Wootten, Herdy Sanders, Barnabas Pace. Wit: Henry Ware, Drewry Pace, Noel Killingsworth.

"Edition to will": will in consideration of my well-beloved wife raising and breeding my children lend her following articles until my eldest son, James Aycock, reaches the age of 21: Negroes that I hadn't given away; the use of my stock and all my household furniture to be kept in the manner plantation until son, James, arrives at full age and then to be put to the uses within mentioned. Wit to edition: Drewry Pace, Noel Killingsworth, David Peace(?).

D: 6 Aug. 1776. P: n.d. R: n.d. Colonial Loose Will Collection.

Thomas Ayres, his mark, St. Paul's Parish. Wife: Mary, executrix, "to dispose of the state," desires that the balance due of the price of the land in South Carolina to be put to the use of schooling my children. Wife also to be given sufficient rites and titles to the purchase of the land laid out to me, tract of 500 acres in South Carolina; rone horse and saddle; one-third of my estate, real and personal, during her widowhood. Sons: Abrham, one grey horse and saddle, tract of 250 acres, being part of the 500 where I now live; Thomas, William, Benjamin, Samuel, Joshua, each to receive from Abrham five pounds Sterling when he comes of age. Daus: Bridget, one bay mare branded thus "T A" and saddle, one cow and yearling; Elizabeth, one cow and one calf. Extrix: wife. Wit: William Mangum, James Ashmore, William Ayres.

D: 1 Feb. 1772. P: 13 July 1773. R: n.d. pp. 41-42 WBAA.

William Backshell, Charles Town, South Carolina, late of London, merchant. All real and personal estate to daughter, Willhelma in England, Spinster. Lands in Georgia, South Carolina, and elsewhere to be sold to pay debts, remainder to go to daughter. Exors: Edmund the third Landgrave Bellinger; James Wright, Attorney General; Anthony Matthews, Esq. Wit: William Allston, Emmanuel Todd, Nathaniel Burt.

D: 8 Jan. 1753. P (as changed): 6 May 1757. R: 20 July 1759.

Codicil to the will: Backshell desires that the exors. permit Susannah O'Neal to take into her possession all my household goods, linens and wearing apparel in consideration of her good offices and services. Appoints Susannah O'Neal executrix of the will. Wit to codicil: Thomas Parker, Charles Pryce.

D (of codicil): 11 Oct. 1756. P (of codicil) 2 Dec. 1756. R: 20 July 1757.

—document in which Susannah (O'Neal) Wemyss, widow of James Wemyss, late of Savannah, carpenter, refuses to accede to the will and refuses to act as executrix for the will of William Backshell as outlined in the will and codicil above. Wit. to this document: Egeston Leigh, James Robertson.

D: 29 May 1759: Sworn to 29 May 1759. R: 20 July 1759. pp. 46-49 WBA.

Joseph Bacon, St. John's Parish, planter. Wife: Mary, during her natural life, use of plantation and 150 acres adjoining, five Negroes named Tirah, Naro, Will, Came, and Rose to be equally divided among the surviving children at her death; to wife forever, one-half of my cattle, a horse named Jack, and one-half my household furniture. Grandson: John Golden, at the age of twenty-one, twenty-one pounds Sterling. Grandchildren: Peter, William, and Abel Golden, at the age of twenty-one, seventy-one pounds Sterling to be equally divided. Children: all "cattle" described in the deed of gift to them. Son: John, the plantation on which he now lives and 280 acres of adjoining land. Tract of land, 140 acres, near Dorchester, South Carolina to be sold, proceeds to pay debts and the residue to be divided equally among the living children. Remainder of the estate to be divided into three parts: one-third for the use of son, Joseph, for his natural life, to be divided among his surviving children at the time of his death; two-thirds to sons, Thomas and William to be equally divided among all children at his death: John, Joseph, Rebecca Quarterman, Thomas, and William. Exors: brothers, Samuel Bacon and William Baker; sons, John Bacon and Thomas Quarterman; friend, John Winn. Wit: James Andrew, Richard Baker, James Baker.

D: 12 July 1764. P: 28 Feb. 1765. R: 5 Mar. 1765. pp. 125-127/117-119 WBA.

Thomas Bailey, his mark, Savannah, Gent. Grandson: Benjamin Farley, six silver tablespoons, six silver teaspoons, one silver strainer, one pair of silver sugar tongs, two fowling pieces, one pewter bedpan, one warming pan, one pair of silver mounted pistols, one pair of gold sleeve buttons, the gold ring by me usually worn, and one pair of plaited shoe buckles, all of which have long been in my family, recommending that grandson do not permit any of them to be sold or disposed of. Ten pounds Sterling to Mrs. Brydie, wife of Dr. David Brydie. Ten pounds Sterling to the poor of the parish of Christ Church. Sufficient sums for suits of mourning to grandson, Benjamin Farley; to granddaughter, Mary Farley; to my sister, Mrs. Francis Robe; and to Miss Mary Milledge. To exors and their survivors, I give a parcel of land containing one hundred feet in front on a street and eighty-five feet in depth at a place called Yamacrau near the Town Common of Savannah, bounded to the west partly on the lands of the number three, and to the southward on a lot purchased of Samuel Pelton, and Isaac Martin by Peter Blyth including my ten Negroes named: Joe, Jack, Pieriot, Nanny, Pienda, Harry, Hannah, Titus, Patrick, and _____; in addition, all estate, real and personal, not before disposed of to the exors and their survivors until Benjamin Farley shall attain the age of twenty-one. Twenty pounds of Sterling to my brother, William Bailey, Birmingham, Kingdom of Great Britain, buckle-maker, each year until Benjamin Farley is twenty-one years old. If my grandson dies before twenty-one, estates are to be sold and the profits turned over to William Bailey. If grandson reaches twenty-one within twelve months he is to give sixty pounds Sterling to William Bailey. Exors: Isaac Young, Esq.; David Brydie of

Savannah, "practioner of physic;" Wit: James Robertson, Thomas Morgan, William Jonston.

D: 25 June 1773. P: 6 Mar. 1775. R: n.d. pp. 128-131 WBAA.

Kenneth Baillie, St. John's Parish, planter. Wife: Elizabeth, Negro wench named Hester; one-half of house and kitching furniture, including silver plate; to live in house until it is sold; the exors to give her a yearly maintenance until my debts are paid. Eldest son: Kenneth, Negro boy named Cuff, one-half of house and kitching furniture, including silver plate, guns, pistols, sword, watch, bridles, wearing apparel, 400 acres of land adjoining Palmer Golden, a part of a tract of my Ryce plantation as now settled on, 100 acres of timberland joining the aforesaid 400 acres and Stephen Clark; also two lots in Sunbury, joining James Stuart, Taylor. Son: Alexander, Negro boy named Joe; one silver-hilted sword; one hundred acres of swampland joining his own marsh and the 400 acres bequeathed to Kenneth; one hundred acres of timberland, joining my said tract and Stephen Colers. Son: Robert Carnibe Baillie, a Negro boy named January, 500 acres in North Newport, adjoining the lands of Matthew Rock, Stephen Clark, and Samuel Burnley. Sons: Kenneth (800) and Alexander (200), 1000 acres of land situated on St. Marys to receive it when they become twenty-one years of age. If the exors judge them capable of managing this land, they may do so at the age of eighteen, but not to dispose of them or sell them until they are twenty-one. Baillie's Island, where I now live, to be sold to the highest bidder. Money to be split as follows: 50 pounds Sterling to wife to build a house on the estate bequeathed to son, Alexander; 50 pounds Sterling to daughter Jean, wife to Andrew Darling, Sunbury, merchant; 50 pounds Sterling to daughter Ann Elizabeth, wife to John Irvin, surgeon, Sunbury; remainder for clothes, education, and maintenance of sons, Alexander and Robert. Daus: Jane, Negro girl named Chloe; Ann, Negro girl named Doll. Exors: wife; son, Kenneth; Andrew Darling; Captain James Mackay, Robert Baillie. Wit: John Osgood, John Winn, Ludovick Anderson.

D: 7 July 1766. P: 2 Sept. 1766. R:22 Jan. 1767.

7

Document giving power to Audley Maxwell, John Simpson, and John Irvine to administer the oath of exor to Elizabeth Baillie, Andrew Darling, and Robert Baillie. Dated 2 Sept. 1766.

Oath of exor signed by Elizabeth Baillie and Andrew Darling.
Dated 1 Nov. 1766. pp. 190-195 WBA.

Rebecca Baker, St. John's Parish. Sister: Elizabeth Luptan, one cow and calf, riding horse, saddle, bridle, three fourths of all my estate, my gold ring. Rebecca Hauskins, a minor, daughter of Isaac Hauskins, deceased, and Barbara Hauskins, one fourth of all my estate, pair of silver shoe buckles. Exors. brother, John Luptan; Thomas Quarterman; John Elliott. Wit: John Osgood, Samuel Jones, William Baker.

D: 7 March, 1767. P: 12 May 1767. R: 18 June 1767. pp. 217-218 WBA.

Richard Baker, St. John's Parish, planter. Wife: Elizabeth, Negro wench named Florow, riding chair and chair horse, side saddle, bridle, feather bed and bed furniture, five head of cattle, her residence on plantation during her widowhood. Son: William, all my lands and real estate, mare named Pleasant, saddle, bridle, feather bed and bed furniture, all cattle in my stock branded "W". Daus: Elizabeth Quarterman, Negro girl named Betty, horse named Diamond, sidesaddle, bridle, feather bed and bed furniture, all cattle branded "E". Lydia McGowen, Negro girl named Murrier, horse named Whistler, side saddle, bridle, feather bed and bed furniture, all cattle branded "L". Mary Way, Negro girl named Abbe, horse named Bendbow, side saddle, bridle, bed and bed furniture, all cattle branded "M". Ann, Negro girl named Sharlot, horse named Button, side saddle, bridle, feather bed and bed furniture, all cattle branded "A". Rebekah, Negro boy named Dick, horse named Grey Tail, side saddle, bridle, feather bed and bed furniture, all cattle branded "R".

Wife is expecting child. If a son, 200 acres of land, 100 acres that I purchased from John Winn, Sr., half of a lot at Newport Landing, one lot in Sunbury, mare named Mouse, saddle, bridle, feather bed and bed furniture, Heifer calf. If a daughter, above lands to go to son William. Dau: to get Negro boy named Sam, mare named Mouse, side saddle, bridle, feather bed and bed furniture, Heifer calf. Remainder of the estate to be equally divided among wife and children. Son, or sons, shall take his, or their, part of the estate at the age of twenty. Archible Christy, son of Thomas Christy, deceased, his maintenance and schooling at a moderate rate to be paid by the exors from the estate until he is of age to be put at a trade. Exors: wife; Benjamin Andrew, Esq.; William Graves, Sr.; Thomas Quarterman; my sons-in-law, Robert Quarterman, Edward Way, Joseph McGowen. Wit: William McGowen, Thomas Boswood, Nicholas Smith.

D: 9 Sept. 1774. P: 16 May 1775. R: 14 June 1775.

Document empowering Parmenus Way, J.P. and James Screven, J.P. to administer oath of exor to Elizabeth Baker, Robert Quarterman, Edward Way. Dated: 16 May 1775.

Oath of exorship. signed by Elizabeth Baker, Robert Quarterman, Edward Way. Dated: 22 May 1775. pp. 165-170 WBAA.

William Baker, St. John's Parish, planter. Wife: Rebecca, whatever estate, real or personal, that was hers before her marriage with me, use of one fifth of my personal and moveable estate, use of one half my house, both during her widowhood. Son: William, two lots of land in Sunbury, known by the numbers 87 and 88, tract of land I now live on, one third of my remaining personal estate, to be given him at the age of twenty years. Daus: Rebecca Jones, wife of Samuel Jones, 250 acres of land joining easterly on land of John Stewart, 100 acres of land joining southerly on land of Joseph Way, one third of my remaining personal estate. Sarah: 250 acres, joining land granted to Josiah Powell, 100 acres of land adjoining the said given tract, remainder of any personal estate (to be delivered to her at marriage or at eighteen years of age). Nieces: Sarah Baker and Elizabeth Baker, daus. of Benjamin Baker, seven pounds and three shillings, Sterling, each (to be granted at marriage or at the age of eighteen). Exors: John Elliott, Esq.; John Stewart; William Graves; son-in-law William Baker. Wit: John Quarterman, John Stevens, Thomas Quarterman.

D: 24 May 1765.

Codicil: William Baker affirms that as of the date of this codicil he has already given to Rebecca Jones the lands bequeathed in the above will. They are to remain in her possession at his death. Also, he grants watch, wearing apparel, and linens to his son, William; gold sleeve buttons and six silver teaspoons to dau. Sarah. These items are not to be accounted any part of my estate in the division of same. Wit: John Winn, Benjamin Baker, John Irvine.

D: 9 March 1767. P(will and codicil): 31 March 1767. R: 15 April 1767.

Document appended empowering John Martin, Parmenus Way, and William Donnom, Esqs. to administer the oath of exor. to John Stewart, William Graves, and William Baker. Dated 31 March 1767.

Oath of exor. attached. Signed by John Stewart, William Graves, and William Baker. Dated 6 April 1767. pp. 208-212 WBA.

Isaac Barksdale, Augusta, Indian Trader. Friend: John Oyston, formerly a partner with my brother, John, and lives now in Charles Town, 500 pounds Sterling to be paid him within eighteen months after my decease; Negro wench named Aba; Negro boy named Johney; Negro girl named Sarah. To Jane Rae, dau. of my now partner, John Rae, 1000 pounds South Carolina currency to be paid her at the age of eighteen; Negro boy named Tom. To John Rae, Jr., one half my 500 acres known by the name of Uchee Island, about sixteen miles above Augusta; Negro boy named Ned. To William Rae, Negro boy named Sambo, my gun and pistols. To Dugald Campbell, my late clerk, 200 pounds South Carolina currency, gold head cain, silver snuff box. Freedom granted to Negro wench named Nancey and her two mulatto children, named Johney and Salley. Full freedom granted to Negro wench named Nanney, whom I partly freed before. To John Rae, partner, remainder of estate, real and personal. Exors: John Rae, John Oyston. Wit: Thomas Vincent, Abraham Croft, James Jackson.

D: 12 June 1757. P: 18 (?). R: 8 Nov. 1757. pp. 30-31, WBA.

Edward Barnard, St. Paul's Parish. Wife: Rebecca, "(in lieu of her Thirds, or Dower)," the house and land on which Doctor Johnson now lives in Augusta, two feather beds, mattresses, bed steads, furniture now standing in the little bedroom below stairs, pillows, six mahogany chairs, the household furniture she brought to me when I married her, a baby horse named Middleton, the chaise, a little grey pacing horse, I lend her for the rest of her natural life, a Negro wench named Sarah and her two children, Peter and Sarah. After wife's decease these Negroes to my younger son, John. Son-in-law: William Goodgion, 50 pounds Sterling, to buy mourning. Eldest son: James Frashier Barnard, house and land in Augusta, containing 450 acres, Negroes named Absolam, Coggie, and Nancy. Sons: James and John, remainder of estate, equally divided. Exors: Wife, William Goodgion. Wit: John Watson, I. Waters, William Little.

D: 13 June 1775. P: 18 July 1775. R: 8 January 1776.

Document empowering James Grierson, John Watson, and John Daniel Hammerer, Esqs., to administer oath of exor. to Rebecca Barnard and William Goodgion. Dated 18 July 1775.

Oath of exor. signed by Rebecca Barnard and William Goodgion. Dated 30 August 1775. pp. 218-222 WBAA.

John Barnard, Wilmington Island, Savannah, Gent. Wife: Jane, all horses, cattle, slaves (except Indian slave, Harry), if she remains a widow she is to get all the profits of all the moneys that shall be raised from the stock and debts which I have in the Indian trade, for the maintenance and the education of my two sons, Timothy and William until they are twenty-one years of age. When the youngest son is twenty-one, each son is to have one fourth of stock and money. Other one half to wife if she remains a widow. On her death her share to be divided between the sons. Son: Timothy, entitled by deed of gift from Richard Kent 500 acres of land on Wilmington Island. Son: William, tract of land, 500 acres, on Wilmington Island. Indian slave: Harry, his freedom, after two years of service to Jane Barnard, or upon her death if it is sooner. Exors: Noble Jones, Esq. of near Savannah; Samuel Marcer, Savannah. Wit: William Stephens, Newdigate Stephens, Charles Watson.

D: 29 Jan. 1747. P: 8 Sept. 1757. R: 9 Sept. 1757.

Document attached signed by Noble Jones and Samuel Marcer in which they "refuse to take upon ourselves the Burthen and Execution" of the will. Dated 2 Sept. 1757. pp. 26-29 WBA.

Mary Bateman, St. John's Parish, widow. Grandsons: Isaac Smallwood, 35 pounds Sterling. Benjamin Smallwood, one lot in the town of Sunbury known by number 252. Granddaus: Sarah Smallwood, one half my silver table and teaspoons. Martha Smallwood, one half my silver table and teaspoons. Dau-in-law: Rebecca Smallwood, one small table, a sugar dish, a table, a tea chest. Daus-in-law: Rebecca and Mary Smallwood, wearing apparel and household furniture equally divided. Remainder of estate, real and personal, to be divided among my six grandchildren (except Mary Smallwood, who is to have one and one half shares), namely, Isaac, Sarah, Benjamin, Martha, Francis, and Mary Smallwood. Exors: sons, Matthew and Robert Smallwood; John Baker, Sr. Wit: John Mitchell; James Williams, his mark; John Baker.

D: 29 April 1772. P: 15 Dec. 1773. R: n.d. pp. 69-70, WBAA.

William Bateman, Savannah Township. Wife: Mary, all estate, extrix. (Remainder of the will is missing.)

D: n.d. P: n.d. R: n.d. (1734 ?) Colonial Loose Will Collection.

Michael Bener, his mark (in German, translation sworn to as accurate by John Martin Griner, 19 Dec. 1775 and Jeremiah Gregory, 5 Jan. 1776), St. George's Parish, planter. Nicholas Streigle, 150 acres of land. "Betsy and her children" the other 100 acres. "Cash, horses and cattle to the two white children and the widow" to be divided among the three. Widow Streigle to have her "Seat upon the Land" as long as she remains a widow. Exor: John Casper Griner. Wit: John Martin Griner, John Casper Griner, Jeremiah Gregory.

D: 3 Dec. 1775. P: 6 Dec. 1775. R: n.d. Colonial Loose Will Collection.

Hannah Biltz, Christ Church Parish, widow. Eldest Dau: Suzanna Gable, "all that half lot whereon I know living," 45 acres of land at Whitebluff, No._____. Youngest Dau: Ann Maly Biltz, "all that half lot whereon my son-in-law now lives," house wench, one town lot at ? bought of the Revt. Mr. Zubly, no._____, bedstead, bed furniture. Exors: John Eppinger, Abraham Gable. Wit: Matthias Ash; George Ducker, his mark.

D: 8 Aug. 1770. P: 14 Sept. 1772. R: n.d. p. 4 WBAA.

Sigismund Biltz, his mark, Savannah, tailor. Wife: Ane, all estate, real and personal. Exors: Wife, John Eppinger. Wit: John Shick, Godfrey Humbert, Joham Georg Moritz (Maritz).

D: 18 July 1765. P: 15 Aug. 1765. R: 15 Aug. 1765. pp. 139-140/131-132 WBA.

John Blenfield, Indian Trader. All estate, real and personal, after debts are paid, to Jane and Mary Rae, daus. of John Rae. Exor. John Rae, Augusta, store keeper. Wit: Isaac Barksdale, Richard Johnston, Dugald Campbell.

D: 24 Oct. 1747. P: n.d. R: n.d. Colonial Loose Will Collection.

Michael Bohrman, St. Matthew's Parish, planter. Wife: Mary Magdalena, 5 pounds Sterling to be raised out of the interest of the 200 pounds Sterling which I now have out, the 5 pounds Sterling to be paid my wife every year until my dau., Agnesia, becomes eighteen years old. Eldest Dau: Hannah, Negro boy named Joe, 66 pounds Sterling of the 200 in interest, one half of all my lands. Dau: Agnesia, 5 pounds Sterling every year to be raised out of the interest and to be applied to clothes and necessaries for her until she becomes eighteen, afterwards 134 pounds Sterling, one half of all my lands. The remainder of the interest which might every year remain always to be laid out on interest again until both become of age and then divided. Exors: Christoffer Kremer, Ja. Casper Walthour of Ebenezer, Jacob Ihle of Goshen. Wit: Jacob Cronberger, Daniel Zettler, Daniel Burgsteiner.

D: 14 Feb. 1771. P: 6 March 1771. R: 7 March 1771. pp. 395-396 WBA.

Henry Lewis Bourquin, Savannah, Doctor. Wife: Henrietta, lot in Savannah whereon I now reside, household furniture, 3 Negroes named Cudjoe, Joe, and Tom. These bequests to be given wife "in lieu and in full satisfaction and recompence which she may have or claim out of my estate by reason of her dower." Nephew: John Lewis Bourquin, son of John Lewis Bourquin, my brother, all that tract of land in St. John's Parish, containing 500 acres. Nephew: John Lewis Dethridge, all that tract of land in St. David's Parish, containing 500 acres; all that tract of land in St. John's Parish, containing 250 acres. Exors: wife, John Lewis Dethridge. Wit: Peter Tondee, Stephen Britton, Henry Bourquin.

D: 5 Dec. 1774. P: 23 Dec. 1774. R: n.d.

Document empowering David Montaigut, William Ewen, and Alexander Wylly, Esqs., to administer the oath of extrix. to Henrietta Bourquin. Dated 22 Feb. 1775.

Oath of extrix. signed by Henrietta Bourquin. Dated 22 Feb. 1775. pp. 116-118 WBAA.

John Martin Boltzius, Ebenezer, minister (in German, translation attached, sworn to as accurate by Christain Rabenhorst, 8 July 1766). Wife: Gertrude Krother Boltzius, wife of 28 years, plantation "Good Harmony" in Joseph's Town, containing 500 acres; small plantation, containing 100 acres, situated near the grist and saw mill (which she had bought with her own money, gained by raising cattle) ; cattle, horses, those moneys at Interest (whereof the two bonds in my packet of receipts are enclosed) ; silver watch; clothes; bedding; whatever else in my temporal estate. Children to split the estate on the death of their mother. If wife dies without a will: "Good Harmony Plantation" to son, Gotthilf Israel or if he should remain in Germany the value thereof together with some cattle, chattles of money. Plantation near the mill, 100 acres, to dau, Catherine Mary, with cattle and money. Parson House to my worthy successor in the ministry. Mentions: Revd. Mr. Lemke, Revd. Mr. Rabenhorst. Boltzius was "most 30 years Servant of the Gosple in the Congregation of Salzburger at Ebenezer". Extrix: wife, Wit: John Flerl, John Casper Wertsh, Theobald Keiffer.

D: 1 June 1763. P: 8 July 1766. R: 8 July 1766. pp. 155-160 WBA.

Adam Bosomworth, St. John's Parish, planter. Wife: Elizabeth slaves, all my lands, cattle, horses, hogs, household goods. Extrix: wife. Wit: John Lettimore; James Maxwell, Jr.; John Handcock, his mark.

D: 29 July 1757. P: 1 April 1765. R: 11 June 1765.

Document empowering The Honorable James Mackay and Elisha Butler, Esqs. to administer the oath of extrix, to Elizabeth Bosomworth. Dated 2 April 1765.

Oath of extrix. signed by Elizabeth Bosomworth. Dated 25 May 1765. pp. 135-137/127-129 WBA.

Samuel Bowen, Christ Church Parish, planter. Wife: Jane, 38 Negroes (named); all my silver plate, household goods and furniture; all my horses, hogs, cattle, carriages, plantation tools, utensils, all money due me by any person in America, Great Britain, or elsewhere; plantation called "Greenwich" whereon I now live, containing 450 acres near Savannah, which I purchased from the Honorable Grey Elliott, Esq; Macao (?) Island, containing 84 acres, which I purchased from John Mulryne, Esq. Extrix: wife. Wit: William Belcher, Samuel Farley, Samuel Stirk.

D: 31 May 1774. P: 12 Sept. 1778. R: n.d. Colonial Loose Will Collection.

Solomon Boykin, his mark, St. George's Parish. Wife: Esther, all that land whereon I now live, containing 300 acres, during her lifetime. This land to go to son, Solomon, after her death. Sons: Hardy, tract of land, 150 acres, on the Beaver Dam in St. George's Parish. Jesse, tract of land, 200 acres, on Briar Creek adjoining the lands of John Wells in St. George's Parish, grant bearing the date 5 May 1767. Francis, Bias, William, 5 pounds Sterling each to secure a tract of land. Daus: Olive, (from this date) one cow, calf, and yearling and their Increase, one cow and calf more at my decease. Doreas, two cows and calves. To the infant with which my wife is now pregnant, three cows and calves. Remainder of estate to wife during her widowhood, to be divided equally among the children if she marrys. Extrix: wife. Wit: David Lewis, Benjamin Lewis.

D: 5 Aug. 1770. P: 31 May 1771. R: 3 June 1771. pp. 406-407 WBA.

Isaac Brabant, Savannah, cutler. Son: Daniel, lot in Savannah, known by the number three "in Sloper Tything Percival Ward," which lot I lately purchased from the Revd. John Joachim Zubly. If Daniel dies before he is twenty-one, the lot to son, William. If William dies before twenty-one, land to daus Harriett and Elizabeth. William, Negro male slaves named Jemmy and Sam. Daus: Harriett, two female Negro slaves named Katey and Minty, one feather bed and furniture. Elizabeth, Negro wench named Rose and her son, to be delivered to her when she becomes eighteen years old. Nieces: Sophia and Christiana Chiffelle, a suit of mourning each. Remainder of estate to be sold, profits to be divided among children: William, Harriett, and Elizabeth. Exors: William Russell, Esq.; Francis Harris, Esq.; Joseph Clay. Wit: George Aland, John Helvenstine, William Young.

D: 22 Nov. 1763. P: 8 March 1764. R: 24 March 1764. pp. 117-119/109-111 WBA.

William Bradley, Lee Street, Red Lyon Square, County of Middlesex, Gent. Wife: Elizabeth, household goods, plate, linen, furniture, all for the extent of her life; to son, William, at her death. Son: William, London, surgeon, all real estate in Georgia, South Carolina, "or any other part of America," all to be sold and profits to William to be divided as he sees fit among himself; my son, Richard; my dau Jane Barnard, widow; Martha Young, wife of Isaac Young, all of the province of "Georgia in South Carolina." Spanish bonds, obligations, other demands upon the crown of Spain amounting together to the sum of 240,000 pounds Sterling and upwards, to be paid son, William. William to divide this amount as he sees fit among the following: my wife, Elizabeth; my son, Richard; my dau, Jane Barnard, widow; my dau, Martha Young; my dau-in-law, Elizabeth Lister Bradley. Remainder of the estate to William. Exor: son, William. Wit: Mary Susan, Thos. Metcalf, W. Creser. (Will "extracted by William Fuller, Proctor in Doctor's Commons.") As last will of William Bradley, late of the Parish of St. George (Georgia).

D: 8 July 1766. P: 28 March 1768. R: 27 Sept. 1769. pp. 321-323 WBA.

Hannah Bradwell, St. John's Parish. To be buried at Mr. Joseph Law's plantation "provided the body of my dau, Mary Law be removed there also, otherwise to be buried there at the Midway Meeting house." Son: Thomas, a tract of land containing 500 acres and another of 300 acres adjoining, in St. Andrew's Parish, to be given him when he becomes twenty-one years of age. Dau: Susanna Dowse, Negro girl named Sibby. Grandchildren: Thomas Elliott, Joseph Benjamin, Charles Law, a Negro wench named Bess and her son, Balam. Remainder of estate to be divided as follows: one sixth to dau, Susanna Dowse; one sixth to son, Thomas; one sixth to be split among grandchildren, Thomas Elliott, Joseph Benjamin, and Charles Law; remaining one half to be equally divided between two sons, John and Given Bradwell. Exors: Gideon Dowse; Jacob Bradwell; my son, Thomas (as soon as he is twenty-one). Wit: Mary Jones, John Kell, John Jones.

D: 22 July 1775. P: ___ Oct. 1775. R: 6 Oct. 1775. pp. 188-189 WBAA.

John Peter Bretton, his mark, Savannah, carpenter. Wife: Mary, use of my house and lot in Savannah during her lifetime. After her death, to be sold, with the profits split between children. My 500 acres of land in the township of Purisbourgh to be sold, profits to be split between son, John, and dau, Priscilla. Exors: wife; sons-in-law, Michael Stutz, James Gallache. Wit: Robert Bolton, James Baillou, Matthew Mauve.

Codicil (same date, same wit): My five-acre lot belonging to my town lot to be sold, with the profits going to my exors.

D: 18 Jan. 1770. P: 16 May 1770. R: 17 May 1770. pp. 343-345 WBA.

William Brisbane (Copy of original which is in the province of South Carolina, sworn to as true by Thomas Skottowe, Esq., Registrar, dated 17 Feb. 1773), Charlestown, South Carolina. Son: William, tract of land containing 1100 acres, partly bounded on Deas Creek, and which I bought at the sale of Hugh Bryan's Estate. Land to confirm deed of gift I gave him, and for two Negro males named Morris and Andrew "least the same should in any manner prove faulty." Son: Adam Fowler Brisbane, Negro wench named Priscilla, who was given to me by Martha D'har-

17

riette. Sons to collect debts. Exors empowered "to put out to Interest 3000 pounds current money on good personal security." Interest on this investment to be paid my brother, Robert Brisbane, every year of his life, and split among my six children at his death. Wife: Eunice, exors to pay 7000 pounds "Current money of this province" within three months after my death; full suit of mourning. Remainder of estate to be divided among my children: William, Adam, Margaret, Hannah, Robert, and Catherine Elliott. Wits: Robert Wells, Robert Murray, John Wells, Jr. Exors: sons, William and Adam.

D: 11 May 1771. P: 15 March 1773. R:n.d. pp. 26-29 WBAA.

James Thomas Brookes, Savannah, mariner. Nephew: John Street, son of John Street "formerly of this place but now of Great Brittain," all my lot of land in Christ Church Parish on the Bay in Savannah, known by the number four in the Second Tything Reynolds Ward, containing 60 feet in front and 90 feet in length. If he dies with no heirs, lot to my sister, Sarah Chapin Cunningham. Hugh Ross and Jacob Oates, both of Savannah, merchants, are appointed guardians of John Street, until he reaches twenty-one years of age. Exor: brother, Cornelius Cunningham. Wit: Sinclair Waters, William Rheny, Aaron Pickeran.

D: 31 Oct. 1770. P: 12 Nov. 1770. R: 14 Nov. 1770. pp. 360-361 WBA.

John Brown (copy of original will which is in the Province of West Florida, sworn to as accurate copy by Alexander Maclellan, Notary Public), merchant. Children: Mary, Katherine, Susanna, 500 pounds South Carolina currency to be divided equally among them, payable within six months of my death. Brother: Samuel Brown, Indian trader," at present in the Choctaw Nation," one-half the remainder of the estate, to be paid him within twelve months of my death. Partners: William Irwin, merchant in Savannah; William Struthers, Indian trader; John McGillavray, merchant in Mobile, other one-half of remaining estate. Exors: William Irwin, William Struthers, John McGillavray. Wit: Robert Crooke, Alexander McIntosh, Daniel Craw.

D: 9 July 1764. P:20 Nov. 1765. R: 1 July 1766. pp. 153-155 WBA.

Elizabeth Brownson, wife of Doctor Nathan Brownson, Newport. To dispose of possessions "by virtue of that power reserved to myself in a marriage settlement." Mother-in-law: Mrs. Jane Donnom, my blue silk gown. Aunt: Mrs. Mary Donnom, widow of William Donnom, my black satin capuchin, hat, my brown silk gown. Remainder of wearing apparel to be divided equally between cousin, Elizabeth Baker (the wife of William Baker), and niece, Mary P. Donnom (dau of my brother, James Donnom, deseased). Husband: Nathan, household goods, horses (except one named "Red Bird"), chair, use of slaves until his death; at that time they are to be given son, James Donnom Martin. Son: James Donnom Martin, horse named "Red Bird." Mentions: John Martin, Esq., my late husband; my brothers, William and Joseph Donnom. Exors: my father, James Donnom; my uncle, John Mitchell, Esq.; in failure of them, husband, Nathan Brownson and brother, Joseph Donnom to act as exors and guardians of my son. Wit: James Dunwoody, Esther Dunwoody, Mary Ann Ladson.

D: 4 March 1775. P: 20 Nov. 1775. R: 22 Nov. 1775.
Document empowering Parmenus Way and James Screven, Esqs. to administer oath of exor. to John Mitchell. Dated 17 Nov. 1775.

Oath of exor. signed by John Mitchell. Dated 20 Nov. 1775. pp. 202-206 WBAA.

Agnes Bryan, Christ Church Parish, spinster. Exors to sell a tract of land, containing 618 and a quarter acres, in Christ Church Parish, to pay debts and funeral expenses. Mother: Mrs. Mary Dawson, remainder of estate, real and personal, for the rest of her life. On Mrs. Dawson's death, the estate is to be equally divided between Mrs. Dawson's children, Richard and Sarah Hatcher Dawson. Exors: mother, Mrs. Mary Dawson; Basil Cowper; Joseph Gibbons. Wit: Anne Cuthbert, William Houstoun, Benjamin Lloyd.

D: 25 Oct. 1775. P: 18 Dec. 1775. R: 12 Dec. 1776. pp. 267-269 WBAA.

Josiah Bryan, Christ Church Parish, Gent. Wife: Elizabeth, one-fourth of all Negroes, moneys, goods, chattels, other personal estate; use of land, containing 450 acres known by the name of Dew's tract on Wilmington Island in Christ Church Parish. Son: Joseph, remaining three-fourths of all my Negroes, possession of plantations and other lands, to receive from guardian (brother, William Bryan) when he becomes twenty-one years old. If son dies without lawful heirs, the lands to be sold, profits equally divided among my brothers, Hugh and William, and my sister, Hannah. Father and Mother, a suit of mourning, each. Also, a suit of mourning to brothers and sister. Aunt: Mrs. Elizabeth Smith, gold mourning ring. Friend: Thomas Ladson of John's Island in South Carolina, gold mourning ring. Negro slave: Peter, "in consideration of the many faithful services performed me," I give him his freedom forever. Remainder of estate to son, Joseph. Mentions: Edward Telfair, Esq. and William Gibbons (to be guardians of son, Joseph, if previously appointed guardian, William Bryan, dies). Exors: brother, William; William Gibbons of Savannah, merchant. Wit: James Robertson, James Adair, Ruthey Jones.

D: 28 Nov. 1774. P: 23 Dec. 1774. R: n.d.
Codicil to will (same date) :

To Anne Cuthbert, a gold mourning ring. To James Robertson, of Savannah, a suit of mourning. Wit: James Adair, Ruthey Jones. pp. 110-113 WBAA.

Mary Bryan, Savannah, widow. Dau: Mary, wife of Jonathan Bryan, tract of land at Ogechee, slave named Peter. Dau: Elizabeth Smith, wife of John Smith, Esq., house and lot in Savannah whereon I now live, household furniture, wearing apparel, slaves named Isaac, Charles, Old George, Young George, Lucy and her dau Magdaline and her son Luke. To children of my deceased son, John Williamson, slaves named Abraham, Billy, Tamarlane, Sue and her son Charles and her dau Peggy, Wintner; six silver spoons. Slaves to remain in the hands of the exors until the children become eighteen. At that time they are to be equally divided. Dau: Ann Cuthbert, wife of Dr. James Cuthbert, 10 pounds Sterling. Grandson: William Henry Williamson, lot at Yamacraw. Graddau: Mary Williamson, 114 pounds, 5 shillings, and 8 pence Sterling, to be paid her when she becomes eighteen. Meanwhile the sum is to be placed at interest. Grandchildren:

Isaac Hayne and Mary, the wife of Doctor William Pillans, 20 pounds Sterling. To exors: 50 pounds Sterling to be placed "as they may think most proper toward the support of the Independant Meeting House in Savannah. Remainder of the personal estate to be equally divided among the children of my deceased son, John Williamson and the children of my dau, Elizabeth Smith. Exors: son-in-law, John Smith, Esq.; dau-in-law, Magdalen Williamson; Joseph Clay. Wit: J. J. Zubly, Noble Wimberly Jones, Matthew Anderson.

D: 14 May 1776. P: 26 June 1776. R: 26 June 1776. pp. 145-148 WBA.

Ann Graham Bulloch, her mark, Mulberry Grove, widow of James Bulloch, Esq. Exors to collect 300 pounds Sterling (as result of indenture dated 1 Jan. 1758) within twelve months after death and put it at interest. Interest to be paid annually to sister, Elizabeth (widow of James Jackson, vintner) in Inverness in North Britain. If sister dies before the stated twelve months, the interest is to be divided equally between nephews, John and Thomas Chisholm, sons of the Revd. Mr. Thomas Chisholm, late minister of the Gospel at Kilmorack. Exors: John Stuart, Esq., Superintendent of Indian Affairs in South Carolina; my cousin, George Cuthbert. Wit: Christopher Dawson, planter; Mary Cuthbert, wife of George Cuthbert of Drakies, Georgia.

D: 17 Nov. 1762. P: 26 June 1764. R: 27 June 1764. pp. 120-121/112-113 WBA.

Barbara Buntz, her mark, St. Matthew's Parish, Town of Ebenezer, widow. Friends: Conrad Frank, 25 pounds, Georgia currency; a rifled gun. Catherine Michael, three pounds, Georgia currency. Sophia Beedenback, four pounds, Georgia currency. Godchildren: John, Ludwig, and Christian Grabenstine, Elizabeth Gnann, 14 pounds, Georgia currency, equally divided. The poor of Ebenezer Congregation, 12 pounds, Georgia currency. Nephew and Nieces: John George Buntz, Christiana Buntz, and Anna Mary Buntz, children of John George Buntz, ten pounds, Georgia currency, equally divided. Remainder of estate, if any, to the Ebenezer School. Exors: Jacob Waldhauer, Lucas Zeigler. Wit: Charles McCay, Daniel Burgsteiner, Jenkin Davis.

D:21 Sept. 1775. P: 23 Nov. 1775. R: 23 Nov. 1775. pp. 206-208 WBAA.

Henry Ludwig Buntz, St. Matthew's Parish, carpenter. Wife: Barbara, all estate, extrix. Wit: Jacob Waldhauer, Lucas Zeigler, Jacob Gnann.

D: 7 July 1774. P: 6 Sept. 1775. R: 20 Sept. 1775.

Document attached empowering John Adam Treutlen and John Stirk, Esqs. to administer the oath of extrix. to Barbara Buntz. Dated 6 Sept. 1775.

Oath of extrix. certified as administered by John Adam Treutlen. Dated 16 Sept. 1775. pp. 184-187 WBAA.

Urban Buntz, St. Matthew's Parish, planter. Wife: Marged, use of plantation where I now live, four Negroes with two Negro wenches and a Negro child during her widowship. Sons: John Christopher, 300 acres of land whereon I now live; 50 acres of land I bought of Frederick Shrempf on Savannah River, joining Conrad Eckort's land. Henry Ludwig, 200 acres of land, 200 acres of swampland granted to Conrad Eckort, 50 acres of land I bought from Jacob Mohr on Savannah River. Daus: Anna Barbara, 200 acres of land on Old Ebenezer Creek, town lot in Ebenezer I have bought of Israel Limburger. Christine, 300 acres of land joining David Unseld's land. Dau-in-law: Marged, 25 pounds Sterling to be paid by the exors within six months after my wife's death. Brother: John George, 25 pounds Sterling to be paid by the exors within six months after my death. Remainder of Negroes and 500 acres of land to be sold, profits placed at interest for wife and children equally divided. Exors: wife, Ludwig Buntz, John Wertsch. Wit: Christopher Fred Triebner; Conrath Rahn; George Buntz, his mark.

D: 24 March 1774. P: 12 Jan. 1775. R: n.d. pp. 118-120 WBAA.

Michael Burkholder (original in German and the translation sworn to as accurate by J. J. Zubly, dated 7 Jan. 1762), Christ Church Parish, Town of Acton, planter. Exors to sell all estate except what is needed by wife. Profits of the sale to be placed at interest to maintain the wife and dau. for the rest of the wife's life. On her death all that remains to be divided among "all my children of the first and second bed" and granddau: Mary Cath-

erine, dau of my dau-in-law, Catherine. Exors: The Revd. Mr.
Zubly, William Russell, Christopher Ring. Wit: John Eppinger,
George Derick.

D: 1 Jan. 1762. P: 8 Jan. 1762. R: 10 Jan. 1762. pp. 75-76
WBA.

Hugh Burn, Christ Church Parish, planter. Mother: Elizabeth
Burn of Sterling in Scotland, 15 pounds Sterling yearly. Nephew:
eldest son of my sister, Elizabeth Burn, now married to _____ ___
_____ of Sterling in Scotland, 10 pounds Sterling a year for
five years for his maintenance and education. When the eldest
son of my sister, Elizabeth, or Hugh Burn, son of my brother
Alexander Burn of Charles Town in South Carolina, becomes
twenty-one years of age, all the estate, real and personal, both in
Georgia and South Carolina, is to be sold by the exors. with the
profits being divided between these two nephews. The one-half
part belonging to the eldest son of my sister, Elizabeth, to be
equally shared with his brothers and sisters. Exors: Joseph Clay
of Savannah, merchant; Joseph Weatherly and William Gibbons
of Christ Church Parish, planters. Wit: John Hubbard, James
Galache, Mathias Avenson.

D: 24 Sept. 1767. P: 30 Oct. 1767. R: 13 (31?) Oct. 1767. pp.
228-230 WBA.

Samuel Burnley, St. John's Parish. Wife: Elizabeth, Negro
wench named Willaby, lot number 233 in Sunbury, riding mare
called Fly, saddle, bridle, feather bed and furniture, use of one
room in my present dwelling house, use of one-third the planting
land of the plantation on which I now live. Sons: Samuel, tract
of land at Newport, containing about 300 acres joining lands
surveyed by Josiah Powell and Phillipa Fenny, Negro slave named
George, riding horse called Diamond, saddle, bridle, feather bed
and furniture, all my carpenter and joiners tools, all of the above
to be delivered to him when he is twenty years of age. Thomas,
one Negro boy named Gershom, young horse called Crickett,
433½ acres of land (part of tract I now live on and one small adjoining tract), all to be delivered him at twenty years of age.
Daus: Sarah, young wench named Lucy, riding horse called Wanton, saddle, bridle, feather bed and furniture, lot number 234 in
Sunbury, all to be delivered her at eighteen years of age or mar-

riage; Elizabeth, Negro girl named Jean, horse called Derick, saddle, bridle, feather bed and furniture, lot number 235 in Sunbury, all to be delivered to her at eighteen years of age or marriage; Mary, Negro girl named Rose, mare called Pleasant, saddle, bridle, feather bed and furniture, lot number 236 in Sunbury. Remainder of estate, real and personal, divided among wife and children. Exors: wife; son, Samuel; Robert and William Quarterman. Wit: Thomas Way; Samuel Stevens, John Winn, Junior.

D: 17 Aug. 1767. P: 24 Nov. 1767. R: 6 Jan. 1768.

Document empowering John Irwin, John Martin, Parmenas Way, and William Donnom, Esqs., to administer the oath of exor. to Elizabeth Burnley and William Quarterman. Dated 27 Nov. 1767.

Oath of exor. signed by Elizabeth Burnley, her mark, dated 15 Dec. 1767. Oath of exor. signed by William Quarterman, dated 21 Dec. 1767. pp. 238-243 WBA.

Richard Burtley, his mark, St. John's Parish. Wife: Sarah, hogs, horses, cattle, beds, furniture, all other household furniture, property. On the death of wife, the entire estate to my granddau, Mary Pritchard. Exors: wife, James Pritchard. Wit: William Morton, Matthew Beard, James Pritchard.

D: 16 Oct. 1771. P: 20 May 1774. R: n.d. pp. 92-93 WBAA.

Joseph Butler, Christ Church Parish, Esq. Son: Shem, 50 pounds Sterling. Dau: Mary Spencer, 500 pounds, Georgia currency; tract of land, containing about 500 acres, that I bought of James Ross, joining Lewis Mutear "on the other side of the river Altamahaw nigh the Ferry." Son: James, my plantation known as White Oak Swamp on Beaver Dam and all the land joining it; the 100 acres I bought of Lewis Mutear at a place called Barbeque Creek, containing about 1500 acres; 100 Negroes; all my cattle at Ogechee. Marget Crocker, seven Negroes; the house and lot in Savannah I bought of ? Miller; 250 pounds, Georgia currency; riding chair; two horses. Girl, Frances Butler, that I had by Marget Crocker, tract of land, containing 460 acres, on the North Branch of South Newport; two lots of land (100 acres) in

24

Maegomery (?) which I bought of Charles Pryce; four Negroes. "Boy called Benjamin Butler," three Negroes; my "Rose Due" plantation; the island I bought from Thomas Perkers. "Boy called Shadrech Butler," four Negroes, 100 acres of land in St. Andrew's Parish nigh the river Altamahaw. "Boy called Masech Butler," four Negroes; two tracts of land, one of 800 acres and the other of 750 acres up Conuchee in St. John's Parish, joining nigh Mitchell Cowpen. "Boy called William Butler," four Negroes; tract of land that I had of my son, James, containing 350 acres on Great Ogechee and one tract of 500 acres not far from it; 300 acres of a 500-acre tract of which I sold my son, James, 200 acres; two tracts in St. Matthew's Parish up Savannah River, containing 300 acres, the whole containing 1450 acres. Marget Crocker and the five children I had by her, all my plate, household furniture, plantation tools at Rose Due, boats, all cattle and hogs at Rose Due, to be equally divided by Marget Crocker and the five children. Each child to have a horse. Marget Crocker shall live at Rose Due until Benjamin is twenty years old. Remaining Negroes to be divided among Frances, Benjamin, Shadrach, Masech, and William Butler. Exors: son, James Butler; William and Edward Telfair, merchants. Wit: Henry Yonge, Joseph Habersham, Samuel Douglass.

D: 22 April 1773. P: 5 Aug. 1780. R: n.d. Colonial Loose Will Collection.

Joseph Butler, Jr., Great Ogechee, planter. Father: Joseph Butler, Sr., all estate, real and personal. Exor: father. Wit: James Butler; Samuel Small; Marget Crocker, her mark.

D: 6 Feb. 1760. P (with codicil): 18 Feb. 1768. R: 20 Feb. 1768.

Codicil-additional bequests to father, Joseph Butler, Sr., tract of land on Great Ogechee River, containing 740 acres which he gave me some time ago by deed of gift. Wit: John Gredire; William Molding, his mark; Michael Mack, his mark. Dated: 5 March 1763. pp. 249-251 WBA.

William Butler, Ogechee, planter. Wife: Elizabeth, all estate, real and personal. Wife to provide for my dau, Mary Elliott Butler, as she shall think proper. Exors: wife, brother-in-law, William Elliott. Exors to act as guardians of the person and estate of dau, Mary, until she is twenty-one years of age. Wit: James Mackay; John Maxwell; Joseph Butler, Jr.; James Maxwell, Jr.

D: 5 Mar. 1759. P: 26 Mar. 1761 and 26 April 1764. R: 23 June 1761. pp. 64-65 WBA.

John Cable, Abercorn, planter. Wife: Ann Barbary, 100 acres of land at Abercorn, house hold goods, money. Son: Abraham, 100 acres of swamp land adjoining lands of Hugh Ross in the district of Abercorn. Daus: Elizabeth, 100 acres of Pine Barren Land; Mary, 50 acres adjoining her brother, Abraham's land. Exor: (not named). Wit: Saml. Pelton, Hugh Ross, John Ross.

D: 5 Aug. 1762. P: 24 Aug. 1763. R: 24 Sept. 1763. pp. 115-116/107-108 WBA.

Robert Campbell, Savannah, planter. Robert McDonald, two Negro slaves named Buck and Ned; rent, remainder and residue of estate, real and personal. Exor: Robert McDonald. Wit: William Lord, John Wason, James Mills (all mariners at sea and unable to appear for the probate). Wit to the handwriting of the will: David Tu Bear (Tobear — T' Bear) of Savannah, gunsmith; Martin Bunn, at present in the Georgia Battalion; Henry Clark, corporal in the Georgia Battalion.

D: 11 Nov. 1776. P: 7 Dec. 1776. R: 19 Dec. 1776. pp. 271-273 WBAA.

Christian Campher, his mark, Christ Church Parish, laborer. Wife: Mary, all estate, real and personal. Son: Jeremiah (on the death of Mary Campher), one lot of land, containing 45 acres in Christ Church Parish, known by number 10 Third Tything Ansons Ward; lot of land number 41 in St. Gall, in Christ Church Parish; lot of land number 223 in Sunbury. Dau: Ann Nichols (on the death of Mary Campher), lot of land number 42 in St. Gall in Christ Church Parish; lot of land number 204 in Sunbury. Exors: son, Jeremiah; John Eppinger. Wit: William Kirk, Jr., of Savannah, Gent.; David Gautier; Elisha Elon.

D: n.d. P: 1 Aug. 1774. R: n.d. pp. 95-96 WBAA.

Joseph Camuse, Savannah, carpenter. To Exor: power to hold lands, rents, issues, in Christ Church Parish, for the use of my two children, Joseph and Elizabeth, when they come of age. Exor: Richard Milledge of Christ Church Parish, carpenter. Wit: Jos. Stanley; Ann Cox, her mark; William Young.

D: 28(?) Sept. 1764. P: 12 Oct. 1764. R: 17 Oct. 1764. pp. 123-126/115-117 WBA.

Richard Cannon (part of will is missing). Son: Duke, my house and town lot, together with my town lot, garden lot and farm lot; in case of his death these to my dau, Clemontine. Wife: Mary. Mentions Trustees for Colony of Georgia. Exor: Joseph Wardrope, Thos. Fawset.

D: n.d. P: n.d. R: n.d. (1735?) Colonial Loose Will Collection.

Mark Carr, St. Patrick's Parish, Esq. Colonel. Sons: William, town lot in Frederica known by the number one North. Thomas, town lot in Frederica known by the number 21 North. Dau: Elizabeth, dau of Elizabeth Rutherford, my island on the North Side of the River Midway; tract of land on the Main fronting on the island, which I purchased of John Cubbage. Dau: Judith, remainder of estate, real and personal. Extrix: dau, Judith. Wit: Grey Elliott, Frederick Holzendorff, William Stephens.
D: 8 June 1767. P: 4 Dec. 1767. R: 27 Jan. 1768.

Document empowering Donald Mackay and John Polsen, Esqs. to administer the oath of extrix to Judith Carr. Dated 4 Dec. 1767.

Oath of extrix signed by Judith Carr. Dated 28 Dec. 1767. pp. 245-247 WBA.

Thomas Carter, St. John's Parish. Wife, Mary, Negroes named Rachel, Bella, Chloe; her chair and chair horse; use of dwelling house and household furniture where I now live along with her maintenance as long as she remains my widow. Sons: Hepworth, James, Charles Thomas Carter, one-third part each of my lands (about 1800 acres in all) in Georgia; one-third part each of my lands in South Carolina and Virginia "the quantity I am not certain of." Dau: Anne Oswald, tract of land, containing 100 acres on Newport River whereon she now lives. Personal estate, consisting of Negroes, cattle, horses, hogs, sheep, etc. to be divided equally among wife, Mary; sons, Hepworth, James, and Charles Thomas Carter; and daus, Anne Oswald and Catherine Mutteair. Exors: sons, Hepworth, James, Charles Thomas Carter; James Cochran of St. Andrew's Parish. Wit: Judah Lewis; Lewis Mutteair; Nicholas Smith of St. Andrew's Parish, schoolmaster.

D: 8 Mar. 1774. P: 17 Mar 1774. R: n.d. pp. 84-85 WBAA.

Christopher Chappell, his mark, Christ Church Parish. Dau: Elizabeth, all estate, real and personal. If she dies leaving no lawful heirs, the estate is to be divided between Mary Temens, dau to Margaret Sackes, and Mary Fisher, dau to David Fisher. Wife: Elizabeth, one shilling Sterling. Exors: David Johnston, James Warden. Wit: Thomas Johnston, Bartholomew Fleming, George Dron(e).

D: 8 Feb. 1774. P: 9 Mar. 1774. R: n.d. p. 83 WBAA.

Thomas Christie, province of South Carolina, "but now bound on a voyage to London." Friends: John and Robert Williams, Jr., all lands, houses, and property in the province of Georgia. Wit: Patrick Laird, Robt. Rutherford, Robert Williams.

D: 16 Aug. 1751. P: 27 April 1751 (?) and 15 Dec. 1758. R: 9 (?) Aug. 1759. p. 51 WBA.

Giles Church, Christ Church Parish, practitioner of physick. Wife: Rebecca, one-half estate, real and personal. Dau: Betsey, one-half estate, real and personal. Wife to act as guardian of the estate of the dau until the dau is married or twenty-one years of age. Exors: wife, Andrew Elton Wells. Wit: Oliver Bowen; Saml. Farley; William Ewen of Savannah, Gent.

D: 9 Aug. 1771. P: 2 Sept. 1771. R: 4 Sept. 1771. p. 417 WBA.

Daniel Clark, Augusta, Indian trader, "but now in Charlestown sick in body." Friends: Alexander Petrie and his wife, 12 pounds South Carolina currency to each for mourning rings, 350 pounds South Carolina currency to be divided equally among their children. John McQueen, his wife and his dau, Ann, 12 pounds current money to buy each a mourning ring; 60 pounds Sterling to be divided among their children, to each child also one horse from my best stock on Shell Creek. George Summers and his wife, 200 pounds current money, a stallion, a mare, a trotting gelding of their choice; 12 pounds current money to buy a mourning ring. To Alexander, son of Mary Dicks, 50 pounds Sterling to be paid him in such manner as my friend Lauchlan McGilvray shall think fit. To Alexander McGilvray and his wife, 200 pounds to buy mourning. To Robert Brisbane and James Parsons, 12 pounds current money to each of them to buy mourning rings. To John McGilvray and William Stuthers, all my wearing apparel, riding saddle, bridle, furniture, swords, belt, guns, and pistols (save one French gun to George Summers), books. To William Stuthers, 50 pounds Sterling. To John McGilvray, 25 pounds Sterling. To Mr. Morrison, minister of the Scotch Meeting house in Charlestown, 25 pounds Sterling. To Charlestown Library, 25 pounds Sterling. Brother: Alexander Clark of Parish of Patty near Castle Stewarth near Inverness in North Britain, 2000 pounds Sterling, or to his children if he is no longer living. Brother-in-law: Alexander Clark, formerly a merchant, at Inverness, 300 pounds Sterling and to his dau, Margaret and her children, 200 pounds Sterling equally divided. Exors: Alexander Petrie, Lauchlan McGilvray, John McQueen, James Parsons. Wit: Hanna Rachable, James Parsons.

D: 19 April 1757. P: 13 May 1757. R: 23 June 1757.

Document in which James Parsons renounces forever the right to act as exor. Wit by John Rutledge. Dated 12 Aug. 1757.

Document empowering Alexander Petrie and Lauchlan McGilvray to act as exors. of the will. Dated 20 May 1757. pp. 22-26 WBA.

Hugh Clark, St. Andrew's Parish, planter. To be buried in the town of Sunbury with my deceased wife and children. Brothers: William, Negroes named Argyll, Rinnah, Jack, and Nancy; one-half my stock of cattle, horses, and hogs; Angus, furniture and bed furniture (except one chest of drawers). Sister-in-law: Sarah Stephens, tract of land on the river St. Mary's. Dau: Barbara, remainder of estate, real and personal. Brother: William, to act as guardian of Barbara until she is of age. Exors: Capt. James Mackay, William Mackintosh, William Clark, and Angus Clark.

Wit to the handwriting signed by Roderick Mackintosh and Robert McKay. Dated 16 June 1773.

D: 15 Oct. 1771. P: 17 June 1773. R: 17 June 1773. pp. 93-94 WBAA.

Lawrence Clark, Savannah, mariner. Wife: Elizabeth, use of the house in Yamacraw facing the street now occupied by William Saunders, during her widowhood. Exors. to give her in addition what they think fit for her support. Also one bed and furniture. Exors. to sell the remaining personal estate, the profits to be placed at interest. Interest from this investment to go to the support of son, Matthew. Son: Matthew, all my real estate. If he dies without lawful heirs, the estate to my three brothers, Morris, Edmond, and John if they shall come to this province. Exors: Philip Box and John Sommerville, both of Savannah, merchants. Wit: Ichabod Higgins, George Hague (Hogue).

D: 19 Sept. 1770. P: 29 Nov. 1770. R: 30 Nov. 1770. pp. 361-363 WBA.

Nathaniel Clark, St. John's Parish, planter. To children of my brother, Stephen Clark, one-half my estate, real and personal, to be put at interest until they are of age and then divided equally. Brother: Joshua Clark, all the money he owes me. Other one-half of the estate for the support of the Gospel Ministry of which the Revd. Mr. John Osgood is Minister. Exors: Brother, Stephen; John Winn. Wit: John Stewart; Elizabeth Sumner; George Fitzgerald, his mark.

D: 20 Aug. 1761. P: 25 Feb. 1763. R: 25 Feb. 1763. pp. 100-101/92-93 WBA.

Patrick Clark, his mark, Augusta. Wife: Sarah, entire estate. Exors: wife, Martin Campbell, Esq. Wit: John Pettygrow, James McHenrey, John Tinley.

D: 21 Sept. 1756. P: 15 Nov. 1756. R: n.d. pp. 18-19 WBA.

John Clubb, St. Simon's Island. Wife: Mary, all estate, after debts are paid; extrix. Wit: James Bruce of Frederica, Gent.; Raymond Demere, Sr.; Raymond Demere, Jr.

D: 25 Sept. 1771. P: 14 July 1772. R: 15 July 1772. p. 449 WBA.

John Coffee, his mark, Savanah. Friend: Adrian Loyer, all estate, exor. Wit: Edward Carlton, James Dixie.

D: 18 Mar. 1759. P: 9 Aug. 1759. R: 9 Aug. 1759. pp. 49-51 WBA.

James Corneck, Christ Church Parish, bricklayer. Sons: John, the old house and half lot; 5 pounds per year for two years to finish construction of the new house. Exors empowered to sell Negro named Tom, with the profits from this sale and the rents from the new house, to be put into repairs of the old house. Joseph, my new house and the other half lot situated on the East End of the half lot bequeathed to son, John. Exors to sell household furniture. Exors: William Ewen, Esq.; John Eppinger; James Nicholas. Wit: Ann Nichols, her mark; William Kirk; Isaac Laroch.

D: 5 Oct. 1773. P: 2 Dec. 1773. R: n.d. pp. 64-66 WBAA.

Heriot Crooke, "widow of Clement Crooke, late of the island of St. Christopher, Esq., at present residing in Savannah." Exors to sell all household goods except the sheeting and two feather beds. One feather bed to Ann Scales of Savannah, spinster. The other feather bed to my two granddaus: Elizabeth Crooke Tannatt and Heriot Cunningham Tannatt. Sheeting, linen to be divided equally among the three of them (In the following bequests, all money in pounds Sterling is the result of a bequest of 2000 pounds Sterling to me from my father, Robert Cunningham, Esq., deceased.) Thomas Boyd Mackinen (son of Charles William Mackinen, Esq.), Negro wench to be chosen for him by his father. Sons: Robert Charles Crooke, 500 pounds Sterling, Negro woman named Chloe and her son Joe. Charles Cunningham Crooke, 700 pounds Sterling. Richard Cunningham Crooke, 300 pounds Sterling; tract of land, containing 500 acres, on island called Burbuda or, Colonel Heru's Island. Daus: Judith Caines, wife of Charles

Caines, 300 pounds Sterling. Frances Graham, wife of the Honorable John Graham, Esq., 130 pounds Sterling. Susannah Wylly, wife of Alexander Wylly of Savannah, Esq., 10 pounds Sterling. Jourdina Cunningham Baillie, wife of George Baillie, Esq., 10 pounds Sterling. Elizabeth Mossman, wife of James Mossman, Esq., 50 pounds Sterling, the use of wench Bauby during her lifetime and said wench then to go to my granddau, Elizabeth Crooke Tannatt. Granddau: Mary Hume, wife of James Hume, Esq., all the monies and legacies whatsoever left me by my son, Clement Crooke, Esq., who died in the East Indies; any Negro of her choice from those I expect from the West Indies upon the sale of my Dower Lands. To Ann Scales, a new Negro of her choice. Granddaus: Elizabeth Crooke Tannatt and Heriot Cunningham Tannatt, lot of land in town of Brunswick; Negro woman named Sophey; remainder of estate, real and personal. Exors: son, Robert Charles Crooke; nephew, Charles William Mackinen; The Honorable John Graham and James Hume, Esqs. Exors to be guardians of the granddaus until they come of age. Wit: James Robertson; John Wood; John Millidge, Jr.

D: 12 Oct. 1774. P (will and codicil): 5 Aug. 1780. R: n.d.

Codicil to the above will: Son, Richard Cunningham Crooke has died since the date of the above will. The 500-acre tract of land has already been given him and thus now belongs to his heirs. The bequeath of 300 pounds Sterling granted him in the above will to go to my son, Charles Cunningham Crooke. Further to Mrs. Mary Hume, Mrs. Elizabeth Crooke Houstoun, Miss Heriot Cunningham Tannatt, and their heirs, my pew in the parish church of Christ Church. Wit: Isabella Mossman, Anne Graham, James Robertson. Dated 22 Aug. 1775.

Colonial Loose Will Collection.

Hariot Crooke, Jr., Savannah, spinster. Sister: Susannah Wylly, Negro wench named Pamela with her two children. Niece: Mary Tannatt, Negro woman called Old Mary. Brother: Robert Crooke, suit of mourning. Remainder of estate to be divided among niece, Mary Tannatt, and the first born child of my sister, Susannah Wylly, and the first born child of my sister, Frances Graham, equally divided. Exors: brothers, Edmund Tannatt,

Alexander Wylly, John Graham. Wit: Heriot Crooke, Andrew Johnston.

D: 18 Sept. 1756. P: 25 Nov. 1756. R: n.d. pp. 19-20 WBA.

Thomas Cross, his mark, Savannah, bricklayer. Dau: Eleanor Sliterman, all my real estate "in Georgia or any other place," all my personal estate. Exors: dau, Eleanor and her husband, Peter Sliterman. Wit: Thomas Lloyd, Samuel Small, William Wylly.

D: 19 June 1768. P: 24 Aug. 1768. R: 25 Aug. 1768. pp. 275-276 WBA.

William Cross (will is partly missing), Savannah. Wife: Elizabeth, use of all estate, real or personal. Upon her death, the estate is to go to William Cross the son of Benjamin Cross, my brother. If he is not living at the time of my wife's death, the estate to Thomas James Doucott, son of John Doucott, late of Annapholis Royall in Nova Scotia. Extrix: wife. Wit: John Teasdale, (John) Clarke.

D: 4 Aug. 1737. P: n.d. R: n.d. Colonial Loose Will Collection.

Henry Cunningham, St. Augustine, province of East Florida, doctor of physick. As all my affairs and concerns in Europe are settled by marriage articles between me and my wife before our marriage, I have nothing to dispose of but what I am possessed of in this part of the world. Wife: Margaret Cunningham, entire estate, real and personal. She is to sell property and effects. Profits to be divided into three parts. One-third to wife; one-third to my son, George Sackville Cunningham; one-third to my dau, Esther Cunningham. Extrix: wife. Wit: Alexander Moodie, John Cherry, William Collins.

D: 9 May 1770. P: 10 April 1771. R: 10 Dec. 1771.

Document in which Margaret Cunningham appoints John Graham, Esq. of Savannah, attorney to administer the will for her. Wit: Henry Pilot, John Forbes. Dated 31 July 1771.

pp. 424-426 WBA.

George Cubbadge, his mark. Wife: Elizabeth, use of house with all furniture, lands, and tenements for the rest of her life; five Negroes named Munday, Sambo, Debborer, Jemey, and Grace. After the death of my wife these Negroes to be divided between my grandsons, George and John Cubbadge. On my wife's death the house, tenements, and land, containing 500 acres, called Linkhorn, to my grandson, George Cubbadge. Son: John, 3 Negroes named Prymis, Cato, and Tom; 20 head of cattle; ten head of "Hors Kind." Exors: wife and son, John. Wit: Joseph Hutton; Samuel Lewis, Jr.; Philip Sutton.

D: 8 Dec. 1758. P: 29 Jan. 1759. R: n.d. p. 53 WBA.

George Cuthbert, Christ Church Parish, Esq. Wife: Mary, annuity of 300 pounds Sterling for the rest of her life; Negro woman named Rose and her child. The above in settlement of our marriage agreement. Cousin: James Chapman, annuity of 50 pounds Sterling for the rest of his life. Remainder of estate to exors. To Joseph Cuthbert, second son of James Cuthbert of Savannah, practitioner in physick, one-half of the remaining estate when he becomes twenty-one years of age. If he is deemed worthy, by the exors, at the age of thirty, he is to have the other half of the estate. But if he has squandered or made ill use of the former half, the second half to George Cuthbert, eldest son of James Cuthbert. Give absolute freedom to woman slave named Christiana. Exors to pay her twelve pounds Sterling yearly for the remainder of her life. Exors: James Cuthbert; Alexander Inglis of Savannah, merchant. Wit: Grey Elliott; David Brydie; Jonathan Evans of Savannah, Gent.

D: 10 April 1767 (1768). P: 16 April 1768. R: 20 April 1768. Document attached in which Grey Elliott, David Brydie and Jonathan Evans swear that the date of the above will was 10 April 1768 and not 10 April 1767.

pp. 263-266 WBA.

James Cuthbert, Drakies, Parish of Christ Church, Esq. Wife: Anne, all estate belonging to her at our marriage; Negro named Charles; plate; jewels; furniture; goods; household stuff; vessels; utensils; implements belonging to my dwelling house, in lieu of all dowers and Thirds and all other Titles, Claims, and

Demands which she may claim; rents, issues, and profits of all personal estate, as long as she remains my widow. Wife to provide for the maintenance of the children until they are of age. Son: George, place called Castle Hill in Inverness, Scotland; all other estates I may have in Great Britain. Rest of estate, real and personal, divided among my wife, and my friends, John Graham of Savannah, Esq. and Alexander Inglis of Savannah, merchant. They shall hold this estate for my sons, George, Joseph, and Lewis Graeme Cuthbert, and my dau, Elizabeth. When the sons are twenty-one years of age and the daughter is twenty years of age or married, the estate to be equally divided among them. Exors: wife, John Graham, Alexander Inglis. Wit: Henry Yonge, Jr.; John Clunie, Adrian Loyer.

D: 14 Aug. 1770. P: 20 Oct. 1770. R: 27 Oct. 1770.

Codicil (same date, same wit): If Alexander Inglis dies before this will is executed, Anne Cuthbert is to be sole extrix. Wife to have, as long as she continues my widow, use and benefit of 500 pounds Sterling.

Document empowering David Montaigut and Thomas Shruder to administer the oath of extrix to Anne Cuthbert. Dated 7 Nov. 1770.

Oath of extrix. signed by Anne Cuthbert. Dated 15 Nov. 1770. pp. 352-359 WBA.

Telamon Cuyler, Savannah, mariner. Wife: Jane, all estate, real and personal. Exor: wife; John Glen of Savannah, attorney at law. Wit: James Philips, John McQueen, John Somerville.

D: 2 Sept. 1772. P: 6 Nov. 1772. R: n.d.

Document in which Jane Cuyler and John Glen renounce the right of exor of the above will. Dated 6 Nov. 1772.

Document in which James Habersham accepts the renunciation of the right of exor by Jane Cuyler and John Glen. Dated 13 Nov. 1772. pp. 16-18 WBAA.

Andrew Darling, Sunbury, St. John's Parish, merchant. Sisters: Euphan, Mary, Katherine (none yet twenty-one years of age), 100 pounds Sterling each, when each comes of age. Wife: Jean, Negro wench named Harriott; use of my dwelling house in Sunbury, with its lot and house furnishings (House, lot, and furnishings to dau Elizabeth on the death of my wife), riding chair, two chair horses. Dau: Elizabeth, Negro girl named Tenor; tract of land containing 500 acres; another tract of 150 acres both in the Parish of St. David. To receive these when she is eighteen or married. Forty pounds Sterling to wife until the estate is settled. Mentions: my mother, Elizabeth Darling; James Fraser, Esq., Provost of Inverness in Scotland. Exors: wife and Simon Munro. Wit: John Goulding, Thomas Quarterman, Alexander Christie.

D: 25 March 1767. P: 5 June 1772. R: n.d.

Codicil (same date, same wit): remainder of estate divided between wife and dau.

Document authorizing Roger Kelsall, Parmenas Way and John Martin to administer the oath of extrix to Jean Darling. Dated 8 June 1772.

Oath of extrix signed by Jean Darling. Dated 6 July 1772.

Codicil number two: to each sister, 50 pounds Sterling instead of 100 because of two more children born to the testator. Fifty pounds Sterling to each of them. House in Sunbury and the furniture to be sold on the death of wife, with the profits divided between the children. Son: Kenneth, my two plantations, the one purchased from Dr. John Irvine. The two tracts of land left dau Elizabeth in the original will to be sold with the profits going to Elizabeth and other dau. (no date, not wit.)

Document including the interrogations of the wits. pp. 5-15 WBAA.

John Davis, Christ Church Parish, planter. Son: John, 200 acres of land known by the name "por Robins Bluff;" nine young cows and calves; one rifled gun; one young sorrol horse (not to receive cattle in less than three years from this time). Eldest dau: Elizabeth, five pounds Sterling, three cows and calves. Youngest dau: Sarah, five pounds Sterling and four cows and calves (not to receive their cattle in less than four years from this day). Wife: Mary, remainder of the estate after debts are paid. Exors: wife, James Anderson, William Howell, Joseph Burton. Loose will includes inventory of the estate of John Davis, deceased, dated 22 Sept. 1761, and signed by Robert Hudson, Christopher Hudson, and Thomas Keesee, appraisers.

D: 12 June 1761. P: 3 Sept. 1761. R: 19 Oct. 1761. pp. 70-71 WBA.

John Davis, St. Philip's Parish, planter. Sons: John, tract of land, containing 450 acres, called the Hanie Swamp in St. John's Parish; five Negroes named Mingo, Adam, Natt, Bob, and Rose; one cherry tree table. William; five tracts of land on the North side of Midway River in St. John's Parish, containing 1150 acres (500, 100, 150, 200, 200 acre tracts); bed and furniture, one large bottle case; eight Negroes named March, Peter, Dick, Cudjo, Lucy, Big Chloe, Jemina, and Paul. Daus: Sarah Jones, four Negroes named Limas, Will, Flora, and Rachel. Catherine Morecock, four Negroes named Joe, Leah, Melinda, and Bob. Rebecca Patterson, four Negroes named Saul, Nan, London, and Bella; bed and furniture. Theodora Davis, five Negroes named Harry, Sauney, Willie, Eve, and Sue; bed and furniture. Grandson: James Davis, tract of land, containing 400 acres at the Spring Branch in St. John's Parish; Negroes named Pompey and Flora; my cattle marked with a crop, a slit, and an under half-penny; all the above to be delivered to him at the age of twenty-one. Remainder of the estate, real personal, to my three youngest children: William (one-half part), Rebecca (one-fourth), and Theodora (one-fourth). Exor: son, William. Wit: James Cochran, John Smith, John Griggs.

D: 13 Dec. 1773. P: 15 Jan. 1777. R: 16 Jan. 1777.

Document attached in which Jonathan Cochran and Thomas Stone, Esqs. are empowered to administer the oath of exor to William Davis. Dated 16 Jan. 1777.

Oath of exor. signed by William Davis. Dated 16 Jan. 1777. pp. 274-278 WBAA.

Robert Davis, planter. Sons: Lewis, two Negroes named Bowlin and Phebe; feather bed and its furniture. Landon, two Negroes named Sam and Sarah; feather bed and furniture. Hugh, three Negroes named Roger, Joe, and Cochena; feather bed and furniture. Nathaniel, 20 shillings Sterling. Robert, 20 shillings Sterling. Wife: Grace, Negro girl named Hannah, feather bed and rest of household furniture; loan of four Negroes named Charles, Peg, Harry, and Jug during her widowhood. Out of the income of these four Negroes the wife is to maintain my son, Hugh, until he is twenty years of age. Daus: Abediah Floyd, 20 shillings Sterling. Elizabeth Sexton, 20 shillings Sterling. Sarah Burke, 20 shillings Sterling. Remainder of estate, real and personal, equally divided among three sons, Lewis, Landon, and Hugh, when the latter is twenty-one years of age. Exors: sons, Lewis and Landon. Wit: Thomas Spell, Mager Spell, Starling Spell.

D: 5 Sept. 1771. P: 9 Nov. 1773. R: n.d.

Document attached in which James Spalding and James Forrester, Esqs. are empowered to administer the oath of exor. to Lewis and Landon Davis. Dated 2 Sept. 1773.

Colonial Loose Will Collection.

Lydia Dean, Savannah, widow. Elizabeth Pye, "what sum of money that remains unpaid in the Hand of the Revd. Mr. John Jehoiakim Zublee being remaining due for my town lot in Savannah, and 45 acres and five acre lots sold to him." Mrs. Wylly, my gold ring. Deborah Houstoun, my black and white callico gown, one pair of Callimanco shoes. Mrs. Truan, my purple gown. Peter Baillou, my bed and bed clothes, 40 shillings Sterling. Poor people of Savannah, 10 shillings Sterling to be distributed in bread to every one a two penny loaf. Nothing at Vandue to be sold. Exor: James Houstoun. Wit: David Truan, John Fitzgerald, James Houstoun.

D: 8 Sept. 1761. P: 20 Oct. 1761. R: 20 Oct. 1761. pp. 71-72 WBA.

John Dearne, Savannah, freeholder. Wife: Jean, all personal estate, my freehold in Savannah, extrix. Wit: Samuel Marcer (Mercer), William Brownjohn, Thomas Salter, William Harris.

D: 25 June 1737. P: n.d. R: n.d. Colonial Loose Will Collection.

Joseph DeFeron (Will is in French), Heiguet (Highgate), "Captain in the service of his majesty the King of Great Britain." Wife (unnamed): all household furnishings, all estate, real and personal, "without which the young child is left nothing in the world except anxiety." to wife also, 50 acres of land "that the Trustees have had the kindness to give me," for the rest of her life, and to the heir, equally divided. This if the King directs it to them; if not, the legacy of the said land will give to Madame de Feron, the mother, 24 (?) pounds Sterling per year through the revenue of the land. Wit: Pierre Morel, Jacob Goy, Charles Gallier, Pierre Fage.

D: 24 February 1734. P: n.d. R: n.d. Colonial Loose Will Collection.

John Baptist Deloney, his mark, Savannah, Christ Church Parish, vintner. Wife: Maryann, Negro wench named Eve, household goods. Son: John Baptist Deloney, Negro named Munday to be delivered to him after he shall be settled in some business in Georgia. Dau: Rose Young, wife of John Young of Savannah, mariner, 10 pounds current money. Youngest dau: Elizabeth, Negro wench named Phillis. Exors: wife and son, John. Wit: Henry L. Bourquin; James Chansat, his mark; Isaac Baillou.

D: 30 June 1772. P: 24 July 1772. R: 31 July 1772. pp. 450-451 WBA.

Raymond Demere, St. Simon's Island, merchant. Betsy Demere, "but the porre little girl she is not my daughter but as she was born under my Roffe I was always willing for to do something for her so that I would not have her to be called a Bastard," about 80 pounds Sterling. Son: Raymond Demere and Nephew: Raymond Demere at Savannah, about 200 pounds Sterling and the remainder of my estate, both equally divided. Exors: John Graham of Savannah; Donald McKay of Frederica, merchant.

Wit: James Forrester; John Polson; William Moore, late of St. Simon's Island and now of Savannah, merchant.

D: n.d. P: 26 June 1766. R: 26 June 1766. pp. 151-152 WBA.

Daniel Demetre, Savannah, mariner. Son-in-law: William Thomas Harris, plantation containing 750 acres on land called Dickenson's Neck in the district of Sappelo and Newport; eight Negroes named Nicholas, Hager, Tony, Prince, Belinda, Dinah, James, and Silvia. Granddau: Ann Harris, 100 pounds Sterling. James Habersham of Savannah, 50 pounds Sterling in trust to be paid by him to the Master and the Warden of the Society of Free Masons in Savannah for the use of said society. Joseph, John, and James Habersham, the younger, the remainder of the estate, equally divided. Exors: James Habersham and Francis Harris. Wit: David Montaigut, Thomas Rasberry, James Mossman.

D: 12 July 1758. P: 10 Aug. 1758. R: 10 Aug. 1758. pp. 34-36 WBA.

Daniel Derizous, St. Paul's Parish. "As my wife Olive Derizous has eloped from me for about six years past I bequeath to her one shilling Sterling for poisoning me." All lands, goods, chattles to be sold by the exors with the profits being divided among my five children, Daniel, Elizabeth, Peter, Stephen, and Michael. Exors: George Galphin of South Carolina and John Morse of Georgia. Wit: Thomas Grubbs and William Harris.

D: 6 Sept. 1766. P: 3 July 1775. R: n.d. Colonial Loose Will Collection.

Thomas DeVall, Indian trader. Nephew: Thomas Morgan of Georgia, tailor, entire estate, real and personal; sole exor. Wit: John Procter, his mark; George Cornal, his mark.

D: 5 Oct. 1758. P: n.d. R: 16 July 1761. p. 69 WBA.

John DeVeaux, Little Ogechee, Christ Church Parish, Esq. Wife: Sarah, six cows and calves, a horse, a riding horse, all of her choice; use of four Negroes named Bob, Rina, Tom, and Betty for her lifetime, after which the Negroes are to be equally divided among my children; use of my plantation containing 500 acres

40

where I now live at Little Ogechee for her widowhood and to dau, Elizabeth, afterwards; one-third of the household goods and furniture. Remainder of the estate to be divided among three children, John, Elizabeth, and Jane, wife of George Delegal. Son: John, 100 acres of land at the south end of Skidoway Island known by the name Balloon's Bluff; 500 acres of a 950-acre tract called Silver Bluff at Great Ogechee. Dau: Jane, other 450 acres. Exors: wife, son, John; Charles Watson of Savannah; and George Delegal. Wit: William Mills, John Mitchell, Joseph Summers.

D: 15 Dec. 1759. P: 6 Jan. 1762. R: 19 Jan. 1762. pp. 73-75 WBA.

Paynter Dickenson, Christ Church Parish, mariner. Wife: Ann, lot at Yammacraw where I now live; tract of land, containing 250 acres on Collin's Creek the north side of Midway River; one mulatto boy named Michael; one four-oared canoe with her tackle and furniture. Son: John Down Dickenson, Negro named Cato. To child or children with which my wife is now pregnant, Negro man named Tom. Wife to keep these Negroes until my children are of age. Dau: Elizabeth Nelmes, wife of Samuel Nelmes of Sunbury, merchant, Negro woman named Beck. Dau: Sarah, Negro woman named Lilly. Son: Thomas, all of my town lots in Sunbury. Remainder of estate to wife: Exors: wife; James Muter of Savannah, cabinet maker; Thomas Fleming of Savannah, carpenter. Wit: William Ewen, Morris Nunes, Samuel Farley.

D: 4 July 1767. P: 13 Oct. 1767. R: 19 Oct. 1769. pp. 327-329 WBA.

Richard Dobbyn, "late of the town of Carrick in the County of Tipperary, but now of Savannah," mariner. Wife: Anastatia, my two houses in Carrick, all personal estate in Savannah. Wit: Adrian Loyer, Thomas Smith, Elizabeth Baugh.

D: 19 Sept. 1759. P: 6 Dec. 1759. R: 20 June 1761. p. 54 WBA.

Robert Donaldson, St. Andrew's Parish, planter. Wife: Christain, one-half real and personal estate. Sister: Margaret Jamieson of the County of Aberdeen in the Parish of Fivey in North Britain. Exors: Robert Baillie, George McKintosh, Esqs. Wit:

William Long, his mark; Michael Lawler, his mark; Nicholas Smith of St. John's Parish, schoolmaster.

D: 19 Dec. 1768. P: 10 Oct. 1769. R: 13 Oct. 1769. pp. 324-325 WBA.

John Doors, Savannah, planter, (also Perukemaker). Son: James, town lot (44' front, 90' deep) fronting on the bay in Savannah, number three, in Wilmington tything, where I now live, which I lately purchased from James Mossman, Esq.; tract of 250 acres in Christ Church Parish, which I lately purchased from Thomas Lee, bounded at the time of the grant in part by the land of John Goldwire; three Negroes named Tom, Penny, and Charlotte; remainder of the estate. Wife: Martha, household furniture, linen, plate, China for her widowhood; these to son, James, on wife's death or marriage. Exors: wife, George McCauley, John Richards, James Dixsee, Wit: Samuel Stirk, Cashman Polock, shopkeeper; Thomas Mills, shopkeeper.

D: 5 March 1777. P: 26 March 1777. R: 26 March 1777. pp. 308-310 WBAA.

David Douglass, Augusta, Esq. Wife: Mary, entire estate if she remains my widow, extrix. If she marries estate to be divided as follows: one-third to wife; two-thirds to the use of my children. Exor in this case: John McQueen. Wit: Thomas Ford, William Day, John Bergeron.

D: 2 Mar. 1759. P: 19 Dec. 1763. R: 23 Dec. 1763. pp. 116-117 WBA.

David Drummond, Savannah, mariner. Wife: Elizabeth, entire estate, particularly lot of land in Savannah with the houses thereon; lot of 45 acres and a lot of five acres in Savannah Township; extrix. Wit: James Houstoun, William Wright, Deborah Houstoun.

D: 17 April 1761. P: 17 July 1771. R: 18 July 1771. pp. 412-413 WBA.

William Dunham, St. John's Parish, planter. Wife: Mary, use of house and furniture during her widowhood; Negro wench named Silvia. Son: John, use of one-third the land and one-ninth the personal estate. Sons: William Charles, Paul James, and the child with which my wife is now pregnant (if it is a boy), all my lands not granted before. Daus: Mary, Esther, Martha, and Hannah, 400 pounds Sterling equally divided. Exors: wife, John Martin, Gideon Dowse, John Sandiford. Wit: Parmenas Way, William Graves, Peter Sallans.

D: 22 Dec. 1769. P: 2 March 1770. R: 29 March 1770.

Document attached in which John Simpson, Andrew Darling, and Roger Kelsall, Esqs. are empowered to administer the oath of exor. to the exors. Dated 2 March 1770.

Oath of exorship. signed by Mary Dunham and John Sandiford. Dated 22 March 1770. pp. 340-343 WBA.

Thomas Eatton, Savannah, merchant. Nephews: John and Thomas Eatton (sons of my brother, Joseph, late of New Jersey, doctor in physick, deceased), 270 pounds Sterling, equally divided when they reach twenty-one years of age. This in settlement of accounts their father transferred to my care on his death. To Elizabeth, the now wife of William Herbert of Georgia, planter, for the rest of her life, annuity of 10 pounds Sterling to be paid out of the rents of my dwelling house on the Bay in Savannah where I now live and which formerly belonged to Captain Isaac Martin. Remainder of the estate to be divided among the following: Nephews: John and Thomas Eatton; my sister, Valeria, wife of Peter LeConte of New Jersey, doctor in physick; my sister, Sarah, wife of Richard Tole of New Jersey, Gent; the heirs of my sister, Lydia, deceased, late wife of Captain John Wanton of Rhode Island; sister, Elizabeth, wife of Captain Thomas Richardson of Rhode Island; sister, Joanna, wife to the Revd. Elihu Spencer of Pennsylvania; sister, Margaret, wife of John Baryan of New Jersey. Exors: Nephews (sons of my sister Valeria): William LeConte of Georgia, Gent., and John LeConte of Georgia, doctor in physick. Wit: Thomas Burrington, Nicholas Nielson, James Port.

D: 9 Feb. 1767: P: 16 Feb. 1767. R: 17 Feb. 1767. pp. 197-199 WBA.

Andrew Elliott, Savannah, mariner. Friends: John Ross of London, merchant, and Thomas Davis of London, mariner, 25 pounds Sterling each. Remainder of estate, real and personal, to Isabella, the dau. of Sylvia Elliott a free Negro woman living in Gambia on the coast of Guinea and "the reputed daughter of me," when she is twenty-one years of age or married. Exors: John Ross, Thomas Davis. Wit: John Holmes, Anthony Ellison, John Green.

D: 8 Sept. 1771. P: 4 Oct. 1771. R: 5 Oct. 1771. p. 420 WBA.

John Elliott, Midway, planter. Wife (not named) : five Negroes named Diannah, Cicero, Nanny, March, and Affey; riding chair and chair horse; one-sixth of my household goods; one-sixth of my cattle (in lieu of her Dower) ; use of one-third of my plantation during her widowhood. Remainder of personal estate to be divided equally among the following children: Ann, John, William, Thomas, Amarantha, when they are twenty years of age. Land to be divided among sons and my lots in Sunbury among my daus. Exors: son, John; brother, John Quarterman; John Winn; John Stewart, Sr. Wit: John Portrees, James Maxwell, William Quarterman.

D: 29 April 1765. P: 30 Oct. 1765. R: 31 Oct. 1765.

Codicil (same date, same wit) : in division of lands, my son, John's share is to include the plantation on which I now live; only three exors do qualify except to fill up the vacancy in case of death.

Codicil number two (dated 26 July 1765) : Whereas I have verbally sold to my brother-in-law, John Sacheveral, a plantation of 400 acres for the sum of 200 pounds Sterling, the exors are to give him title to the land when he pays for it. Wit: John Osgood, Lydia Sanders, John Portrees.
pp. 142-145 WBA.

William Ely, his mark, Savannah, waggoner. Wife: Catherina, and dau: Elizabeth, entire estate, real and personal, equally divided. Exors: wife and brother, Jacob Ely. Wit: William Stephens, Thomas Reid, John Britton.

D: 25 May 1775. P: 26 Mar. 1777. R: 26 Mar. 1777. pp. 306-307 WBAA.

David Emmanuel, St. George's Parish, planter. Sons: Amos, David, Levi, and Asa, 5 shillings Sterling each, within six months of my death. Daus: Elizabeth, Rebeckah, Martha, and Ruth, 5 shillings Sterling each, within six months after my death. Sons: Amos, three cows and calves and two sows and pigs. David, three cows and calves and two sows and pigs. Asa: value of 20 pounds Sterling in cattle and horses. Levi, tract of land, containing 200 acres where I now live. Dau: Ruth, three cows and calves. Sons: Amos, David, Levi, and Asa and daus: Martha and Ruth, all my books equally divided. Exors are to sell tract of land, containing 200 acres in St. George's Parish on a creek called Chevis's Creek, to pay debts. Remainder of estate to son, Levi. Exor: son, Levi. Wit: David Lewis; Thomas Lewis; Thomas Lewis, Jr.

D: 22 Nov. 1768. P: 6 Mar. 1769. R: 5 Aug. 1769. pp. 302-304 WBA.

John Emmanuel, St. George's Parish. Brothers: Levi, tract of land, containing 100 acres adjoining land of Andrew Hampton on Brier Creek; my cloak. Amos, tract of 150 acres on Rocky Comfort. David, one suit of clothes, saddle, and a yearling heifer to his little son. Asa, my watch. Sisters: Elizabeth Nowland and Rebecca Walker, five shillings each. Martha Duehart, all the money her husband, John, owes me, my silver shoe buckles, and a yearling heifer to her dau Ruth and a black pacing horse to herself, branded "IE." Ruth, her choice of my cows and her calf, a sorrel filly of two years old branded with a B crossways. Remainder of estate to be equally divided between my father and my brother, Levi and my sister, Ruth. Exor: father, David Emmanuel. Wit: David Lewis, Jacob Lewis, Evan Davis, his mark.

D: 21 Mar. 1768. P: 16 June 1768. R: 17 June 1768. pp. 271-273 WBA.

John Eppinger, Savannah, bricklayer. Wife: Barbara, two adjoining lots in Savannah whereon I now live, 500-acre lot at Hampstead formerly belonging to Hysler, all my Negroes. Son: John, half lot in Savannah; 300 acres in St. Matthew's Parish. Daus: Margaret, Hannah, Veneford, and Sarah, 350 acres of land in St. Matthew's Parish, and 50 acres in Christ Church Parish at Acton, equally divided; four five-acre tracts in Christ Church Parish being part of a tract of 80 acres, equally divided. Sons: John, James, George, and Matthias, 60 acres, part of the aforesaid tract of 80 acres; 150-acre tract at Hamstead in Christ Church Parish, equally divided. Children: Margaret, Hannah, Veneford, John, Sarah, James, George, and Matthias, 250 acres of land in St. George's Parish, equally divided. Dau: Margaret, Negro wench named Pender. Exors: wife, sons John, James, George, and Matthias (the latter when they are twenty-one). Wit: Frederick Fahm, Smith Clarendon, Joseph Goldwire.

D: 12 Jan. 1777. P: 8 Jan. 1777. R: 28 Jan. 1777.

Document attached in which William Ewen is empowered to administer the oath of extrix to Barbara Eppinger. Dated 8 Jan. 1777.

Oath of extrix signed by Barbara Eppinger, her mark. Dated 28 Jan. 1777.

pp. 278-282 WBAA.

William Ewen (will partly missing), Savannah. To the poor of Christ Church Parish, 10 pounds Sterling. Nephew: Richard Ewen (son of my eldest brother Richard Ewen) one shilling Sterling. To Jacob Waldhauer of Ebenezer, my wife's brother, tract of 350 acres of land; town lot in Brunswick number forty-nine. Mary Jones, the dau of Col. Noble Jones of Savannah, one mourning ring valued at 10 guineas. Priscilla Holman, wife of John Holman of South Carolina, one mourning ring. Mary Saunders, wife of William Saunders of Savannah, a mourning ring to the value of 40 shillings. Wife: Margaret, all household goods, wearing apparel, cattle, horses, chair, harness, bonds, books, papers, plate, money, accounts, Negroes named Pender, Diana, Hester, Jemmie, Johnny, and others; garden lot in Savannah, number 38 by deed of conveyance from David Unseld to me; my town lot in Ewensburgh; other real estate. Five hundred pounds Sterling to charity

46

school for boys of St. Andrews, Holborn, city of London, to raise a fund for the maintenance of the poor children, as in Christ Hospital. Priscilla Jones, of South Carolina, and Mary Saunders, of Savannah, all money remaining from the sold part of the estate, equally divided. Exors: Wife, The Honorable Archibald Bulloch; William O'Bryen, Esq. Wit to handwriting: Edward Langworthy and Nehemiah Wade.

D: 30 Sept. 1776. P: 20 June 1777. R: n.d. Colonial Loose Will Collection.

Benjamin Farley, planter. Dau: Mary, town lot in Savannah known by the number 9 in Laroche Tything; lot at Yamacraw which I purchased from John Joachim Zubly. Exors to sell horses and cattle (except those needed on the plantation) with the profits to be put at interest for son, Benjamin and dau, Mary. Estate to be kept together by the exors for the maintenance and the education of the children. To be divided equally between them when they become twenty-one. Son: Benjamin, plantation whereon I now live, containing 362 acres; two tracts of land at South Newport, containing 500 acres adjoining lands granted to James Heart. Exors: Joseph Gibbons; William Gibbons; John Bacon of Midway, planter; Joseph Clay of Savannah, merchant. Wit: John Milledge; Thomas Baillie, his mark, of Savannah, blacksmith; Charles Watson.

D: 26 Sept. 1765. P: 25 June 1766. R: 26 June 1766. pp. 148-151 WBA.

John Farley, his mark, Savannah, carpenter. Wife: Elizabeth, use of town lot during her life and after her death the value of it to be equally divided among my children; cattle stock; household goods; remainder of personal estate. Exors: wife, Robert Bolton, Christopher Ring, and The Revd. Mr. Zubly. Wit: Jonathan Bryan, Alexander Sheppard, J. J. Zubly.

D: 27 Dec. 1763. P: 6 Mar. 1764. R: 14 April 1764. pp. 119-120 WBA.

George Faul, St. Matthew's Parish, blacksmith. Wife: Rebeckah, entire estate, including: 100-acre tract of land where I now live two miles below the town of Ebenezer bounding northwest

47

on land of George Glaner and on other sides on vacant land at the time of the survey; personal belongings; sole extrix. Wit: John Wertsch; John Flerl, Jr.; Soloman Zand.

D: 12 Mar. 1767. P: 15 Nov. 1768. R: 22 Nov. 1768. pp. 277-278 WBA.

Martin Fenton, White Bluff. John Houstoun, son of the late Sir Patrick Houstoun, deceased, three Negroes named Prince, Cuffy, and Lucy. Priscilla Houstoun, widow of Sir Patrick Houstoun, remainder of estate, real and personal. Exors: Priscilla Houstoun and Sir Patrick Houstoun (?). Wit: Ann Stuart, John Glenn, James Houstoun. Martin Fenton was too feeble to sign his name to the will and it was signed for him by John Glenn before the other witnesses.

D: 7 Dec. 1768. P: 16 Dec. 1768. R: 29 Dec. 1768. pp. 286-288 WBA.

Joshua Ferguson, planter. Sons: John and James, personal estate, equally divided. Exor: Thomas Cooper of Savannah. Wit: Thos. Carter, John Hoggatt, Benjamin Sheffield.

D: 8 Dec. 1777. P: 2 Jan. 1778. R: n.d. Colonial Loose Will Collection.

Nicholas Fisher (translation from the Dutch sworn to as accurate by John Martin Greiner, dated 13 Feb. 1769). Sister's dau: 200 acres of land. The cattle to be sold to buy a Negro to live with the children. Mentions: Michael Bower (Bener). Wit: John Martin Greiner; Elizabeth Roberts (?), her mark; James Roberts.

D: 8 Jan. 1769. P: 18 Feb. 1769. R: 4 Mar. 1769. pp. 304-305 WBA.

John Fitch, Christ Church Parish, planter. Wife: Anne, use of the entire estate for the rest of her life; the same to be given my cousin, Bryan Kelly, on wife's death. If Bryan Kelly is not living at that time the estate is to go to my three nieces, Mary Ann, Mary, and Ann Perinoue, daus. of Isaac Perinoue, deceased, equally divided. Cousin: Bryan Kelly, all my wearing apparel, long gun, silver mounted pistols. Brother: Tobias Fitch, ten cows and calves, six mares and two young horses. Extrix: wife. Wit: Thomas Gegg; Ezekiel Harlan; John Lamboth, his mark.

D: 3 Nov. 1762. P: 27 May 1763. R: 4 April 1763. pp. 111-112 WBA.

James Fitzsimmons, Savannah, tavernkeeper. Wife: Mary, entire estate, real and personal. Exors: wife and Peter Francis Greniere. Peter Francis Greniere, wearing apparel, watch. Martha Greniere, my wife's mother, suit of mourning apparel. Wit: Benjamin Prime, Thomas Ried, John Heffernan (Heffarnan).

D: 15 Mar. 1769. P: 29 Mar. 1769. R: 4 April 1769. pp. 305-307 ᵥBA.

Joseph Fitzwalter, his mark (will partly missing), Savannah. Wife: Pennellopy, town lot number 8 in Wilmington Tything Derby Ward; my garden lot number 37 lying east of the ....; farm lot number 9; personal estate. After wife's death I bequeath the above lands to my children (now in England) by my former wife, Mary Fitzwalter, provided any of them come to Georgia within two years of my wife's death. If none comes, the bequest to John Horton and Elizabeth Wright. My tract of land on the east of St. Augustine's Creek formerly called ...., together with the stock of hogs thereon to be included in the above estate. Wit: John Pye, (John?) Robe.

D: 18 Oct. 1742. P: n.d. R: n.d. Colonial Loose Will Collection.

Penelope Fitzwalter, Savannah, widow. Francis Robe of Savannah, widow, all personal estate. In the event of her death, the bequest to John Milledge, Esq. Mary Elizabeth Milledge, dau of John Milledge, town lot in Savannah in Wilmington Tything Darby Ward, number 7; farm lot. John Milledge, Jr., town lot in Savannah in Frederic Tything Darby Ward, number 10; farm lot. Exor: John Milledge, Esq. Wit: Lewis Warner, his mark; John Leonard Niess; Charles Watson.

D: 7 Oct. 1765. P: 19 Nov. 1767. R: 30 Nov. 1767. pp. 233-235 WBA.

Charles Flerl, his mark, Ebenezer, St. Matthew's Parish, planter. Wife: Mary, all estate, including two 50-acre tracts, town lot and garden lot, cattle, horses. Extrix. Wit: John Wertsch; George Heckel, his mark; Philip Portz.

D. 1 May 1764. P: 14 Aug. 1767. R: 14 July 1767(?) pp. 221-222 WBA.

John Flerl, St. Matthew's Parish, planter. Wife: Dorothea, two Negroes named Peter and Catherina, use of my land where I now reside for the remainder of her life. Son: Israel, 150 acres of land where I now reside after my wife's death. Dau: Mary, my town lot in Ebenezer which I received of my father-in-law, Matthias Brandner; Negro child named Salome. Exors to sell: 100-acre tract I bought from Hanne and Elizabeth Unseld; 100-acre pine barren joining Thomas Soveighofers land; my horses, cattle, and part of my household goods, all to pay my debts. Remainder of personal estate equally divided between wife and two children. Exor: John Wertsch of Ebenezer. Wit: Nathaniel Briesser; Matthew Zettler; Andrew Seckinger, his mark.

D: 27 Sept. 1776. P: 16 Jan. 1777. R: 31 Jan. 1777.

Document attached in which John Adam Treutlen and Jacob Casper Waldhauer are empowered to administrate the oath of exor to John Wertsch. Dated 16 Jan. 1777.

Oath of exor. signed by John Wertsch. Dated 16 Jan. 1777. pp. 285-287 WBAA.

Mary Flerl, her mark, wife of Charles Flerl, deceased, of Ebenezer, St. Matthew's Parish. Son: John Gruber, son of my second husband, Peter Gruber, deceased, entire estate after debts are paid; exor. Wit: John Wertsch; John Martin Paulitz; Andrew Seckinger, his mark.

D: 18 June 1764. P: 14 Aug. 1767. R: 14 July 1767(?) pp. 222-223 WBA.

John Forbes, Gent. Janet, a free girl now at my household, 200 pounds Sterling. To a mulatto girl of Babet's dau in Charles Town named Dyna, her freedom, also a trust fund of 100 pounds

Sterling to her to be administered by the exors. Uncles: George Forbes of Bermuda, physician and Benjamin Forbes, an officer in France, remainder of estate, equally divided. Exors: Roger Kelsall; Edward Telfair; John Simpson of Charles Town, merchant; Charles Ogilvie of London, Esq. Mentions: Basil Cowper of Savannah, "Jericho" (residence of the testator).

D: 25 Feb. 1775. P: 17 April 1775. R: n.d. pp. 148-150 WBAA.

Magdalene Fountain, her mark, widow. Dau: Jane Cary, personal goods. John Cary, Junior, town lot in Savannah, and its garden lots, total of 50 acres, temporal estate. Exors: John Cary, Sr. and his wife. Wit: Matthew Mauve, John Pye.

D: 15 Sept. 1754. P: 14 Oct. 1755. R: n.d. pp. 11-12 WBA.

Benjamin Fox, Christ Church Parish, planter. Son: Benjamin (when twenty-one or married), plantation on which I live in Christ Church Parish, containing about 1300 acres; one fourth of all my Negroes. Household goods, horses, hogs, and cattle to be divided equally among son, Benjamin and daus: Ann, Elizabeth and Mary. Daus. also to have one third each of the remaining real estate. Brother: John, shirts. Brother-in-law: Joseph Raynes, my silver watch. Wearing apparel to be divided among my brothers: George and James Fox, and Joseph Raynes. Exors: John, William, and George Fox, Joseph Raynes. Mentions: John McMahan.

D: .... 1773. P: 2 July 1773. R: 27 July 1773. pp. 44-48 WBAA.

David Fox, Christ Church Parish. Wife: Catherine, Negro girl named Hannah. Lands, slaves, moneys, and stocks all to be equally divided among wife and children: William, Joseph, John, and David (to receive when twenty-one or married). Exors. wife; brothers, John and William Fox. Wit: Christopher Dawson, John MacLean, Lauchlin McGillvray.

D: 11 Dec. 1766. P: 7 Jan. 1767. R: 7 Jan. 1767. p. 189 WBA.

David Fox, Sr., his mark, Little Ogeechee. Wife: Elizabeth, household furniture, use of all goods and real estate, except

51

Negro boy named Primas that I gave my son, Benjamin, for her lifetime. On her death the estate is to be divided as follows: Sons: Benjamin, Richard, James, and George, all real estate, equally divided. Six children: Jonathan, Benjamin, Richard, James, George, and Ann, cattle and horses equally divided. Children: Benjamin, Richard, James, George, Nancy, all Negroes equally divided. Exors: sons, Benjamin and Richard. Wit: Richard Warren, Edward Delegal, Francis Pary.

D: 30 Mar. 1760. P: 11 Nov. 1762. R: 11 Nov. 1762. pp. 86-88 WBA.

James Fox, Christ Church Parish, planter. Wife: Ann, 10 pounds Sterling, my house, my worst feather bed, one third my household furniture. Dau: Mary, Negroes named Cuffy and Juda, second best feather bed, one third household furniture. Son: James, three Negroes named London, Jack, and Betty, best feather bed, one third household furniture. Exors to sell tract of land, containing 300 acres in St. George's Parish and use the profits to buy a Negro for son, James. If he dies before coming of age, his share of the estate to my niece and nephew, Mary Ann and Richard Fox, son and dau of my brother, William Fox. Exors: brothers, William and Jonathan. Wit: John McMahan, Joseph Raynes, James Cook.

D: 25 Oct. 1773. P: 13 Dec. 1773. R: n.d. pp. 67-68 WBAA.

Richard Fox, Christ Church Parish, planter. Brothers: William of Christ Church Parish, planter, tract of land whereon I now live, containing 326½ acres, in Savannah; all my horses, hogs, cows, and calves. George, of Christ Church Parish, planter, two tracts of land in St. David's Parish on the Buffalo Swamp, containing about 800 acres; five Negroes. Benjamin, four Negroes. John, two Negroes. Jonathan, 5 shillings Sterling. James, 5 shillings Sterling. Sister: Ann, use of Negro woman during her lifetime, the same woman to nephew, Richard Fox, son of William on her death. Niece: Mary Fox, dau. of James, one Negro. David Fox, son of John Fox, one Negro. Exors: brothers, William and George. Wit: Isaac Baillou, Hugh Sym, Samuel Clarke.

D: 15 April 1771. P: 27 Mar. 1772. R: 28 Mar. 1772. pp. 432-434 WBA.

Benjamin Francis, his mark. Sterling Francis and John Francis, entire estate, real and personal, equally divided after paying 25 pounds Sterling to Frederick Francis as a legacy to him. Exors: Isaac Perry and Joseph Gresham. Wit: Frederick Francis; Mary Francis, her mark; Mary Wade.

D: 21 Aug. 1774. P: 30 Sept. 1774. R: n. d. p. 104 WBAA.

William Francis, of Grantham, Christ Church Parish, Esq. Thomas Palmer of Savannah, 100 acres in Christ Church Parish (part of a grant of 589 acres received by grant from King George, dated 7 Nov. 1758), adjoining land of Lewis Johnson. This tract to his son, Thomas Palmer, on his death; also one half of my wearing apparel. To Thomas Palmer, Jr., six cows, six calves, two steers, one grey horse called Sauguah. Peter Slighterman, planter, 100 acres adjacent to tract given Thomas Palmer; six cows, six calves, two steers, my black horse named Pacer, one half my wearing apparel. To Peter Slighterman in trust, 100 acres for William Slighterman, son of Jeremiah Slighterman of Christ Church Parish, blacksmith, until William is twenty-one years of age, also six cows, six calves, one mare colt, all in trust. Mary Smith of Savannah, my town lot known by the number three in Digby Tything Deckers Ward in Savannah; wharf lot under the Bluff in Savannah; Negro man named George; black riding horse; strawberry roan paceing mare; whatever money will remain due me in the hands of Thomas Lloyd of Savannah, merchant; suit of mourning clothes; a mourning ring. Nephew: Harry Wolford, son of my sister Sarah, 100 pounds Sterling at the age of twenty-one. Brother: John Francis of London, leather dresser and glover, remainder of the 589 acres; other tract of 559 acres in Christ Church Parish, adjoining the lands of Isaac Young; tract of 500 acres in Ogeechee District, Christ Church Parish, bounded by lands granted to William Elliott; tract of 133 acres adjoining the last tract on the northwest; tract of 300 acres on Mill Island in St. Matthew's Parish bounded on the southwest by Christian Rabenhorst; tract of 200 acres in Christ Church Parish; town lot in Hardwick; total aggregate of 1981 acres; also stock of slaves; Indian slave whom I hereby emancipate; all the above provided that my brother comes to Georgia within two years to claim it and reside on it. If he fails to come to Georgia within two years the above bequests are to go to my cousins Walter and James Port of London. In the latter

53

case, brother John Francis, is to receive 100 pounds Sterling. Joseph Ottolenghe, Esq., suit of mourning and a mourning ring. William Ewen, Esq., suit of mourning and a mourning ring. Remainder of estate divided between persons taking over the estate (one half part) and Peter Slighterman in trust for William Slighterman (one fourth part) and Thomas Palmer (one fourth part). Exors: Joseph Ottolenghe, William Ewen, Mary Smith. Wit: John Ludwig Mayer, James Whitefield, William Clifton.

D: 14 Aug. 1762. P: 10 Mar. 1763. R: 30 Mar. 1763.

Codicil (dated 26 Feb. 1763, same wit): Brother, John Francis has died. Either James or Walter Port, (whichever comes first) shall have the estate. Additional exors: James and Walter Port. Exors to sell a thousand weight of "Indico" with the profits to be divided among the following: Matthias Slighterman, John Slighterman, Peter Slighterman (in trust for Jeremiah Slighterman), one part for erecting a font or Baptistry in the new church about to be built in Savannah, and the residue to the poor of Christ Church Parish.

pp. 94-102 WBA.

George Fraser, his mark, Abercorn, planter. Friend: Hugh Ross, entire estate, exor. Wit: Isaac Gibbs; John Stuart; Isaac Gibbs, Jr.

D: 14 June 1751. P: 30 July 1755. R: n.d. pp. 7-8 WBA.

George Fraser, Savannah, practitioner of physick. Wife: Margaret, 1100 acres of land in Georgia, one third of my Negroes, use of household goods during her widowhood. Children: Susannah, Sarah, and Thomas William Fraser, 500 acres of land each, two thirds of my Negroes, equally divided. Remainder of estate to be equally divided among wife and three children. Exors: William Moss of Savannah, merchant; James Houstoun of Savannah, practitioner in physick; and William Miller of Savannah, merchant. Wit: Mary Stephens; Deborah Anderson; Henry Yonge, Jr.

D: 6 Dec. 1775. P: 15 Dec. 1775. R: 15 Oct. (Dec.??) 1775. pp. 215-218 WBAA.

Thomas Frazer, Christ Church Parish, planter. Wife: Catherina, entire estate including: houses, lands, household goods, plantation tools, apparel, horses, hogs, cattle, poultry, Negro fellow named David; extrix. Wit: Peter Theiss; Jacob Theiss, Sr.; Jacob Theiss, Jr.

D: 13 Sept. 1772. P: 23 Dec. 1774. R: 6 July 1775.

Document attached in which Clement Martin and John Stirk are empowered to administer the oath of extrix to Catherina Frazer. Dated 10 Dec. 1774.

Oath of extrix. signed by Catherina Frazer. Dated 25 Feb. 1775.

pp. 174-176 WBAA.

Samuel Fulton, St. Andrew's Parish, planter. Son: Paul, tract of land, containing 400 acres, on the Alatamaha bounded east by land of Mary McClelland, west by lands of Daniel Witherspoon, south by lands of John McClelland, and north by lands vacant at the time of the survey which land I have already made over to my son, Paul Fulton; Negro woman named Judy, already in his possession; I have already given him that part of the estate of John Crawford, deceased, that was due him. Grandson: Samuel Bennet (son of my dau Jane Bennet, deceased), Negro girl named Phebe, Negro boy named Pero, both of which are now in the possession of his father, William Bennet. Also to William Bennet, all that part of the estate of John Crawford, deceased, that belonged to Jane Bennet. Dau: Margaret, wife of Josiah Osgood, Negro woman named Pegg, now in her possession, Negro boy named March. Wife: Christian, one third of my moveable estate, use of my house and household goods during her lifetime. Sons: Samuel and John and dau: Mary McClelland, two thirds of moveable estate, equally divided. Sons: Samuel and John, three tracts of land containing in the whole 624 acres on Cathead Creek in St. Andrew's Parish, equally divided by a North-South line (Samuel to have the east half). Exors: Wife; sons, John and Samuel; brother-in-law, John McClelland. Wit: Benjamin Shuttleworth, Peter Sallens, Reuben Shuttleworth.

D: 24 May 1775. P: 16 Jan. 1776. R: 5 Dec. 1776.

Document attached in which Sir Patrick Houstoun, Bart. and Robert Baillie, Esq. are empowered to administer the oath of exor to the exors. Dated ___ July 1775.

Oath of exor signed by the four exors. Dated 16 Jan. 1776. pp. 263-267 WBAA.

Alexander Fyffe (a confusing, unclear will), Savannah, merchant, "the youngest lawfull son to James Fyffe of Dron being designed to go abroad and considering the certainty of death." Exors: sisters: Magdalen and Elizabeth Fyffe of Dundee in North Britain. Exors to sell all the estate to pay debts. Exors to pay to James Fyffe, my nephew, son of John Fyffe, merchant in Dundee, 30 pounds Sterling. Mentions: Pat Chrichton, Notary Public; George Johnson; James Anderson, Notary Public. Wit: Robert Dick, James Jobson, William Smith all writers in Dundee.

D: 8 Sept. 1756. P: 29 Dec. 1766. R: 13 Mar. 1767.

Document attached in which the exors appoint Doctors Charles Fyffe and William Fyffe both surgeons in Georgetown Wynyade in South Carolina lawful attorneys to execute the will of Alexander Fyffe, their brother. Dated 20 Sept. 1756.

Document attached in which Doctors Charles Fyffe and William Fyffe acknowledge the letter of attorney above and appoint the Honorable John Graham and Samuel Douglas both of Savannah, merchants, as substitute exors. Dated 29 Dec. 1756. pp. 204-208 WBA.

John Gallache, Christ Church Parish, gunsmith. Brother: James Gallache, 100 acres of land in Christ Church Parish (as a grant recorded in the Register's Office 5 Sept. 1760(?); four head of horses branded "Gp", a stone horse branded "A--", a horse known by the name Diamond, branded "Z--", all the remainder of the estate, exor. Wit: Anthione Gautier, John Stanton.

D: 5 May 1755. P: 30 Oct. 1767. R: 5 Aug. 1769. pp. 301-302 WBA.

Richard Gambell, his mark. Sister: Hannah New, wife of John New of the city of Cork, entire estate, after debts are paid. To the governor's Negro woman in consideration of her care for me, 5 pounds Sterling. Wit: W. Jones, Abraham Gay.

D: 2 April 1770. P: 25 July 1771. R: 26 July 1771. pp. 413-414 WBA.

Gasper Garbut, Savannah, Christ Church Parish, carpenter. Wife: Christiana, use of town lot in Savannah known by the number three in the Fourth Tything Anson Ward. After her death this town lot to dau Mary Garbut. Also to wife, Negro wench named Sarah and her two children, Joe and Jem, plate, linen, household goods, kitchen and furniture. Son: George, town lot in Savannah known by the number five in Sloper Tything Percival Ward (this lot was granted to Isaac Baillou by grant bearing the date 6 Dec. 1757 from the king. By deed of 26 May 1769 he conveyed the same to me and it now in the occupation of   Mick Widow); tract of land, including 200 acres in St. Matthew's Parish, bounded on the southeastward by lands of Frederick Herb, southwestward by Great Ogechee River, and on every other side by land vacant at the time of the survey; Negro man named Peter; my carpenter tools. Frederick Fahm and John Richards both of Savannah, half town lot in Savannah, number seven in the Fourth Tything Anson Ward, containing 45 acres, to hold in trust and to sell on my wife's death and divide the profits among my children, George and Mary. Son, George, to be put at a trade of his choice. Exors: wife, John Richards, Frederick Fahm. Wit: Charles Pryce; Henry Preston; C. Pryce, Jr.

D: 9 April 1772. P: 22 Nov. 1776. R: 22 Nov. 1776. pp 253-257 WBAA.

James Garvey, Christ Church Parish, Gent. Dau: Elinor Garvey of Edgeworth Town near Mulingar in the Kingdom of Ireland, all estate, real and personal. Exor: Garret Allen of Savannah, lawyer. Wit: James Lowe, Patrick McCann, Cornelius Driscoll.

D: 21 Sept. 1772. P: 9 Oct. 1772. R: n.d. pp. 80-81 WBAA.

Anthione Gautier (Gotere), Savannah, laborer. Wife: Jean, house and lot in Savannah, farm lot containing 45 acres, garden lot containing five acres in Purysburg, South Carolina, town lot at Purysburg, household goods, furniture, debts and moveables, all for her natural life, Extrix. Dau: Jane, the wife of George Fox, 25 pounds Georgia currency; my wife's wearing apparel after her death. Children: David Gotere and Jane Fox, after wife's death, all household goods, furniture, and moveables, equally divided. Son: David, house and lot in Savannah, wearing apparel. Wit: John Eppinger, John Spencer, George Basil Spencer.

D: 26 Mar. 1772. P: 11 Jan. 1774. R: n.d. pp. 73-74 WBAA.

Michael Germain, Savannah, mariner. Wife: Priscilla, temporal estate, including town lot number four in Jeykil Tything Derby Ward, with the farm lot and the garden lot belonging to it; Negro man named Piero; Negro boy named Sippio, all my cattle branded "MGS Anchor," horses. Mother: Ann Emery, use of one room in my aforesaid house in Savannah. Wit: John Pye, Ann Young, John F. Triboudete.

D: 23 July 1753. P: 5 Jan. 1769. R: 7 Jan. 1769. pp. 295-296 WBA.

John Gibbons, Christ Church Parish, planter. Son: John, tract of land, containing 200 acres in Christ Church Parish. Sons: Thomas Gibbons and John Barton, tract of land I now live on and one other tract of one hundred acres adjoining the aforesaid tract, to be cultivated for the benefit of my estate during the minority of my children. Dau: Susannah, 10 pounds yearly of my estate, until my debts are paid and then 125 pounds Sterling to be taken from my estate and put to interest, with the annual interest to my dau Susannah. Son: John, one Negro named March. Wife, one sixth of the remaining moveable estate, my house during her widowhood. Remainder of the estate to be kept together for the benefit of the other children (five youngest— not including John and Susannah). Exors: brother, William Gibbons; friends, Joseph Gibbons and his brother, William Gibbons; my two sons, John and Thomas. Wit: William Fox; George Fox; William Gibbons, Jr.

D: 8 Nov. 1770. P: 19 Dec. 1770. R: 20 Dec. 1770. pp. 368-370 WBA.

Joseph Gibbons, Christ Church Parish, Esq. Son: Joseph, 1500 acres of land (enumerated). Son: William, 1562 acres of land (enumerated); water lot under the Bluff or Bank at Savannah to the East of Bull Street. Son: Thomas: 2772 acres of land (enumerated). Son: John, 1000 acres of River Swamp in Christ Church Parish which I purchased of Richard Cox the Elder by Alexander Inglis and Nathaniel Hall, his attorneys. Dau: Hannah, tract of land containing 500 acres on the South side of Newport adjoining the public landing at Donnam's Mill; two hundred acres of PineLand, heretofore granted to Andrew Way; town lot in Savannah I purchased of William Russell, Esq. Daus: Sarah and Mary, 1000 acres of land lying on a branch of the Buffalo Swamp on the fourth side and near the Alatamaha River. Ann, 500 acres of land on the Lake Swamp above Fort Barrington near the Alatamaha River, Negro girl named Sue. Wife: (not named) town lot and garden lot in Savannah, which I purchased of Charles Bowler. Lots at Yamacraw to be divided as follows: son, Thomas, one lot near the Bluff or Savannah River; son, John one lot near the Bluff or Savannah River; dau, Ann, one lot; dau, Sarah, one lot; son, Joseph, one lot; dau, Mary, one lot. Dau: Sarah, Negro girl named Sabina. Exors to keep the personal estate together until the children are of age, and then to be equally divided among the children and my wife. Exors: wife; brother, William; friend, John Martin, Esq.; sons, Joseph and William (when they are twenty-one). Wit: J. J. Zubly, Alexander Inglis, David Brydie.

D: 16 July 1769. P: 25 July 1769. R: 28 July 1769.

Codicil (dated 17 July 1769, same wit): Sum of 507 pounds and ten shillings Sterling granted to son, Joseph, to purchase Negroes, shall be deducted from his share of the personal estate. Dau: Hannah, Negro girl named Charlott. Dau: Mary, mulatto girl named Leah. Additional exors: son, Thomas (when of age) and brother John.

pp. 313-320 WBA.

William Gibbons, Christ Church Parish, planter. Sons: William, tract of land containing 500 acres in Christ Church Parish purchased by me of Joseph Parker; piece of land (south end of tract of 365 acres) adjoining Newington Village in Christ Church

Parish. Barak, tract of land, containing 90 acres on which my dwelling house now stands; tract containing 265 acres (part of the 365 acres adjoining Newington Village), tract of 73 acres; two other tracts containing 300 acres purchased of James Baillou. Sons: James Martin Gibbons and Joseph Gibbons, two tracts of land on Great Satilla River, containing 872 acres. Wife: Sarah, town lot in Savannah for the remainder of her life and to son, Joseph on her death, Negro wench named Winter, a house wench, chaise, any two horses. Son: Josiah, two tracts of land, containing 720 acres on the Newport River in St. Matthew's Parish. Son: James Martin Gibbons, water lot under the Bluff or Bank at Savannah to the west of Bull Street. Daus: Sarah, Negro girl named Silvia. Mary, Negro girl named Tamar. Mentions: James Habersham, Bartholomew Zouberbuhler, Benjamin Singleton, Gouvernor Ellis. Exors: wife; brothers, Joseph and John; kinsman, John Martin; sons, William and Josiah Gibbons. Wit: N. Jones; Joseph Gibbons, Jr.; J. J. Zubly.

D: 6 Mar. 1769. P: n.d. R: n.d. pp. 382-391 WBA.

William Gibbons, Christ Church Parish, planter. Son: Josiah, tract of land, containing 530 acres; another tract, containing 220 acres; both tracts are on Newport River in St. Andrew's Parish. If child with which my wife is now pregnant is a boy, then he and Josiah are to hold the above tracts as tenants in common. Personal estate divided equally among my wife and all my children. Mentions: my two brothers, Joseph and John Gibbons, both deceased, son, William. Exors: The Reverend John Osgood; The Reverend John Joachim Zubly; John Winn, Esq.; nephews, William and Joseph Gibbons; wife; John Martin. Wit: William Young, John Davis, William Brabant.

D: 8 Feb. 1771. P: 26 Feb. 1771. R: n.d.

Document attached in which Jonathan Bryan and Noble Wimberly Jones are empowered to administer the oath of exor to Sarah Gibbons and John Martin. Dated 27 Feb. 1771.

Oath of exor signed by Sarah Gibbons and John Martin. Dated 27 Feb. 1771.

Colonial Loose Will Collection.

William Gilbert, Island of Wilmington, planter. Son: John, lot of land number 310 in Beaufort, South Carolina; Negro man named Lewis; Negro boy named Nimrod. Son: William, tract of land containing 500 acres, on Great St. tilley known by the name Round About; Negro man named Will; Negro girl named Maryann. Dau: Elizabeth, 100 acres on Wilmington Island, which is part of a 200-acre tract I now live on; Negro woman named Moll and one girl named Lindy. Dau: Sarah, one hundred acres on Wilmington Island, the other part of a 200-acre tract I now live on; Negro woman named Sibbe; Negro girl named Ameali. Wife: use of all my estates during her lifetime; Negro girl named Chloe. Remainder of estate, at my wife's death, I give to the use and the maintenance of my daus, Elizabeth and Sarah. Exors: wife, Sarah; friends, Louis Turner of Whitmarsh Island; Christopher Ring of Savannah. Wit: Timothy Barnard, John Barnard, Jane Barnard.

D: 15 Dec. 1768. P: 4 Sept. 1775. R: 6 Sept. 1775. pp. 182-184 WBAA.

John Giovanoli. Sons: David, Nicholas, Samuel, 50 pounds Sterling each (to be paid one year after my death), all my wearing apparel. Dau: Hannah, all my late wife's wearing apparel, 10 pounds Sterling. Remainder of the estate divided among my six children: Hannah, Joseph, Benjamin, John, Jonathan, and Helena (as they come of age). Exor to be guardian of the children and the estate. Exor: John Joachim Zubly. Wit: Jonathan Peat; Thomas Flyming; John Van Rensselair.

D: 22 Feb. 1770. P: 2 Sept. 1771. R: 4 Sept. 1771. p. 416 WBA.

Thomas Goldsmith, Sr., Golden Grove, St. Philip's Parish, Esq. Son: Thomas, one half of entire estate, real and personal. Wife: Hannah, one half of entire estate, real and personal. Her half of the estate to son, Thomas, on her death. Exors: wife, and son, Thomas. Wit: Henry Yonge, Jr.; George Herdman; The Reverend Timothy Lowthen.

D: 7 May 1772. P: 10 March 1774. R: n.d. pp. 87-88 WBAA.

Benjamin Goldwire, Christ Church Parish, carpenter. Wife: Ann, use of town lot number one in Holland Tything during her lifetime. After her death this lot is to go to my eldest son, Benjamin. Other lands divided equally among other children: eldest dau Mary, youngest dau Amy, second son Joseph, youngest son John. Also to wife: one third personal estate, Negro woman named Frank, and her children. Remainder of the personal estate divided among my children. Son: Benjamin and son-in-law: Peter Morel, my carpenter tools, books of architecture, and pump tools, equally divided. Exors: wife, John Smith, Thomas Vincent, David Fox, John Goldwire, John Morel. Mentions: Ann Cuthbert. Wit: Noble Wimberly Jones, Jasper Shargots Whitehart, John Morel, Francis Colson.

D: 30 May 1766. P: 9 July 1766. R: 9 July 1766. pp. 161-163 WBA.

John Goldwire, Sr., St. Matthew's Parish. Son: John, tract of land, containing 300 acres in St. Matthew's Parish near Buck Creek, joining lands of Captain Phillip Howel; three Negroes named Tom, Caesar, and Prymis; one half my stock of cattle (ranging around Mount Pleasant). This bequest to my granddau, Sarah King, if John dies without lawful heirs. Dau: Sarah King, use of the labor of ten slaves (named), use of one tract of land, containing 300 acres in St. Matthew's Parish (which was conveyed to me by James Nelson); one half my stock of cattle and hogs; three horses; carriage, household furniture (except my clock and mahogany tables). This bequest to her children when they come of age. Son: James, tract of land, containing 200 acres, in St. Matthew's Parish, where he now lives; another tract of 600 acres; three tracts at Mount Pleasant whereon I now live, containing 400 acres; a tract of 500 acres in South Carolina on the Savannah River, opposite Mount Pleasant; 14 slaves (named), one half the hogs and horses; wearing apparel; my clock, watch, and mahogany tables; my books and firearms. Grandson: John King, 9 slaves (named); one tract of land on Ogechee River in Christ Church Parish, containing 300 acres; one tract in St. Matthew's Parish joining lands of Peter Tondee, containing 400 acres; a tract joining the above mentioned tract, containing 50 acres; two horses. Granddau: Sarah King, Negro girl named Bat. Ann Goldwire of Savannah, widow and her children: Ann Goldwire (10 pounds Sterling); Benjamin Goldwire (20 pounds Sterling); Mary Morell and her children (30 pounds Sterling) ; Amy McGilvery (20 pounds Sterling) ; Joseph Goldwire (20 pounds Sterling) ; John Goldwire (20 pounds Sterling) ; total of 120 pounds Sterling to be raised out of my estate. Exor: son, James. Wit: Charles Parkes, his mark; William Hammond; James Goldwire; William King.

D: 10 Aug. 1774. P: 8 March 1775. R: n.d. pp. 135-138 WBAA.

James Goodall, St. George's Parish in Halifax, planter. Son: Pleasant, tract of land, adjoining land of William Macdanniels, which he now lives on. At death of my wife, all the personal estate to be divided equally among children: Clary Moore, William, Martha, Sarah, Pleasant, Francis, Mary, Elizabeth. Wife: Mary, use of remainder of my estate during her lifetime, to be divided among my children at her death. Exors: wife; son, William; and Andrew McCorrie. Wit: Benjamin Williamson, Robert Williamson.

D: 13 April 1768. P: 17 June 1768. R: 23 June 1768.

Document attached to loose will which includes an inventory of the estate of James Goodall signed by John Green, John Casper Greiner, John Casper Hersman.

pp. 274-275 WBA.

Mungo Graham, Savannah. Estate to be divided equally among my children: James Graham, Elizabeth Butler, and Alice Fullalove, and Mungo Fonlayson, my nephew. James Love and his wife, 10 pounds Sterling each. Exor: James Love. Wit: John Teasdale, Thomas Flyming, Robert Kirkwood.

D: n.d. P: 3 Dec. 1766. R: 3 Dec. 1766.

Document attached to loose will which includes an inventory of the estate of Mungo Graham at the time of his decease. Signed Robert Kirkwood and Thomas Flyming.

p. 178 WBA.

Patrick Graham, Josephs Town. Brother: David, all my lands in Redford in the Shire of Perth in North Britain, 100 pounds Sterling. Mungo Graham, tract of land on Pipemaker's Creek, containing 450 acres. Wife: Ann, remainder of estate, real and personal. Sister: Mary Graham, relict of John Grenly (Gunly), deceased, 150 pounds Sterling. Niece: Ann Graham, dau of my brother Thomas Graham, deceased, 100 pounds Sterling. Extrix: wife, Wit: Patrick Mackay, Isab. Mackay, George Cuthbert.

D: 26 May 1755. P: 27 Aug. 1755. R: n.d. pp. 9-10 WBA.

George Gray, St. Andrew's Parish, planter. Negroes and chattels to be sold to pay debts. The tract I now live on may not be sold under 2000 pounds Sterling, unless necessary to pay debts, in less than five years from the date of this will. Remainder of estate to be divided between my brothers and sisters. To Catherine Morrison, Negro wench called Betty. Exors: William Gray, Esq. of Jamaica; The Honorable James Mackay of Georgia; George McIntosh, planter, of Georgia. Wit: Ann Morrison, Catherine Morrison, Margery Morrison.

D: 15 April 1766. P: 4 April 1777. R: 8 April 1777. pp. 310-311 WBAA.

Rosannah Gregory, her mark, Christ Church Parish, widow. Dau: Mary Rouvier (by Simon Rouvier, my first husband), entire estate, real and personal. If dau dies without heirs, the bequest to my son, James. If son dies without heirs, the same to the children of .... Cander (sister of my late husband Simon Rouvier), equally divided. Exor: James Muter of Christ Church Parish, planter. Wit: Benjamin Weddall, William Kynnier, John Hunter.

D: 1 Jan. 1774. P: 21 Jan. 1774. R: n.d. pp. 76-78 WBAA.

John Grover, "one of the Fellows of King's College, Cambridge, but now of the province of Georgia." Richard Potinger, Esq., clerk of the Privy Seal now living in Cork Street Burlington Gardens, London, entire estate, real and personal, to be kept in trust for my mother, Carolina Grover for the rest of her natural life and then to the said Richard Potinger. Exor: James Hume. Wit: Mary Hume, Elizabeth Tannatt.

D: 9 July 1772. P: 12 Aug. 1774. R: n.d. pp. 96-97 WBAA.

James Habersham, Sr., Savannah, Esq. Son: James, plantation called "Silk Hope," containing 500 acres; tracts of land, containing the following number of acres: 118, 100, 300, 80, 500, 500, 500, 71, 197, 175, 82, and 300, total of 3423 acres in the district of Little Ogechee in Christ Church Parish. Also three other tracts of 500, 500, and 800 acres in St. George's Parish; all household furniture and books at "Silk Hope," gold repeating watch, 600 pounds current money. Son: Joseph, tracts of land containing the following number of acres: 900, 150, 40, 300, 250, 229, 103, 100, and 100, total of 2172 acres in the district of Little Ogechee in Christ Church Parish. Also three other tracts of 340, 332, and 328 acres on the south side of Great Ogechee River in St. Philip's Parish. Also lot in Savannah known by the number six in Wilmington Tything Derby Ward and the farm lot belonging to it. Another town lot in Savannah, known by the number seven in Wilmington Tything Derby Ward, lot number 32 in Hardwicke, household furniture in Savannah house, silver plate, gold rings. Son: John, plantation containing 500 acres called "Dean Forrest;" tract of 382 acres; tract of 118 acres; all in Christ Church Parish. 2160 acres in St. Mary's Parish. Lot in Savannah known by the letter "L" in Ellis Square Digby Tything, which I purchased of Henry Ellis, three farm lots, gold watch, Negro woman named Jenny, 400 pounds current money. Joseph Clay (son of my nephew Joseph Clay), lot number 35 in Brunswick. James Clay (also son of my nephew Joseph Clay), lot number 85 in Brunswick. Sister: Mary Bagwith of Yorkshire in Great Britain, 50 pounds Sterling. Nephew: Joseph Clay, and his wife, 25 pounds Sterling for a mourning suit each. Bro-in-law: Robert Bolton, 10 pounds Sterling for a mourning suit. Granddau: Mary (dau of son, James), Negro girl named Fatima. To her brother Alexander at her death. Remainder of estate, equally divided among my three sons. Mentions: Jonathan Bryan; Miss Esther Rasberry; Lachlan McGillivray; Rudolph Pury; Alexander Wylly; Richard Fox, Philip Delegal, Sr.; Elizabeth Deveaux; William Gibbons, Jr.; James Sunier; Peter Guirard; Henry Bourguine; Charles Watson; Noble Wimberly Jones; Charles Burnett; James Wright;

Thomas Netherclift; William Thomas Harris; Daniel Demetre; John Giovanoli; Mordecai Sheftall; Thomas Burrington; Alexander Crighton; Revd. Mr. George Whitefield, a friend for 33 years. Exors: sons, James, Joseph, and John Habersham. Wit: John Jamieson, John Storr, John Fox.

D: 8 May 1775. P: 23 Nov. 1775. R: 13 Sept. 1776. pp. 232-246 WBAA.

Henry Hamilton, Savannah. Children: Thomas, Charles, Elizabeth, and Francis, 10 pounds Sterling each (when of age). Wife: Francis, all my lands, houses, tenements in Savannah, Hardwick, or elsewhere. Land to be divided among sons on the death of my wife. Remainder of personal estate to wife. Exors: wife; The Honorable Noble Jones; William Spencer. Wit: Bartholomew Zouberbuhler, Hugh Ross, Daniel Steuart (Stewart).

D: 7 June 1760. P: 23 Oct. 1760. R: 22 June 1761. pp. 58-59 WBA.

Francis Harris, Savannah, Esq. Son: Francis Henry Harris, lot in Savannah number one in Frederick Tything Darby Ward; plantation at Little Ogechee called "Mear (?)," containing about 1300 acres; one-half of all my Negroes, horses, cattle, hogs, sheep, goats and all other personal estate; tracts containing 3400 acres on Little Ogechee (to pay his sister Elizabeth one-half the value of these tracts). Dau: Elizabeth Harresall, tracts of land, containing 1150 acres at Great Ogechee called Bushy Park, adjoining lands of Joseph Wright and William Elliott; one-half of all my Negroes, horses, cattle, hogs, sheep, goats, all other personal estate. Mentions: my late brother, Thomas Harris of London; Joseph Clay of Savannah, merchant. Nephew: William Harris and his wife, John Field and his wife, and _____ Brown and his wife, all of London in England, 10 pounds Sterling each for a mourning ring. Exors: The Honorable James Habersham, Esq.; Philip Delegal, Esq.; Joseph Clay; son, Francis Henry Harris (when he is of age). Wit: William Young, William Watt, William Brabant.

D: 15 July 1771. P: 29 Oct. 1771. R: 1 Nov. 1771. pp. 422-424 WBA.

William Harvey, his mark, Williamsburgh on Ogechee River, "belonging to Captain John Williams' Troop of Rangers." Exor: Henry Green, a Ranger. Estate to Henry Green and his wife who have taken care of me during this sickness. Wit: Charles Maran, Jonathan Smithes.

D: 10 Mar. 1744/5. P: 13 Sept. 1745. R: n.d. Colonial Loose Will Collection.

John Harwell, "late of Augusta," planter. Wife: Ann, entire estate, real and personal. Exors: wife and Daniel Nunas. Wit: J. Barnard, Andrew Johnston, Ambrose Bart.

D: 3 Aug. 1755. P: 11 Aug. 1755. R: n.d. p. 8 WBA.

Marguerite Jean Henri, her mark, Purisburg. (Will is in French). Exor: The Revd. John Joachim Zubly. Wit: Hannah Stirk, Samuel Stirk, Elizabeth Farley.

D: 30 Nov. 1772 (?). P: 23 April 1773. R: n.d. Colonial Loose Will Collection; p. 31 WBAA.

James Herron, St. Paul's Parish, planter. Wife: Anne Martilina Herron, entire estate, real and personal. At her death the entire estate to dau, Elizabeth. My estate was purchased of Richard Womack. To wife, one-fourth of the profits of a sum of money I daily expect to receive from Germany. Dau: Elizabeth, one-fourth of the money from Germany. Anne Tinley, one-fourth of the money from Germany, one black mare and mare colt. Mary Smith, my wife's dau, one-fourth of the money from Germany, one bay mare with a horse colt. Father: John Herron, residing in Ireland, 10 pounds Sterling for the rest of his life. Sisters: Mary Herron and Elizabeth Chambers, 10 pounds Sterling each, yearly. Cousin: Joseph Caughran, all my wearing apparel. Exors: Robert Rae, James Rae, George Whitefield. Mentions: Aunt Tennet Rae of Ireland.

D: 20 Aug. 1771. P (by oath of Robert Rae): 21 June 1774. R: n.d.

Document attached in which Edward Barnard, Thomas Waters, and John Daniel Hammerer are empowered to administer the oath of exor to James Rae. Dated 21 June 1774 and 6 Aug. 1774.

Oath of exor signed by James Rae. Dated 22 Aug. 1774.
pp. 98-103 WBAA.

George Heyd, St. Matthew's Parish, planter. Wife: Maria Magdalena, a black-speckled cow with a white face and her calf, all the cattle she owned before our matrimony; all the household furniture she then had. Remainder of the furniture to be equally divided between my sons, Christian, Israel, and Abiel. Exor: David Steiner of Ebenezer. Wit: George Schweiger, his mark; Christian Steiner; Jacob Cronberger.

D: 29 Oct. 1770. P: 7 Nov. 1770. R: 9 Nov. 1770. pp. 359-360 WBA.

William Hickson (Hixon), his mark. St. Paul's Parish. Wife: Elizabeth, my plantation whereon I now live for her widowhood; at her decease plantation to my son, Timothy. Also to wife, one bed and furniture, two cows, two sows and pigs. Son: John, 60 acres of land in the Garvey's, an improvement I had of George Murrow, containing 300 acres. Dau: Elizabeth, loom and furniture. Son: William, one-half my land. Son: Timothy, other half my land. Dau: Ann, one heifer, a year old next spring. Daus: Mary and Kashiah, 5 shillings each. Exors: wife and eldest son, John. Wit: Richard Smith; Phebe Smith, her mark; John Still.

D: 19 Sept. 1770. P: 23 May 1772. R: 12 June 1772.

Document attached in which Joseph Maddock and John Oliver, Esqs. are empowered to administer the oath of exor to Elizabeth and John Hixon. Dated 7 Jan. 1772.

Oath of exor administered by Joseph Maddock. Dated 13 May 1773.

pp. 441-443 WBA.

John Hobson, St. Paul's Parish. Entire estate to be divided among the following after debts are paid: my mother, Agnes Gillam; my three brothers, Matthew, Nicholas, and William; my sisters, Elizabeth Bugg, Mary Bilbon, Obedinee Bacon, Agnes Bacon, Sara Hobson, and Margret Hobson. Exors: brothers, Matthew and Nicholas Hobson and Richard Gilliam. Wit: Nehemiah Wade, John Bacon, George Jackson Powell.

D: 28 Oct. 1767. P: 6 Jan. 1768. R: 8 Jan. 1768. pp. 243-244 WBA.

Samuel Holmes, his mark, planter. Wife: Helena, all my lands, lots, buildings, Negroes, household furniture, goods, chattels, for her lifetime. After her death the bequest is to be divided as follows: wife's son: John Tobler, Negro wench named Chloe, Negro boy named Will. Her son: Ulric Tobler, lot of building at Yamacraw where his mother now lives; tract of land on Turkey Creek in South Carolina, containing 100 acres, four Negroes. Helena Holmes Gray, dau of James Gray of Augusta, four Negroes. Ann Tobler, dau of Ulric Tobler, one mourning ring, one suit of mourning clothes. Extrix: wife. Wit: David Zubly, Michael Meyer, John Sturzenhegger.

D: 13 April 1772. P: 20 Feb. 1775. R: n.d.

Document attached in which James Grierson and John Daniel Hammerer, Esq. are empowered to administer the oath of extrix to Helena Holmes. Dated 10 Feb. 1775.

pp. 151-153 WBAA.

Frederick Holzendorf, Savannah, sadler. Wife: Mary Ann, 50 pounds, Georgia currency; my best bed and furniture. Daus: Sarah and Mary, remainder of estate, equally divided. Exors: wife; brother-in-law, Bolzer Miller. Wit: Thomas Moodie; Philip Hughes; Joseph Wood, Jr.

D: 28 Dec. 1767. P: 12 April 1768. R: 14 April 1768. pp. 261-263 WBA.

Benjamin Horn, his mark, St. George's Parish, planter. Wife: Mary, lands, mill, Negroes, horses, hogs, and cattle. Son: Benjamin, one shilling Sterling. On death of wife, entire estate to be divided among my grandchildren. Exors: Edward Weathers and John Anderson. Wit: Edward Weathers, his mark; John Anderson.

D: 6 Nov. 1775. P: 12 Dec. 1776. R: 12 Dec. 1776. pp. 269-270 WBAA.

Nicholas Horton, Savannah, vintner. Wife: Mary, all estate, real and personal. Exors: wife, John Stirk, William Young. Wit: David Montaigut; Chris. F. Ring; Jno. Detheridge.

D: 6 Feb. 1774. P: 9 Mar. 1774. R: n.d. pp. 82-83 WBAA.

Sir Patrick Houstoun, Savannah, Bart. Wife: Priscilla, entire estate, real and personal. Exors: wife, brother-in-law, Captain George Dunbar. Wit: Hugh Ross, Ann Steuart, John Ross.

D: 11 Feb. 1761. P: 15 April 1762. R: n.d. pp. 83-84 WBA.

Priscilla Houstoun, Savannah, widow and relict of Sir Patrick Houstoun. Dau: Ann, wife of George McIntosh, Esq., Negro girl named Chloe and her son, George; my rings and wearing apparel. Son: Sir Patrick, silver plate. Miss Ann Stuart, suit of mourning and mourning ring. Son: James, Negro boy named Abraham. Son: John, Negro wench named Hannah and her son. Exors to dispose of Negroes and remainder of estate. Following legacies to be paid out of the profits: Son: William, 500 pounds, Georgia currency when he is twenty-one or married. Son: George, 500 pounds, Georgia currency. Dau: Ann McIntosh, 500 pounds, Georgia currency. Rest of the money to be equally divided between sons, James and John. Exors: sons, George and John. Exors to pay debt of 100 pounds, Georgia currency to Messrs. Johnston and Simpson of Charlestown, merchants, for articles provided by them for my son, John, while he was at his education in Charlestown. Wit: Thomas Ross, James Simpson, William Ross, James Beverly.

D: 10 June 1772. P: 8 Mar. 1775. R: n.d. pp. 131-134 WBAA.

John Howell, St. George's Parish. Son: David, 10 pounds Sterling, my gun or fowling piece. Dau: Abigail, two pounds, 10 shillings Sterling. Son: James, two pounds, 10 shillings Sterling. Dau: Sarah, eight pounds Sterling, three blankets which I bought of Thomas Lewis, Esq., a cow and her yearling, another young cow (the calf of which I gave to my granddau: Mary, dau of David Howell). Son: John, two tracts of land in St. George's Parish whereon I now live, remainder of my estate. Exor: son, John. Wit: Benj. Lewis, Jacob Lewis, Myrick Davies.

D: 1 April 1771. P: 6 Sept. 1773. R: n.d. pp. 57-59 WBAA.

David Hughes, St. George's Parish, schoolmaster. Friend: Nehemiah Tindall, debts and moveable effects; tract of land, containing 100 acres on Savannah River. Exor: Nehemiah Tindall. Wit: James Roberts, his mark; Richard Jones; Thomas Gun, his mark.

D: 7 Oct. 1764. P: 21 Jan. 1765. R: n.d. pp. 256-257 WBA.

James Huston, Christ Church Parish, laborer. Wife: Elizabeth, use of a lot to the westward of Savannah during her widowhood. Dau: Mary Lambert, 10 pounds. Son: James, 5 pounds Sterling. On death of wife, entire estate to be sold with the profits being divided among dau, Rachel, and sons, John and William (when each becomes twenty-one). Exors: wife; William Ewen, Esq.; Doctor Henry Lewis Bourquin. Wit: William Kirk, Jr.; William Townsend; William Norton.

D: 25 Nov. 1774. P: n.d. R: n.d. p. 114 WBAA.

John Jagger, planter. Housekeeper: Rosannah Giles, four Negro slaves of her choice, 50 head of cattle of her choice, to be chosen out of slaves and cattle in Georgia. William Strode of Musketor Shore, Gent., Negro slave named Hansome Cuffy, my Logwood Work near the New River Lagoon Barr, in the Bay Honduras. Mary Allen of the Musketor Shore*, Negro named Nancy. Samuel Miller of Georgia, Gent., four Negroes of his choice, two chosen out of slaves on Musketor Shore and other two out of slaves in Georgia, my Logwood Work on the Western Shore in the New River Lagoon in the Bay Honduras, together with my Pit Pans, Darrys, and Sailing Crafts which I have in Bay Honduras. Deborah, Rebecca, and William Jones (children of Basil and Margaret Jones of the Musketor Shore), one-third of the remainder of the estate when they are twenty-one, both real and personal, in Georgia or elsewhere; should any or either die before age of twenty-one, the survivor(s) shall have the deceased's share, equally alike; I appoint the aforesaid Basil Jones guardian of his said children's share of my estate, until they are twenty-one and then to account with them for the same. Remainder of estate, both real and personal, in Georgia or elsewhere, to William Richardson of the city of New York, mariner, and to all his heirs, executors, administrators, and assigns. Exors:

*See footnote, p. 154.

71

Jonathan Bryan and James Habersham of Georgia, merchants and planters; William Richardson of New York City, mariner; Basil Jones of Musketor Shore. Wit: William Webb, George Bull, Robert Winchester.

D: 27 June 1760. P: 28 July 1760. R: 23 June 1761.

Addition on back of will in which Robert Winchester, Musketor Shore, practitioner in Physick & Surgery, declares to witnessing of will. Statement made at Black River on the Musketor Shore, dated 28 July 1760. Wit: R. Jones, Superintendent and Chief Magistrate of the Musketor Shore. (Honduras). pp. 62-63 WBA.

D: 27 June 1760. P: 28 July 1760. R: 23 June 1761. pp. 62-63 WBA.

David John, St. George's Parish, blacksmith. Son: David, plantation and tract whereon I now live (when he is twenty-one years of age). Son: Joseph, five shillings Sterling (when he is twenty-one years of age). Wife: More, remainder of estate, real and personal, extrix. Wit: David Emanuel, Sr.; David Lewis; Phebe Davie.

D: 11 Oct. 1764. P: 5 Mar. 1765. R: 5 Mar. 1765. pp. 131-132 WBA.

Francis Jones, his mark, St. Matthew's Parish, planter. Wife: Elizabeth, Negro wench named Jude, feather bed and furniture, three cows, three yearlings, gray mare. Sons: John, Negro boy named Seaser, Negro wench named Beack, feather bed and furniture. Philip, Negro boy named Sharper, Negro named Peter, feather bed and furniture. Sons: Philip and John, copper still, 18 head of cattle, 32 head of hogs, equally divided. Son: Francis, Negroes named Jeff and Phillis, feather bed and furniture, three cows and calves, 16 head of hogs. Dau: Elizabeth, Negro wench named Lucy, five cows and five yearlings. Dau: Suckey, Negro wench named Lettuce, six head of cattle. Son: Matthew, one shilling Sterling. Son: Richard, two cows and calves. Son: William, two cows and calves. Sons: Francis and James, my manner plantation whereon I now live and my mill, equally divided. Exors to sell 300 other acres of land, Negro boy named Davy and all other movable household furniture and stock of cattle, hogs, and horses

72

to pay debts. Any remaining money to be divided equally among my wife and children. Deed of gift given my two sons, John and Philip, for a tract of land in St. George's Parish, including a mill, formerly the property of John Lotts. Exors: son, John and Benjamin Lanier. Wit: Thomas Mills, Daniel Bonnell, Valentine Hollingsworth.

D: 10 Mar. 1774. P: 30 Mar. 1774. R: n.d. pp. 88-89 WBAA.

William Jones, St. Andrew's Parish, Gent. Brother: Charles, tract of land on St. Mary's River, six Negroes, my roan horse. Sister: Sally and Susannah, all my part of the Negroes belonging to my mother's estate, all my stock of cattle marked with an under keel in one ear and a slit in the other ear, freedom to a Negro named Primus. Nephews: Charles and William Middleton, plantation whereon I now live (including several tracts of land and Negroes I purchased of William Middleton's estate); stock of cattle marked with an upper keel in one ear and an under keel in the other ear, equally divided. Friend: John Webb, little boy I bought of Samuel Elbert. Friends: Jonathan Cochran and James Cochran, a horse each of their choice. Remainder of estate equally divided among my brothers and sisters. Exors: brother, Charles Jones; Jonathan and James Cochran. Wit: John Stewart, Simon Munro, Stephen Williams.

D: 18 Feb. 1768. P: 12 Aug. 1775. R: 6 Sept. 1775. pp. 180-182 WBAA.

Bryan Kelley. Following slaves are granted their freedom: Negro man named Dick, his wife, Juno, their three children (Paris, Venus, and Tulip). Ann Fitch: 19 pounds Sterling to purchase a suit of mourning and one mourning ring. Catherine Cashell, three pounds Sterling for a mourning ring. Exors to sell entrie real and personal estate to pay debts with the residue to George Galphin and Francis Macartan. Exors: George Galphin and Francis Macartan. Wit: Edward Eckles; Robert Gordon, his mark; James Grierson.

D: 13 Mar. 1766. P: 23 April 1766. R: 25 Nov. 1766.

Document attached in which Edward Barnard, James Jackson, and Edmund Cartlidge, Esqs., are empowered to administer the oath of exor to George Galphin and Francis Macartan. Dated 2 July 1766.

Oath of exor signed by George Galphin. Dated 12 Aug. 1766. pp. 176-177 WBA.

John Kelly (will partly missing), his mark. Son: John, town lot in Savannah, and a five-acre lot. Son: William, two cows, 45-acre lot. Dau: Sarah. Wife: Ann, household goods and effects. Exors: wife and Christopher Horton (?). Wit: Peter Joubert, Lydia Dean, _____ _____(?).

D: 18 Jan. 1741. P: n.d. R: n.d. Colonial Loose Will Collection.

Darby Kenedy, St. George's Parish, planter. Friend: Cartin Campbell of Charlestown, South Carolina, merchant, one-half of my lands at Stony Bluff on Savannah River, one-half tract above Augusta in St. Paul's Parish, one-half my personal estate. Nephew: John Kennedy, other half of my estate (if the exors deem him worthy). Exors: James Herbert and Donald Fraser of St. George's Parish. Wit: Thomas Chasser, John Williams, Isabell Chasser.

D: 31 Jan. 1777. P: 13 Feb. 1777. R: 13 Feb. 1777.

Document attached in which John Wereat and William Ewen, Esqs. are empowered to administer the oath of exor to James Herbert. Dated 13 Feb. 1777.

Oath of exor signed by James Herbert. Dated 13 Feb. 1777. pp. 295-298 WBAA.

Henry Kennan, Joseph's Town, Gent. Tract of land, containing 400 acres on Mill Island in St. Matthew's Parish to be sold for payment of debts. Wife: Susannah, remainder of estate, real and personal. On her death the estate to be divided among my children: Henry, James, Elizabeth, and Marianne. Exors: wife, Patrick Mackay, and George Cuthbert of Christ Church Parish, Esqs. Wit (to handwriting): John Kennan (9 Mar. 1767).

D: 30 April 1763. P: 9 Mar. 1767. R: 9 Nov. 1767. pp. 235-238 WBA.

Susannah Kennan, Christ Church Parish, widow of Henry Kennan. Entire estate, after debts are paid, to my children: Henry, James, Elizabeth, and Marianne. Exors: James Cuthbert of Castle Hill, Esq., and Stephen Bull of Sheldon, South Carolina. Wit: Mary Tobler, Ann Wilson, William Grome.

D: 30 Nov. 1769. P: 11 July 1770. R: 8 Aug. 1770. pp. 351-352 WBA.

William Kennedy, his mark. Brother: Hugh, entire estate, real and personal, after debts are paid. Wit: Owen O. Carter, James Roche.

D: 27 Jan. 1769. P: 10 Mar. 1769. R: 13 Mar. 1769. p. 305 WBA.

Charles Keys. Cousin: Susannah Roberts, to administer the estate of Charles Keys and to make an inventory. Dated 5 Nov. 1754. p. 1 WBA.

Theobald Kieffer, Ebenezer (will unsigned). Daus: Elizabeth, tract of 350 acres which I have bought of Thomas Baxley on the Island of Pathmos, Negroes named King and Sarah. Hannah, 400 acres of land in St. George's Parish, Negroes named Peter, Old Gags, and Gloi. Dorothe, town lot in Ebenezer (opposite garden lot of Andrew Seckinger), Negroes named Peter, Ernest, Martha, Adam and Catherine, Judy Christiana, other twon lot in Ebenezer and also one in Ewenburgh, Negroes named Jonas and Mary. Sons: Israel, my half plantation whereon I now live on the southeast side; half my 300 acres on the Island across the river with the dwelling house and the Negroes named Jack and Marther. Emmanuel, other half of lands above; Negroes named Adam and Judy. Five pounds Sterling for the support of the Lutheran Church and School at Ebenezer. All my movables to be divided among my children. To Israel, my great Bible. To Emmanuel, John Arnds Psalm Book. Exor: _____. Handwriting witnessed by Christain Rabenhorst and John Flerl (25 Feb. 1767).

D: n.d. P: 5 Mar. 1767. R: 9 Mar. 1767. pp. 201-203 WBA.

John Kitt, St. George's Parish, planter. Wife: Ann, entire estate, real and personal. Wife to provide for my son, Wade Kitt. Exors: wife and Lachlan McGillvray. Wit: Thomas Morgan, Neh. Wade, James Whitefield.

D: 18 Mar. 1761. P: 11 June 1761. R: 25 June 1761. p. 68 WBA.

Roger Lacy, Thunderbolt, planter. Brothers: James and Theophilus, to each a guinea to buy a ring. Sister: Grace, 20 pounds Sterling to buy her mourning. Wife: Mary, all the rest and remainder of estate, extrix. Wit: George Tyrrell, Charles Collyer, John Chapman.

D: 9 Oct. 1736. P: n.d. R: n.d. Colonial Loose Will Collection.

Edward Larking, his mark. Martin Bynn of Savannah, entire estate, exor. Wit: Bruce Wynsley; James Byrns, his mark.

D: 3 July 1777. P: 17 July 1777. R: n.d. Colonial Loose Will Collection.

William Lavery, Savannah. Paul Cheeswright, personal estate. John West of Darby Ward, town lot and garden lot and 45 acres more. Robert Hows, a brown coat and waistcoat and looking glass. Thomas Tipet, my red great coat. Edward Johnson, carpenter, a pair of shoes. Wit: William Waterlund; Nehemiah Wickes; Thomas Cross, his mark.

D: 20 Dec. 1733. P: n.d. R: n.d. Colonial Loose Will Collection.

Thomas Lee, Savannah, Gent. Wife: Mary Ann, household furniture, bedding, all monies at interest, my two horses, Negroes named Affa, Diana, Clarissa, and Bob. Brother: William, two lots in St. Philip's Parish, containing 650 acres, all my working tools, mechanical instruments, all my wearing apparel. Sister: Ann, two tickets in the lottery of the United States of America, if they bring money. Godson: Isaac Weddall, tract of 300 acres near lands of Luke Mann. Friend: John McLuer, my bay horse, my military sash. John Lyon, Jr., 50 pounds Georgia currency. Mentions: sister, Rebecca Lee. Remainder of estate to wife. Exors: wife; William Fox, Jr. (my father-in-law); John McLuer and William Stephens. Wit: Mary McLuer, Henry Cuyler, Joseph Goldwire.

D: 11 Feb. 1778. P: n.d. R: n.d. Colonial Loose Will Collection.

John Lester, "late of the city of Exeter in Great Britain, but now of the Town of Savannah," Gent. (son of John Lester, late of Exeter, hosier, deceased). Brother: Henry, of Exeter, farm called Coombes in Parish of St. Thomas the Apostle, near Exeter in the County of Devon, all other real estate in Great Britain, all personal estate. Exors: Thomas Burrington, Matthew Roche, both of Savannah, Gents. Wit: William Patterson, Alexander Mackay, Michael Germain.

D: 27 Dec. 1761. P: 21 Jan. 1762. R: 25 Jan. 1762. pp. 77-78 WBA.

Abraham Lewis, St. John's Parish, planter. Entire estate, after debts are paid, to be divided among my brothers and sister: Joseph, Judah, Elijah, and Demmes. Brother Isaac's share to be given him at the discretion of my exors. Exors: brothers, Joseph, Judah, and Elijah. Wit: John Bacon, Edward Ball, Sampson Ball.

D: 17 June 1774. P: 19 Aug. 1774. R: n.d. pp. 97-98 WBAA.

Evan Lewis, St. George's Parish, planter. Son: Thomas, tract of land, containing 150 acres in St. George's Parish at the mouth of Stalking Head Branch. Dau: Ann, two cows and calves, two breeding sows, six pounds and five shillings Sterling. Son: Jacob, 125 acres of land, being part of a tract I now live on; all the shoemaker's tools I now have. Son: Evan, 100 acres of land, being part of the tract I now live on; all my cooper's tools. Dau: Mary, one grey two-year-old horse colt, a cow and a calf. Wife: Mary, mare called Fly, she shall be maintained by my son, Joseph, during her widowhood. Exors: wife and son, Jacob. Wit: David Lewis; David Emanuel; Thomas Lewis, Jr.

D: 23 Aug. 1766. P: 16 Dec. 1766. R: 16 Dec. 1766. pp. 180-181 WBA.

Jacob Lewis, St. Andrew's Parish, planter. Mother: Mary Lewis, annuity of 20 pounds Sterling, use of Negro girl named

Janny. Brothers: Isaac, and his son, Joseph, use of one-sixth my estate. Judah, Negro man named Tom. Elijah, Negro man named Dick. Sister: Demmis, Negro girl named Mariah. Remainder of estate to be equally divided among my brothers and sisters, Abraham, Joseph, Isaac, Judah, Elijah, and Demmis. Exors: brothers, Abraham, Joseph, Judah, and Elijah. Wit: Andrew Way; Albert Duynmier; Thomas Dawsey, his mark.

D: 10 Feb. 1774. P: 17 Mar. 1774. R: n.d. pp. 85-86 WBAA.

John Lewis. Entire estate to father, Samuel Lewis, now living in the province of Georgia, exor. Wit: Demmis Lewis, Abraham Lewis, Joseph Lewis.

D: 9 Aug. 1763. P: 13 Dec. 1764. R: 13 (?) June 1765.

Document attached in which Robert Baillie and George McIntosh, Esqs. are empowered to administer the oath of probate to Demmis Lewis. Dated 30 Mar. 1765.

Oath of probate signed by Demmis Lewis. Dated 1 June 1765. pp. 137-139 WBA.

Isaac Lines, St. John's Parish, planter. Wife: Martha, four Negroes, her riding horse, saddle, and furniture, feather bed and furniture, watch, use of tract of land whereon I now live during her widowhood, an equal part of all my neat cattle with my children, marked with a crap and slit in one ear and an under keel in the other branded "TL". Child with which my wife is now pregnant (if a boy, at the age of twenty-one), tract of land I now live on, Negro girl named Jenny, six cows and calves. If a girl, only to draw an equal share with the rest of the children of my movable estate. Son: Samuel, one-half a tract of land in St. Andrew's Parish, bay horse, writing desk, equal part of movable estate. Son: Morgan, other half of this tract of land, one bay mare. Dau: Mary, one gray mare, saddle, furniture, equal part of movable estate. Dau: Rebecca, gray horse colt, equal part of the movable estate. Daus: Marthe and Hannah, equal part of movable estate. Exors to sell lot in Sunbury and divide the profits among my children. Exors: Nathan Taylor and John Sandiford. Wit: William Baker, John Goulding, Palmer Goulding.

D: 5 Feb. 1766. P: 17 Sept. 1766. R: 18 Sept. 1766. pp. 168-170 WBA.

Moses Linus (includes a copy taken from the original will), St. George's Parish in the province of South Carolina, tailor. Sons: Charles, Thomas, and John (when they become twenty-one), entire estate, equally divided. Exors: Whitmarsh Fuller, William Mill, William Norman. Wit: Sarah Marquiss, John Barker.

D: 12 June 1767. P: 28 Aug. 1767. R: n.d.

Document attached in which John Jones and James Hitching, Esqs. are empowered to administer the oath of exor to John Elliott, Joseph Way, and Mary Norman. Dated 12 April 1775.

Oath of exor signed by Mary Norman, John Elliott, and Joseph Way. Dated 24 April 1775. pp. 146-148 WBAA.

Thomas Lloyd, Savannah, merchant. Wife: Rebecca, all lands and tenements, silver plate, furniture, goods and household stuff. Son: Thomas, 500 pounds Sterling at the age of twenty-one. Benjamin, Edward, and Rebecca Holmes (children of my wife), remainder of my estate, equally divided. Exors: wife and brother, Benjamin. Wit: James Edward Powell, Thomas Vincent, Charles Pryce.

D: 25 May 1765. P: 13 Oct. 1766. R: 13 Oct. 1766. pp. 173-175 WBA.

John Long, Wheat Marsh Island, (Whitemarsh?) fisherman. James Huston, of Wheat Marsh Island, planter, exor, to pay debts by selling personal estate and tract of 150 acres in Beckley County on the north side of the Seludy River in South Carolina, if necessary. Any money left over to go to the exor. Wit: Richard Floide (Floyd), his mark; Margaret Floyd; Ann Smith.

D: 15 Nov. 1773. P: 22 Dec. 1773. R: n.d. pp. 72-73 WBAA.

James Love, Savannah, cabinet maker. Wife: Elizabeth, house in Savannah; town lot adjoining the lot of Noble Wimberly Jones, Esq.; five-acre garden lot; forty-five acre farm lot. Sons: James, town lot, garden lot and farm lot in Savannah, Negro man named Jacob. John: town lot in Savannah (now in the possession of William Wright of Savannah, goldsmith), farm lot, my man slave (a Spaniard) called Henry. Walter: two tracts of land in St. (Matthew), containing 250 acres each, Negro girl called Pegg, half of town lot in Savannah held by my wife and Mrs. Jane Blyth (wife of Peter Blyth) as co-heirs of their late father, John Evans, deceased. Remainder of estate to wife. Exors: wife and Peter Blyth. Wit: Andrew Starks; Elizabeth Kaner, her mark; Charles Pryce.

D: 28 April 1768. P: 6 June 1768. R: 10 June 1768. pp. 269-271 WBA.

Thomas Loyd, St. Paul's Parish, planter. Eldest son: John, Negro boy named Jonny, horse called Jack, feather bed, two mares, a two-year-old colt. Wife: Patience, remainder of estate for her widowhood. Children: Elizabeth, Thomas, Samuel, Francis, James, Jane, and Patience, personal estate on the death of my wife. Exors to sell 300 acres on which I now live and a tract of 100 acres adjoining on which Margerate Proctor now lives. Profits from this sale to be equally divided by my children. Exors: wife, Hugh Middleton, Mordecai Sheftall. Wit: Edmund Cartlidge, J. P.; Reuben Blanchard, Mordecai Sheftall.

D: 11 July 1771. P: 25 May 1772. R: 30 June 1772.

Document attached in which Edward Barnard, James Jackson, John Francis Williams, and Edmund Cartlidge, Esqs. are empowered to administer the oath of exor to Patience Loyd, Hugh Middeton, and Mordecai Sheftall. Dated 30 April 1772.

Oath of exor signed by Patience Loyd, her mark; and Mordecai Sheftall. (not dated). pp. 444-446 WBA.

John Luptan, (Midway). My well-beloved Susannah Baker (dau of Benjamin Baker), Negro wench named Jean, with her sons, Bob and Jack, feather bed and furniture, my riding horse called

Ball. Remainder of estate to be divided into six parts, one part to each of the following: Susannah Baker; my sister, Elizabeth Luptan; my nephew, William McDowell (son of John and Lucretia McDowell); one part divided among by nephews and niece: William McGee, Elizabeth Conner, and Benjamin Johnston, the children of Ann Johnston; one part divided between my nieces, Mary and Elizabeth Grace (daus. of William and Hannah Grace); one part divided between my niece, Sarah Hauskins and my friend, Benjamin Baker, Exors: Samuel Jones, Benjamin Andrew, John Quarterman, and Thomas Quarterman. Wit: Henry Barfield, Nathaniel Plomer, Sarah Plommee (Plomer).

D: 18 April 1767. P: 12 May 1767. R: 18 June 1767. pp. 215-217 WBA.

Philip Delegal, Esq., Captain in Lieutenant General Parson's Regiment of Invalids, St. Peter's Port, Island of Guernsey. Wife: Eleanor, living at Philip's Bluff, South Carolina, plantation already transferred by deed of gift to wife: Eleanor, son: Edward, and dau: Sophia; also 200 pounds, now at interest in Bank of England, to wife and her heirs, for the rest of her natural life, if she survives me. If she does not, to dau: Catherine, wife of Hugh Campbell, South Carolina, mariner. If she dies before I do, this to her legal heirs, equally divided. Eldest son: Philip Delegal, Little Ogechee, Georgia, Gent.: (200) pounds now at interest in Bank of England, gold watch, swords, plate, jewels, linnen, wearing apparel; if he dies before I do, this to his legal heirs, equally divided. Son: John Delegal, South Carolina, mariner, 200 pounds now at interest in Bank of England, if he dies before I do this to his legal heirs equally divided. Sons: George and Edward Delegal, Georgia, planters, "all that my tract of Land laying and being situate near unto the Lands of my eldest Son Philip, at Little Ogechee," containing about 500 acres, the grant for which in wife Eleanor's name, equally divided, or to the surviving heirs of either, entailed to them and their heirs forever. Son: George, also 100 pounds now at interest; if he should die, to his legal heirs. Son: Edward Delegal, also 100 pounds now at interest; if he should die then to his legal heirs, equally divided. Eldest dau: Catherine, another 100 pounds now at interest; if she die, to her legal heirs, equally divided. Dau: Margaret, wife of _____ _____, South Carolina planter, 100 pounds now at interest, if she die to her legal heirs, equally divided. Youngest dau: Sophia, living with her mother in South Carolina, 100 pounds now at interest, if she die, to heirs, equally divided. Ten Shillings to the Poor of St. Peter's Port, to be paid within six months of my decease to the proper Officers of said Parish for the use of the said Poor. Remainder of estate, real and personal, to be sold to pay legal debts and funeral expenses. If any be left, divided thus: wife, Eleanor, one-fourth: son, Philip, one-half; other one-fourth to other six children or their heirs, equally divided. If any of my children die without heirs, their share to go to other children and their heirs, equally divided. Exors: wife, Eleanor, and son, Philip. If either should die, sons, Edward and George to take his or her place as exor. Executorship to descend to the next eldest son. As exors. are all "dwellers beyond the seas," and cannot take immediate care of all my affairs, I appoint Sir John Mylne, Barronet Lieutenant Governor of Guernsey, and Elisha Tupper, joint trustees, to correspond with the exors and take care of my affairs. To them, one guinea each for a mourning ring. Wit: Andre Migault, George Hawley, Edward Knight.

D: 22 Jan. 1762. P: 4 Jan. 1769. R: 5 Jan. 1769. Sworn statement by Elias Crespin to signature of Philip Delegal, dated 6 Jan. 1763 . . . Vicedean of the Island of Guernsey. pp. 288-294 WBA.

NOTE: Will also admitted for probate in Guernsey on 31 Dec. 1762, per Royal Archivist of the Island of Guernsey, Great Britain.

Laughlin McBean(e), his mark, Augusta, planter. Sons: William and John, house and plantation whereon I now live, containing 500 acres of land; all personal estate. Exors: sons, William and John; David Douglass, Esq.; and Laughlin McGillvray, Gent.; both of Augusta. Wit.: James Paris, Edward Barnard, Joseph Oaks.

D: 23 Sept. 1756. P: 11 Nov. 1756. R: n.d. pp. 17-18 WBA.

Robert McClatchie, Savannah, schoolmaster. Mathew Mauve, of Christ Church Parish, planter, silver watch and seal. Brother: Alexander of London, tailor, all my new books. Jane Mauve (wife of Matthew Mauve), three pounds Sterling. Joseph Dunlap of

Savannah, carpenter, three pounds Sterling. Robert Bolton, of Savannah, Gent., five pounds Sterling. Thomas Barber, of Savannah, Gent., five pounds Sterling. Exors. to sell the rest of the estate to pay debts and legacies. Excess money to brother, Alexander. Exor.: Robert Bolton. Wit.: John Houstoun, Jacob Williams.

D: 1 Dec. 1766. P: 17 Dec. 1766. R: 18 Dec. 1766. pp. 182-183 WBA.

Robert McDonald (nuncupative will). (Savannah, Vintner). Sons: James and Robert, entire estate, equally divided. Margarette Goodall to have the use of the same for her and the children as long as she "doesn't keep company with any man." Sons: James, Negro (?) named Buck; Robert, Negro (?) named Ned. Exors.: Mathias Ash, Doctor David Brydy.

(D: 1778.)

Colonial Loose Will Collection.

John McFarlane, Savannah, tailor. Wife: Susannah, my two several messuages or tenements in Savannah, Christ Church Parish, one of which is in my possession and one in the possession of Mr. Hugh Simm, sadler; also to my wife, 500 acres adjoining Indian Bluff, four Negroes, all my household furniture. Use of all the above during her widowhood. To children, after her death or marriage. Exors.: George Baillie and Philip Box, both of Savannah. Wit.: Ambros Barr of Savannah, senior yeoman; Sarah Dean; J. Bulloch.

D: 20 Nov. 1766. P: 21 Sept. 1767. R: 25 Oct. 1767. pp. 225-228 WBA.

John McGilvery, his mark. Son: Lauchlin, 12 head of cattle, three mares, three colts, parcel of corn, Negro named Glasco. Heremiah Knott, a Neat of land payable by William Graves for 100 pounds currency. Mentions: Flower Mitchel. Exors: David Douglass, Lauchlin McBean. Wit.: James Paris, John Wisely, Flower Mitchel.

D: 24 Feb. 1748. P: n.d. R: n.d. Colonial Loose Will Collection.

Edward McGuire, his mark (late of Midway, planter). Son: Joseph, 10 shillings Sterling. Wife: Mary, all remainder of estate, real and personal. Exors: wife and Andrew Way. Wit.: Benjamin Baker, James Harley.

D: 2 April 1761. P: 4 Feb. 1762. R: n.d. pp. 79-80 WBA.

Mary McGuire, St. John's Parish. William Sallett, of St. John's Parish, 20 pounds Sterling (at the age of twenty-one). Nephew: John Bacon, son of William Bacon, 40 pounds Sterling (at the age of eighteen). Exors to make the best possible use of the remainder of the estate. Exors: John Bacon, Sr.; William Bacon, Jr. Wit.: Joseph McGowen, Richard Spencer, William Girardeau.

D: 7 Oct. 1773. P: 15 Dec. 1773. R: n.d. pp. 70-71 WBAA.

James McHenry, Savannah, innkeeper. Eldest son of my brother, Morris McHenry in Ireland, 60 pounds Georgia currency, tract of 500 acres of land on Great Ogechee River. The children of the late Thomas Gordon of Charlestown, South Carolina, four guineas to purchase them mourning rings. Wife: Ann, all remainder of estate, including: household furniture, Negroes, lands and houses, extrix. Wit.: Jonathan Cochran, Mordecai Sheftall, John Van Rensselaer.

D: 1 Sept. 1767. P: 20 April 1768. R: 21 April 1768. pp. 266-267 WBA.

Donald Mackay, Frederica, St. James Parish, merchant. Natural Dau.: Elizabeth (eldest dau. to Elizabeth Leman (Lamon) wife to James Leman, trader on Great Sittilly River), Negro girl (now in the hands of Ann Stuart of Savannah), 200 pounds Sterling when she is of age or married, 20 pounds Sterling annuity during her minority. Elizabeth Leman, Negro woman. James Leman, 40 pounds Sterling for the care of my daus. Natural Dau.: Sarah (second dau. to Elizabeth Leman), Negro girl now in the hands of James Leman, 200 pounds Sterling when she is of age or married, annuity of 20 pounds Sterling during her minority. Captain James MacKay, his wife, and Miss Sally Stevens, 10 pounds Sterling, each to buy a suit of mourning. Nephew: John Mackintosh, enough money to keep him at school. Mother: Barbara Mackay, remainder of estate. Exors: brother-

84

in-law, William Mackintosh; partner, James Spalding. Wit.: James Cuthbert, James Mackay, Allen Stuart.

D: 29 Jan. 1768. P: 4 Mar. 1768. R: 8 Mar. 1768. Codicil (30 Jan. 1768, same wit.) : If both daus. are dead, their shares to be divided among the children of my sister, the wife of William Mackintosh.

pp. 253-256 WBA.

In Ye Name of God Amen.

I **John Mackay** being at this time sick and weak, but by God's great blessing of perfect sense & memory, but yet uncertain how soon my change may come, do therefore make this my last will & Testament in mannr & form following (Viz)

Imprimis. I bequeath my body to ye. Ground decently to be interd in ye usual buring Ground of Savanna in ye (Province of) Georgia. And my Soul unto God that gave it, _____ of a glorious _____ unto life _____ all but I give unto Joseph (Stanley) _____ _____and make him or them Sole Executors of _____ & Testament in Witness whereof I have _____ hand in ye presence of three Witnesses this 25 Day of July in ye sixth year of Reign of our Sovereign Lord George by ye Grace of God _____ Great Britain France & Ireland King Defender of ye _____ Ano Dom 1733.

Published & Declard in ye presence of us
William Waterlund
Richard Cannon
     his
Francis X Mugridge
    mark
                     [JOHN MACK_____]

D: 25 July 1733. P: n.d. R: n.d.

Colonial Loose Will Collection

Patrick Mackay, Sunbury. Brother: John, 10 pounds Sterling. Wife: Isabella, entire estate, extrix. Wit.: Allan Stuart, Simon Munro, Andrew Darling.

D: 6 June 1768. P: 13 Feb. 1777. R: n.d.

Document attached in which John Wereat and William Ewen, Esqs., are empowered to administer the oath of probate to Allan Stuart, Simon Munro, and Andrew Darling. Dated 13 Feb. 1777. pp. 289-300 WBAA.

Alexander McKertney, his mark. Kinsmen: George and Henry Megumery, entire estate after debts are paid. Exor: George Galphin. Wit.: George Jackson, William Atchison Finlay.

D: 8 Sept. 1741. P: n.d. R: n.d. Colonial Loose Will Collection.

William McKenzie, Savannah, Esq. Estate to be kept together by exors until my youngest son, John, shall arrive at the age of twenty-one. At that time the exors shall have an evaluation made of the estate and divide it as follows: one-third to my wife, Christiana; two-thirds divided equally among all my children. Exors: wife, John Simpson (who hath intermarried with my dau., Anna), and John Jamieson of Savannah, Esq. Wit.: John Houstoun, Francis Knowles, George Macaulay.

D: 16 April 1773. P: 17 May 1773. R: n.d.

Codicil (same date, same wit.): Authorizes the exors to sell my house and lot in Sunbury, my sloop and boat, my Negro named Prince, with the profits going to my estate. Son: George, my riding horse, my gun, sword, pistols, and other arms.

pp. 32-34 WBAA.

John McLean, Little Ogechee, Christ Church Parish, Gent. Wife: Elizabeth, seven Negroes, annuity of 20 pounds Sterling during her widowhood, one-eighth of my household goods, riding chair and chair horse, use of my dwelling house for her widowhood. Son: John, one-eighth of my household goods, one shilling Sterling. Dau: Elizabeth, wife of Alexander Crighton, six Negroes, town lot in Savannah on Broughton Street, one-eighth of my household goods. Dau: Margaret, 500 acres of land on the north side of Great Sattily River, adjoining lands of Benjamin Farley. Son: Josiah, plantation, containing 200 acres, whereon I now live, adjoining lands of Christopher Dawson and David Delegal; 500 acres on Buckhead, joining lands of Hooker. Sons: Andrew, Jervey, and dau, Sarah, all my lands on the south side of Great Satilla River, that is, 500 acres to Sarah, and the remainder to be divided equally between two sons. Children: Margaret, Josiah, Sarah, Andrew, and Jervey, all my other slaves, stock of cattle, household goods, equally divided when they are all twenty-one years of age. Exors: The Honorable James Read; Joseph Clay, Esq; James Butler (son of Joseph Butler) ; James Habersham, Jr. Wit: I. Baillou, James Mercer, Tabitha Baillou.

D: 21 July 1773. P: 14 Jan. 1774. R: n.d. pp. 74-76 WBAA.

Roderick McLowd, his mark, St. Andrew's Parish, planter. Wife: Margaret, 200 acres in St. Andrew's Parish, household goods, moveable effects. Exors: wife, George Mackintosh, Esq. Wit.: Mark Noble; Alexander McDonald, his mark.

D: 8 Jan. 1775. P: 20 Feb. 1775. R: n.d.

Document attached in which James Mackay is empowered to administer the oath of extrix. to Margaret McLowd. Dated 17 May 1775.

Oath of extrix. signed by Margaret McLowd, her mark. Dated 18 May 1775.

pp. 122-125 WBAA.

William McPherson, St. John's Parish. Brother: John, annuity of 7 pounds, 3 shillings Sterling. Wife: Mary, remainder of estate, real and personal, extrix. Wit.: John Baggwell, Josiah Serjeant, James Lord.

D: 10 Jan. 1761. P: 5 Feb. 1761. R: 23 June 1761.

Document attached in which Francis Arthur, James Fisher, and Lyman Hall are empowered to administer the oath of extrix. to Mary McPherson. Dated 5 Feb. 1761.

Oath of extrix. administered to Mary McPherson on 14 Feb. 1761. pp. 60-62 WBA.

Pierre Maillier (will in French with translation attached). Wife: Aymie, entire estate, after debts are paid. Exors: wife and her father, Gedeon Mallet. Wit.: Pierre Joubert, Jeremie .... Alletten (?), Jean Seillie.

D: 18 Dec. 1742. P: 29 Dec. 1742. R: n.d. Colonial Loose Will Collection.

Henry Manly, his mark, Frederica. Son: Peter, estate in Hemick Town in Devon, estate in Dunkswell called Abby Wood, my estate called Little Cruff and Big Cruff, lying on the east side of Dunkswell Abbey. Wife: Sarah, use of above listed estates until son, Peter, is twenty-one years old. Daus: Elizabeth, Sarah, Deborah, Mary Ann, 20 pounds Sterling, each, on their day of marriage. Exors: wife, and William Abbott of Frederica. Wit: James Billinghurst, John Cassie, Mary Cassie.

D: 17 Oct. 1746. P: n.d. R: n.d. Colonial Loose Will Collection.

Charles Maran, St. John's Parish. To all my relations, except John Couper, one shilling Sterling. John Couper, all my lands, Negroes (except Dinor, who I give her freedom), my cattle, horses, hogs and all other estate. Exors: James Butler, Jr. and John Couper. Wit: James Ducker; James Barron; James Taylor, his mark.

D: 30 Mar. 1772. P: 11 May 1772. R: 13 May 1772. pp. 438-439 WBA.

Clement Martin, Sr. Son: Clement Martin, "six dunghill fowls for having cheated me out of six thousand pounds, by my keeping no account against him." Dau: Susannah (wife of Thomas Anderson of Georgia, carpenter), Negro woman named Delia, son named Tom Fountain, boy named Punch. Grandson: Clement Jacob Simpson (son of John Simpson of Savannah and my late dau., Elizabeth Simpson), 900 acres (when he is twenty-one). Remainder of estate to be equally divided between my son, John, my daus: Jane and Ann. If they die with no heirs, estate to go to the Honorable Lewis Johnson and his wife Lateah, and their children. Son: Clement, nor any of his heirs shall claim any right or property therein. Exors: The Honorable James Habersham; The Honorable Anthony Stokes; The Honorable

Lewis Johnson, Esq.; George Baillie; James Habersham, Jr. Wit: George Houstoun, William Moore, John Bard Randell.

D: 9 Sept. 1771. P: 12 Dec. 1775. R: 12 Oct. 1775. pp. 212-214 WBAA.

Clement Martin, Jr. Children, sum not to exceed 20 pounds annually each for maintenance. Alexander, the son of Elizabeth Jackson, whom I acknowledge to be my son, all my Abercorn lots, wearing apparel, arms, watch, cane, pineland containing 100 acres I bought from Ports (?) , my island called Abercorn Island, remaining Negroes after those given later in will. Ann, dau. of Elizabeth Jackson, whom I acknowledge to be my dau., 600 acres of land on the Altamaha River, 12 Negroes, feather bed, mattress, bolster, two pillows, a counterpane, pair of blankets. Dorothy, dau. of Elizabeth Jackson, whom I acknowledge to be my dau., 600 acres of land on the Altamaha River, 12 Negroes, feather bed, mattress, bolster, two pillows, a counterpane, one pair of blankets. Elizabeth, dau. of Elizabeth Jackson, whom I acknowledge to be my dau., 600 acres of land on the Altamaha, 12 Negroes, feather bed, mattress, bolster, two pillows, a counterpane, one pair of blankets. William, son of Elizabeth Jackson and whom I acknowledge to be my son, my sword, tract of land, containing 500 acres in St. John; tract of land, containing 300 acres on Briar Creek in St. Matthew's Parish; all my lands south of Thompson's Creek. (These tracts originally granted James Pelten, and the other to Philip and Isaac Gibbs.) ; 50-acre lot I lately bought from Sybella Sthaley; 11 Negroes. Debars father and all his children, John Martin, more especially, from making any claims on his estate. Exor: son, Alexander. Wit: Andrew Law, Peter Edwards, Henry Cuyler.

D: 29 Sept. 1775. P: 17 Oct. 1775. R: 17 Oct. 1775. pp. 190-194 WBAA.

(copy of the original, dated 31 Dec. 1772)

John Martin, St. John's Parish. Exors to sell lands south of Altamaha River, containing 900 acres, adjoining lands of Thomas Hutchinson and Daniel Blake, Esqs. and lands of Gideon Dowse and John Stacey; profits to pay debts. Nephew: James Martin Gibbons, son of Sarah Gibbons, my other tract of land on the south of Altamaha River, containing 200 acres, joining lands of Gideon Dowse, Michael Stutze. Son: James Donnom Martin, all my lands in St. John's Parish, known by the name of Boyn (Boin(e)) Swamp, containing about 1500 acres (my wife Elizabeth shall have use of all the cleared land during her widowhood). Wife: Elizabeth, 11 Negroes, given me by her father, James Donnom, my riding chair and two horses. Remainder of movable estate to son, James (when he is twenty-one). If he dies a minor, the estate to be divided as follows: Nephew: John Gibbons, son of Hannah Gibbons, 200 acres of land. Remainder of swampland (about 1300 acres) to nephew, James Martin Gibbons. Exors: father-in-law, James Donnom of South Carolina; my two nephews, Joseph and William Gibbons; William Graves, Sr.; John Stewart; Thomas Quarterman; Thomas Bacon, son of Marsey Bacon. Mentions: James Mossman, Thomas Way, William McLaughlin, Barrack Gibbons. Wit: John Portress; Thomas Cater; John Davis.

D: 1 Feb. 1772. P: 30 Dec. 1772. R: n.d. pp. 21-24 WBAA.

Thomas Mathers, his mark (Christ Church Parish). Exors to sell tract of land, containing 200 acres, at Ogechee, to pay debts. Wife: Ana, use of town lot and farm during her life; land to sons: William and John, after death of my wife. Exors: wife, and Richard Fox. Wit: J. J. Zubly, David Brydie, William Gibbons.

D: 3 Jan. 1769. P: 8 Feb. 1769. R: 10 Feb. 1769. p. 299 WBA.

Jacob Matthew(e)s, Savannah, Indian trader. Wife: Mary, entire estate, real and personal, in Georgia and South Carolina, or any other place in America. Extrix, sisters: Sarah (one-quarter), Elizabeth (one-quarter), and Mary (one-half), Matthews, now in England, entire estate, real and personal. Wit: John Pye, John Keeler.

D: 15 Jan. 1740. P: n.d. R: n.d.

Colonial Loose Will Collection.

John Mathewson (fragment of will), Westbrook in Georgia. Wit: Frances Mugridge.

D: 3 June 1734. P: n.d. R: n.d.

Colonial Loose Will Collection.

George Maurer, his mark, St. Matthew's Parish. Wife: Maria Sevell, 100 acres of land, 3 cows, all my effects and one mare. John Mauer, Jr., one yearling haffer black bitted. George ...., one calf. Wit: Christopher Cramer, John Mauer, John Glanir.

D: 5 April 1775. P: 25 April 1775. R: n.d.
p. 150-151 WBAA.

Matthew Mauve, Savannah, shopkeeper. Robert Bolton, Jr. (son of Robert Bolton of Savannah, Gent.), tract of land in town of Hardwicke. Wife: Jane, lot number ten, near the bluff or bank of Savannah River, east of Bull Street (at present occupied by William Moore at the yearly rent of 50 pounds Sterling) ; on her death, this lot to Mauve John Moore, son of William Moore of Savannah by Susannah, his wife. If Mauve John Moore dies before twenty-one, this lot to his brother, William Moore, Jr. Profits arising from estate to be used toward liberal education for William Moore, the younger. To the trustees of the independent meeting in Savannah, 5 pounds. Remainder of estate to wife, Jane. Extrix: wife. Wit: James Alexander, Alexander Brodie, James Robertson.

D: ___ Aug. 1770. P: 30 June 1775. R: 30 June 1775.

Signed statement attached in which Matthew Mauve declares that above is his last will and testament. Wit: J. Zubly, Natha. Adams, Ann Adams.

pp. 171-173 WBAA.

Audley Maxwell, St. John's Parish, planter. Wife: Hannah, Negro woman named Patty, horse and chair, bed and furniture, kitchen furniture. Son: James, tract of land whereon he now lives, Negro girl named Betty, one-third of my black cattle, an equal part of my movable estate. Son: Andrew Elton Wells, one-half a 350-acre tract of land in Newport, adjoining land of John Mitchell, Matthew Smallwood and John Davine; Negro girl named Siby; one-third of my black cattle. Son: John Sandiford, other one-half of tract mentioned above, Negro girl named Beck, eleven cows and calves. Grandson: Audley Maxwell, tract of land on Midway, containing 150 acres, adjoining lands of Kenneth Baillie and Audley Maxwell, Jr., deceased. Granddau: Elizabeth Maxwell, one-third of my black cattle, as was mentioned in my deed of gift to her father, Audley Maxwell, Jr., deceased. Son: Josiah Powell, 10 shillings Sterling. All remaining real and personal estate equally divided among three sons: James Maxwell, Andrew Elton Wells, John Sandiford. Exors: Sons, James Maxwell, Andrew Elton Wells, John Sandiford. Wit: Jonathan Evans, James Alexander, Richard Wylly.

D: 22 May 1769. P: 22 Nov. 1776. R: 22 Nov. 1776. pp. 246-248 WBAA.

John Maxwell, St. Philip's Parish, planter. Sale of two tracts of land on Great Ogechee River to John James of the Island of St. Croix be confirmed as soon as he fulfills the agreement made. Sons: Elisha and John, entire estate, real and personal, equally divided when they are twenty-one; if both sons die before twenty-one, the estate to my brothers, James and William. Exors: James Parsons of Charlestoun, South Carolina, Esq.; Elisha Butler, Esq.; my brothers, James and William. Wit: James Maxwell, Allan Stuart, James Guthrie.

D: 8 Dec. 1767. P: 2 April 1768. R: 5 April 1768.

Authorization for the inventory of the estate of John Maxwell is attached. Appraisers: James Mackay, Esq.; Jonathan Cochran, Esq.; William LeConte, Esq.; John Man(e); dated 2 April 1768.

pp. 260-261 WBA.

Mary Maxwell, St. Philip's Parish, widow and relict of James Maxwell, deceased. Grandson: Morgan Sabb, Negro boy named Stephen. Granddau: Mary Caldwell, Negro girl named Maria. Grandson: Elisha Maxwell, Negro boy named Peter. Grandson: James McKay Maxwell, Negro boy named Tom. Granddau: Ann Jackson Maxwell, Negro wench named Patty. Grandson: James

Benjamin Maxwell, mulatto boy named Sam. Sons: James and William, my stock of black cattle (save those marked with the two proper ear mark of my son, John, lately deceased), my stock of sheep, my horses, mares, and colts. Grandsons: Elisha and John Butler Maxwell, cattle marked with the proper ear-mark of my son, John, deceased. Son: William, my stock of hogs. Son: James, and dau: Jane Gray, one feather bed, mattress, bolster, pillows, sheets, to each. Son: William, all rest of household furniture. Remainder of Negroes and other slaves to sons: James and William and daus: Mary Esther Nichols, widow; Elizabeth, the wife of Thomas Young, Esq.; and Jane, wife of Joseph Gray; all equally divided. Exors: sons, William and James; The Honorable James Read and James McKay, Esqs. Wit: Elisha Butler, Elizabeth Jackson, Nathan Taylor.

D: 30 May 1770. P: 1 Nov. 1774. R: n.d.
pp. 108-110 WBAA.

John Ludwig Meyor (Mayer), practitioner in physick, (Ewensburgh, Christ Church Parish). Wife: Barbara, use of house I now live in during her widowhood. Eldest son: Gottlieb, house (with condition that wife be allowed to occupy for her widowhood). Exors to add 150 pounds Sterling that I have, to the 300 pounds Sterling already at interest, profits to widow and family for their maintenance. If wife remarries, give her 150 pounds Sterling, rest to be divided among my children. Wife to have use of two Negroes, Will and Betsy, during her life, also use of household goods during her widowhood. 300 Florins I have in Germany to be equally divided between my two sons when they come of age. Exors: wife (during her widowhood), The Reverend Mr. Zubly. Wit: George Sherous, Sigismund Biltz, John Eppinger.

D: 9 Sept. 1764. P: 15 Oct. 1764. R: 16 Oct. 1764.
pp. 122-123 WBA.

Louis Michel, his mark, Village of Newington, Christ Church Parish, planter. Anthony Pages of Savannah, baker, entire estate, real and personal. Wit: David Montaigut, Thomas Gegge, John Bourquin.

D: 24 Sept. 1762. P: 14 May 1767. R: 17 May 1767.
pp. 214-215 WBA.

Richard Milledge, his mark, Savannah, carpenter. Land at Tuckasee Kings to be sold, and any other of my estate to pay debts. Exors to keep the remainder for the benefit of my wife and four sons. Wife: Mary, Negro wench named Hate. Exors: John Milledge and Philip Box. Wit: Richard Floyd, his mark; Mary Wilson, her mark; William Stephens.

D: 15 Nov. 1768. P: 5 Jan. 1769. R: 9 Jan. 1769.

pp. 294-295 WBA.

Boul Miller, St. Matthew's Parish. Wife: Elizabeth, two cows and two calves, all my sheep, all my hogs, horse called Diamond, plows, gard, ax, what she wants of house furniture. Sons: Frederick Miller, 50 acres of land whereon I now live and 50 acres of that tract I hold in "the Swamp boun Bear Crick," one ax, one cow and calf; John Boul Miller, 100 acres in the Swamp, one hafer calf, and two toun lots in Ebenezer, garden lot; "but if my wife should gite one Son more by me" son, John Boul Miller, to have only 50 acres of the 100 above mentioned, "but if my wife should gite a daughter, she is to have no land," and my personal estate is to be sold, profits (after debts are paid) to be divided among my wife, my children, my nephew Christopher Miller. Exors: The Revd. Mr. Christopher Tribener, Mr. John Flerl, Mr. Salmen Zant. Wit: Christopher Cramer, Fridrich Lackner, Israel Lackner.

D: 20 Oct. 1773. P: ___ May 1775. R: n.d.

pp. 153-154 WBAA.

Elias Miller, St. George's Parish. Wife: Martha, one-third of my personal estate. Children: Aligil and William, other two-thirds of personal estate. Son: William, 200 acres of land on Brier Creek. Exors: wife and brother, Nathaniel Miller. Wit: John Brunson; William O'brian, his mark; Moses Miller.

D: 3 Nov. 1769. P: 21 Feb. 1770. R: 23 Feb. 1770.

pp. 337-338 WBA.

James Miller, his mark. Brother's children, my lot in Savannah, 100 acres of land at Ogechee. Michael Stutz, my working tools. John Stuart and Peter Breton, my wearing apparel. Mrs. Ross and the Stuarts, a shilling a piece. Michael Stutz, remainder of estate. Exors: Benjamin Goldwire, Michael Stutz, Edward Davidson. Wit: Jean Pierro Breton, George Ulland, Alexander McKay.

D: 15 May 1762. P: 1 Sept. 1762. R: 1 Sept. 1762.

pp. 84-85 WBA.

John Boul Miller, his mark, St. Matthew's Parish, planter. Wife: Anna, four cows and calfs. Son: Christopher, two cows and calfs. Bro-in-law: John Lang, one cow. Mother-in-law: Catarina Seckinger, one cow and calf. Exors to sell my tract of land, containing 200 acres in the swamp, to pay debts. Remainder of personal estate to wife. Exors: Salomon Zant, Christopher Cramer. Wit: George Ziegler; Andrew Seckinger, his mark; Benjamin Glaner.

D: 18 Feb. 1772. P: 3 June 1772. R: 5 June 1772.

pp. 440-441 WBA.

Palser Miller, Savannah, sadler. Exors to settle the estate of my bro-in-law, Frederick Holzendorff, late of Savannah. Wife: Susannah, all my estate, personal and real (except lot number 10 in Savannah), rents of excepted lot until my niece, Mary Holzendorff, is sixteen, at which time my niece shall inherit this lot. Mentions: my sister, Mary Strable. Exors: wife and friend, William Kirk, Jr. Wit: William Stephens, Raymond Demere.

D: 14 Jan. 1771. P: 12 April 1771. R: 18 April 1771.

pp. 401-402 WBA.

Robert Miller, St. John's Parish. Granddaus: Martha and Magdalene Miller, 20 shillings Sterling each. Remainder of estate equally divided among my seven children: James, Samuel, Daniel, Elizabeth Clark, Judith, Mary, and Hariot. Exors: Sons: Samuel and Daniel, Parmenas Way. Wit: Josiah Powell, Parmenas Way.

D: 29 Nov. 1773. P: 8 Feb. 1774. R: n.d.

pp. 78-79 WBAA.

Abraham Minis, Savannah. Sons: Philip and Joseph, all stock of horses and mares, equally divided. Daus: Leah, Esther, Judith, Hannah, and Sarah, all my black cattle, equally divided. Wife: Abigail, remainder of estate, real and personal, extrix. Mentions: Joseph Phillips, Benjamin Sheftall of Savannah. Wit: Edmund Tannatt, Thomas Parker, Charles Watson.

D: 21 Oct. 1754. P: 5 May 1757. R: n.d.
pp. 20-21 WBA.

Joseph Money, St. Paul's Parish, township of Wrightsborough, yeoman. Son: John, my land on south side of Upton's Creek, adjoining William Mill's land, containing 275 acres; plantation which I now live on, (when he is twenty-one), on the northwest side of Upton's Creek, supposing to be 175 acres. Wife: Mary, one-third the benefits of my plantation; half-acre lot in town of Wrightsborough known by number 27; all household goods, horses, cattle, hogs, sheep, all personal estate. Wife to pay 10 pounds Sterling to daus: Mary Hickson, Deborah, and Martha Money (when the latter comes of age). Exors: wife and John Stubbs. Wit: James Ryn, John Moore, Richard Moore.

D: 20 Sept. 1774. P: 25 Feb. 1775. R: n.d.

Document attached in which Joseph Maddock and Jonathan Sell are empowered to administer the oath of exor to Mary Money and John Stubbs. Dated: 8 Feb. 1775.

Oath of extrix signed by Mary Money. Dated 25 Feb. 1775.
pp. 125-128 WBAA.

Ann Monford, her mark, Savannah, widow. Dau: Anne, the wife of David Guindre (Guinter), entire estate, real and personal. "I cut off and disinherit my sons, Simon and John Rouvier with one shilling each." Wit: Christian Levenberg, his mark; Adam Kubeler, his mark.

D: 4 Jan. 1762. P: 12 Mar. 1762. R: n.d.
pp. 82-83 WBA.

Alexander Moon (translation of his will). Will made in Mr. Penrose's Schooner. Exors: James Mackay and John Gordon. Exors to sell all but my land. Eldest son: Alexander Moon, my plantation at Combahoo, Negro boy named Tom, 100 pounds Sterling. Remainder of estate divided between wife, Sarah, and Alexander, and the rest of my children: Duncan, Peggy (I give her besides one Negro girl named Miloy), and Rachael Moon, equally divided. Wit: Benjamin Sheftal, Michael Walthoe (Walthour).

D: 2 Jan. 1747/8. P: n.d. R: n.d.

Colonial Loose Will Collection.

William Moore, St. Matthew's Parish. Exors to sell all lands, lumber, cattle, horses (except two wagon horses and my wife's riding mare). Profits to pay my debts. Son: John, one shilling Sterling. Wife: Elizabeth, use of all my full-grown slaves and horses excepted above, household goods, tools. Her share of estate to my son, Aaron, on her death. Granddau: R(e)achel Weston, slave boy named Toney and his sister Dinah (at age of sixteen). Granddau: Sarah Moore, dau. of Aaron Moore, slave girl named Tamer. Exors: wife, John Goldwire, Aaron Moore. Wit John Morris; Michael Joyce; Jemima Joyce, her mark; Katherine Morris, her mark.

D: 9 April 1762. P: 17 May 1765. R: 17 May 1765.

pp. 133-134 WBA.

Andrew Moorman, his mark, St. Matthew's Parish, planter. Sons: Gideon, Cornelas, and Andrew, Jr., land I now live on, equally divided. When each arrives at age of twelve years, shall have one cow and calf. Eldest son: Gideon, my rifle gun. Wife: Cataran (Catherine), remainder of estate, real and personal, sole extrix. Wit: Thomas Keesee; Townsend Robinson; Sophero Robinson, her mark.

D: 20 Nov. 1761. P: 6 Dec. 1762. R: 8 Dec. 1762.

pp. 88-89 WBA.

John Morel, Christ Church Parish, planter. Sons: Peter Henry, and John (by my first wife, the dau. of Henry Bourquin, Esq.), and Bryan and Isaac, my sons by my present wife, the dau. of Jonathan Bryan, Esq., all my islands called Ossabaw in St. Philip's Parish, to be held as tenants in common, all my stock of horses, cattle, hogs, plantation tools, Negroes, divided equally when they reach the age of twenty-one. Dau: Mary, by my first wife, and her two sisters, Esther (Hetty) and Anne Bryan, by my second wife, 1000 pounds Sterling each, when they are married or eighteen years old. Wife: Mary, 1000 pounds Sterling, in settlement of her Dower, 150 pounds Sterling to be laid out in furniture, or otherwise as she shall think proper, best carriage, two horses, annuity of 50 pounds Sterling, 3 of my house Negroes, both during her widowhood. Eldest son: Peter Henry Morel, lot at Yamacraw adjoining the Common of the Town of Savannah, known by the number one, formerly the property of James Box, Esq., deceased; whose lot in Savannah, number ten west of Bull Street, originally granted Grey Elliott, Esq. Son: John, lot number two in Savannah. Son: Bryan, lot number three in Savannah. Son: Isaac, 200 acres on Great Ogechee in St. Matthew's Parish. Four sons: tract of 500 acres on Vernon River in Christ Church Parish, originally granted to William Stephens, Esq., named Bowlie (Beaulie) (Beaulieu), to be held as joint tenants. All remaining estate, real and personal to exors to be sold for best prices available. Money to be put at interest until children are of age and then equally divided. Exors: wife, (during her widowhood); Henry Sheall, now of London, my late clerk and bookkeeper; Doctor Henry Louis Bourquin of Savannah; four sons, Peter Henry, John, Bryan, and Isaac Morel (at the age of twenty-one). Wit: William Young; David Zubly, Jr.; Robert Watts.

D: 23 June 1774. P: 9 April 1777. R: 10 April 1777.

Codicil (dated ____ Jan. 1775. Wit: John Cosson, John Pinkerton, John Detheridge); Four sons: two tracts of land containing 1900 acres, in St. Andrew's Parish. Exors to sell plantation at Bowlie (Beaulie), on Vernon River. Exor Dr. Henry Louis Bourquin is dead. Appoint, John McQueen of South Carolina, Esq., an exor.

pp. 312-322 WBAA.

Peter Morel, Savannah, victualer. Eldest son: John, tract of land containing 500 acres on Pipemaker's Creek, provided that son gives my wife for her use a town lot, number two in Try Konnel Tything in Darby Ward, with lot number 63 (5 acres) and farm lot number 8 (45 acres). Wife: Mary, one-third of my personal estate. Wife and children, use of John Penrose's farm lot where I now dwell. Eldest dau: Mary Ann, toun lot number 1 in Digby Tything Deckers Ward; five-acre lot number 40, farm lot number 8 (45 acres), the latter two which are mortgaged to me by Caleb Davis of Georgia, mariner, but now in England. Youngest son: Peter, 50-acre farm in Abercorn. Remaining two-thirds of personal estate equally divided among all my children: Mary Ann, John, Jean, Mary, Peter, Judah. Exors: wife, William Ewen of Savannah, Thomas Rasberry of Savannah. Wit: William Russell, William Bull, Anthony Camuse.

D: 15 Oct. 1752. P: 27 Oct. 1752. R: n.d.

Colonial Loose Will Collection.

Capt. Martin Morland, London, mariner. Wife: use of plate, linen and household furniture during her widowhood; bequest to dau: Dorothy, after death of wife. All remainder of estate to friends, Thomas Horne of Ratcliff in Middlesex County, shipwright, and Walter _____ sun of the same place, apothecary to be sold, profits given to my children. Exors: Thomas Horne and Walter _____ Sun. Wit: Joseph Heaton, George Green.

D: 4 June 1751. P: n.d. R: 22 June 1761.

p. 57 WBA.

John Murphree, St. George's Parish. Sons: William and Josiah, one shilling Sterling each. Son: James, two cows and calves. Wife: Martha, use of my plantation and land and all my personal estate during her widowhood. After her death or marriage, plantation to son Mills, personal estate to be divided among my children: Wright, Demsey, Sarah, and Mills. Exor: son, William. Wit: Francis Pugh, Demsey Murphree, Wright Murphree.

D: 24 Sept. 1770. P: n.d. R: n.d.

Colonial Loose Will Collection.

David Murray, Christ Church Parish, Esq. Wife: Lucia, plate, furniture, household goods. Rest of personal estate to wife; brother, John Murray of Philipbaugh in Scotland: Charles Murray, late of Island of Maderia, Esq., John Graham of Savannah, Esq., William Telfair and Edward Telfair of Savannah, merchants. Above as exors. Exors to sell lands on Little Ogechee and plantation called Hermitage, to pay debts. To hold rest of estate until my dau., Charles, is 18, at which time she shall have the estate. Wit: James Edward Powell; Henry Yonge, Jr.; George Walton.

D: 17 Feb. 1770. P: 21 May 1771. R: 4 June 1771.

pp. 409-412 WBA.

(Charles Murray I, brother of David; Charles Murray II, daughter of David.)

Malcolm Nelson, Savannah. Brother: Thomas, and sisters: Jane Russell and Jennet Nelson, two tracts of land in Effingham County, containing 400 acres, to be held as tenants in common; three Negroes named Combernold, Glascow, and Adam, equally shared. Mother: Jane Nelson and brother: William, 100 pounds Sterling, now at interest in Scotland, equally divided. Exors: William Watt and Alexander Cunningham. Wit: James Jones, James Storie, Seaborn Jones.

D: 3 April 1778. P: n.d. R: n.d.

Colonial Loose Will Collection.

Robert Nichols, St. John's Parish, planter. Sister: Sarah, spinster, 5 Negroes, bed, bedstead and bedding now in her possession, six silver tablespoons, one large mahogeny dining table, six silver teaspoons, my pictures, my large leather portmantue trunk, 1000 acres of land in St. David's Parish on Turtil River. Stepson: Morgan Sabb, wearing apparel. Plantation called "Springfield" in St. John's Parish to be sold with my stock of cattle, horses, sheep, hogs, plantation tools and utensils, four Negroes (Sam, Hecter, Primus, and Nancy) to pay debts. Money left over to wife, Mary Esther. Also to wife, 12 Negroes, bed and furniture, blue chest, one dining table, tea table, seven silver tablespoons, sugar tongs and strainer, large soup spoon. Exors:

Simon Munro, Andrew Darling, Roger Kelsall, and John Irvin, Esq. Wit: Simon Munro, John Gibbons, Jr., Donald Fraser.

D: 17 Sept. 1768. P: 20 Dec. 1768. R: 21 Dec. 1768.

pp. 282-284 WBA.

Barak Norman, St. John's Parish, (carpenter). Exors to sell entire estate at public sale to pay debts. Remaining profits to be put at interest for maintenance of my dau: Elizabeth Norman, until she is eighteen, when she is to have the remaining principle. Mentions: father, Barak Norman; brothers, Thomas, William, and sister, Elizabeth. Dau: Elizabeth shall live under the care of her grandmother: Prysillah (Priscilla) Girardeau as long as she may live. Exors: John Stewart, Jr.; my uncle, Richard Spencer; and my brother, Thomas Norman. Wit: James Andrew, Rebekah Girardeau, Elizabeth Sumner.

D: 22 Jan. 1765. P: 28 Feb. 1765. R: 5 Mar. 1765.

pp. 127-129 WBA.

William Norman, St. John's Parish, planter. Wife: Mary, one-fourth of my personal estate, riding chair, two horses, Negro boy named Plymouth, residence on my plantation during her widowhood. Dau: Mary, one-third of my personal estate (at age of eighteen or marriage). Dau: Renchy, one-half my personal estate (at age eighteen or marriage). Son: William, remainder of personal estate, at age of eighteen, either one of my tracts of land. Other tract of land to be sold at that time and money divided among my wife and children, Mary, Renchy, and William Exors: wife, John Elliott, Joseph Way. Wit: Lazarus Mallard; John Bacon, Jr.; Rebekah Elliott.

D: 3 Mar. 1773. P: 3 April 1773. R: n.d.

Document attached in which Parmenas Way and Audley Maxwell, Esqs., are empowered to administer the oath of extrix. to Mary Norman. Dated 3 April, 1773.

Oath of extrix. signed by Mary Norman. Dated 21 April, 1773.

pp. 35-37 WBAA.

Charles Odingsell, Christ Church Parish, planter. Wife: Sarah, all that I had by her, both what was left her by her former husband, Lurngston, and what fell to her by the death of her dau, Dory, household furniture, 2 horses, Negro boy named Alex, sum of 1500 South Carolina currency, (all above in settlement of my wife's Dower). Dau: Mary Screven, 2 Negroes. Son: Charles, six Negroes. Son: Benjamin, seven Negroes. Dau: Elizabeth, one Negro wench with her two children. Dau: Sarah, eight Negroes. Freedom and new suit of clothes annually to Old Mimah and Amoses in exchange for 5 shillings annually. Exors to sell two tracts of land where Mr. Screven now lives, known by name of Rest Park and London Derry, with two tracts opposite one bought of Johnson and Alex Wylly, and lands in South Carolina to pay debts. Remainder to be divided among my children. Sons: Benjamin (when twenty-one), and Charles to divide, by lot, land granted me in St. David's and St. Andrew's Parishes. Exors: son-in-law, James Screven; Anthony Toomer of Charlestown, South Carolina. Wit: John Stack, Mary Ash, John Screven.

D: 27 July 1770. P: 10 Jan. 1774. R: 11 Jan. 1774. pp. 375-378 WBA.

IN THE NAME OF GOD, AMEN, **I, CHRISTOPHER ORTON,** minister at Savannah, being infirm in health, but of perfect mind and memory, do make this my Last Will and Testament in manner following — Imprimis, I commend my soul into the hands of Almighty God, trusting in his mercy, thro' the merits of my Dear Redeemer for all my sins, and my body I commit to be buried at the discretion of my dear neighbours — I also give and bequeath to my servant Ann Kelly whatsoever clothes of mine are in her custody, and if Mr. Bosomworth shall not chuse to accept of one matress bed in my house I also leave it to her, the said Ann Kelly — Item, I give and bequeath to Colonel Stephens any book he shall please to accept of in my library. Item, I give and bequeath to my dear brother Rowland Orton of Sheeby nigh Richmond in Yorkshire, whatsoever is within one large chest of Mr. Bosomworth's now in the custody of Capt. Patrick Mackay, provided that the silver plate belonging to the Church of Savannah, one surplice, one folio book belonging to the library, and one silver pint belonging to his Excellency, Genl. Oglethorp, which Mr. Peter Jouboy (Joubert) is under condition to ingrave according to the directions given him, for which he has already rec'd of me to the value of forty shillins by Genl. Oglethorp's order and which I hope his Excellency will repay to Mr. Thomas Bosomworth — Lastly, I nominate and appoint my dear friend Thomas Bosomworth, sole Executor of this my last will and testament desiring him to receive what is due to me from the honourable trustees (viz) my salary and my servants allowance, due from ye 14th day of June last and I will and desire that he (Mr. Bosomworth) do pay of(f) as far as effects will suffice, all my debts and funeral expences — part of which I desire about six pounds Sterling to Capt. P. Mackay, one pound, more or less, to Mr. Campbell, and 5 shillings to Mr. Bromfield. I also am indebted to ye said Mr. Bromfield for one fowling piece and some other things belonging to it which I desire he will please to accept again for ye value.

To Mr. Bosomworth I also give the choice of all my manuscripts and books, desiring only that he will reserve a few(e) of the small family books and tracts for a token to my dear father and friend. I hereby declare this my last will, made this 24th day of July in ye year 1742.

(CHRISTOPHER ORTON)

Colonial Loose Will Collection.

John Osgood, St. John's Parish, preacher. Wife: Mary, in lieu of Dower, 10 Negroes and 50 pounds Sterling, riding chair, harness, chest of drawers, feather bed and furniture, silver tablespoons and teaspoons, all my hogs and sheep, one-third of my cattle, my gold sleeve buttons, my ring, silver watch. Nephew: John Baker, 20 pounds Sterling. John Osgood Harley, son of James Harley, 5 pounds Sterling. Nephew: Thomas Baker, Negro named Jack, who now works with him at the carpenter's trade, town lot in Sunbury, number 57. Grandchildren: John and William Quarterman, 20 pounds Sterling a year toward their education, if the exors of the will of John Quarterman see fit. Dau: Sarah Way, one-third of my remaining estate for her lifetime, after her death, to her children. Grandchildren (children of said dau.): Sarah, Elizabeth, John, William, and Elijah Quarterman, one-third of my remaining estate. Grandchildren: Mary and Joseph Way, other one-third of my remaining estate. Mentions: Mary Baker, Dau. of my wife's sister, Elizabeth Baker; John Godfrey, son of Hannah Alexander, formerly Hannah

Godfrey; Susannah Andrew, dau. of Benjamin Andrew; Mary Bacon and Saunders Andrew, children of Joseph Andrew; sister-in-law: Lydia Winn. Exors.: wife, dau., Sarah Way; John Winn, Sr.; Benjamin Andrew; Robert Quarterman; my nephews: William and Thomas Baker. Wit: Samuel Salters, John Stacy, John Elliott.

D: 2 June 1773. P: 27 Aug. 1773. R:

Codicil (18 June 1773, same wit.): appoints son-in-law Parmenas Way an exor. of above will. Exors. granted permission to sell any part of estate that would prove advantageous to heirs.

Document attached in which James Screven, John Mitchell, and John Baker, Esqs., are empowered to administer the oath of extrix. to Mary Osgood and Sarah Way. Dated 27 Aug. 1773.

Oath of extrix. signed by Mary Osgood and Sarah Way. Dated 6 Sept. 1773.

pp. 53-57 WBAA.

Josiah Osgood, Senior, St. John's Parish, planter. Wife: Barbara (in lieu of her lawful Dower), one-third of my personal estate; use of 50 acres on this tract of land I now live on, adjoining land now the property of my son, Josiah; use of one-half my dwelling house. Son: Josiah, 200 acres of land, adjoining lands formerly laid out to Rebecca Quarterman and Joseph Way, north of this tract I now live on. Son: John, 150 acres, part of tract I now live on, adjoining lands of Richard Spencer and land laid out for my son, Josiah. Son: Thomas, tract of 250 acres on the Mortar Swamp in St. Andrew's Parish. Daus: Sarah Fulton, Mary Osgood, and Elizabeth Osgood, 10 pounds Sterling each. Remainder of estate equally divided among my six children. Sons to have their share of my estate at age twenty, daus., at eighteen or marriage. Exors: sons, Josiah and John. Wit: Thomas Way, William Willson, Richard Shave.

D: 23 June 1770. P. 3 July 1772. R: 4(?) July 1772. pp. 447-448 WBA.

John Owens, his mark, Savannah, Christ Church Parish, joiner. Wife: Ann, all estate, real and personal, for her life. After her death estate to Barbara Wright, wife of Benjamin Wright, Savannah, carpenter. Extrix.: wife. Wit: I. (Isaac) Baillou, William Lesslie, Jacob Mock.

D: 11 Oct. 1775. P: 13 Nov. 1775. R: 13 Nov. 1775. pp. 200-202 WBAA.

John Paddero, his mark, Ebenezer District, planter. Son: Solomon, tract of land, containing 100 acres, adjoining the Savannah River and the tract of land where I now live; tract of land, containing 200 acres where I now live; Negro man named Rogger, wagon, furniture, yoke of oxen, four cows and calves, four sows and pigs, my black horse, saddle, bridle, gun, wearing clothes. Wife: Margit, use of manner plantation during her widowhood. Remainder of personal estate to be divided among wife and other children. Exors.: wife; John Frail, (Flerl (?)) Esq.; John Gasper Wertsch of Ebenezer. Wit: Edward Boykin; William Rogers, his mark; William Deloatch.

D: 10 Oct. 1761. P: R: 5(?) Aug. 1763. pp. 112-113 WBA.

Margaret Pages, Savannah, widow. Alexander Wylly of Savannah, Esq., and Richard Wylly of Savannah, Merchant, entire estate, real and personal, to act as exors. Son: Michael Lucas, my estate, during his life. After his death to Susannah Wylly, wife of Alexander Wylly, and then to her children. Exors. to clothe, maintain, and educate in such beneficial trade, my mulatto slave named Peter, until he is twenty-one when he shall be manumitted. Wit: Henry Louis Bourquin, John Storr, Grey Elliott.

D: 10 Dec. 1768. P: 14 Dec. 1768. R: 16 Dec. 1768. Codicil (same date, same wit.): I give and bequeath to Peter Tondee of Savannah, carpenter, Negro wench named Comba. p. 280-282 WBA.

Capt. George Palmer, Savannah. Wife Mary Ann: entire estate, real and personal for her lifetime; after her death, the estate to my son, William, and my dau., Elizabeth, equally divided.

105

Exors.: Lyman Hall, John Glen, and Job Pray. Wit.: W. Stephens, Moses Nunes, Amadeus Chiffelle.

D: 24 Nov. 1771. P: 16 Feb. 1778. R: n.d.

Colonial Loose Will Collection.

Mary Palmer, Savannah, spinster. Brother: Samuel Palmer (born in Northampton, England, if he is still living), 10 pounds Sterling. If he is dead, the 10 pounds Sterling to my sister, Elizabeth, wife of Emanuel Western of London. Children of Elizabeth Western: Samuel and Sarah, 10 pounds sterling each. Wearing apparel to Elizabeth Western, also. Chinz counterpane to Sarah Western. Friends: Wakelin Welsh of Matlin Street in London, tobacco merchant, his wife; and Thomas Vincent of Savannah, Esq., his wife; Elizabeth Rook; one Guinea Sterling each. Remainder of estate equally divided between my brother, Samuel Palmer and my sister, Elizabeth Western. Exors.: Wakelin Welsh and Thomas Vincent. Wit.: Robert Bolton, William Ritch.

D: 18 Nov. 1761. P: 28 Mar. 1763. R: 30 Mar. 1763. pp. 110-111 WBA.

Margaret Papot, Christ Church Parish, her mark, widow. Grandchildren: John Weddale, 100 pounds Sterling, when he comes of age and Isaac, 50 pounds when he comes of age. Son: James Papot, 50 pounds Sterling. Granddau.: Jane Judith Papot (dau. of my son, James), 50 pounds Sterling, when she is eighteen or married, Negro wench named Lucy, bed and furniture, two pair of sheets, one quilt, two large silver tablespoons, chest of drawers, dressing table, tea table. Susannah Papot, 20 pounds of Sterling. Granddau.: Jane Papot (dau. of my son, Peter Papot), 20 pounds Sterling, when she is eighteen or married, bed and furniture, sheets, quilt, four large table spoons. Grandson: Peter, 20 pounds Sterling, when he comes of age. Dau: Sarah Papot, wife of my son, Peter, Negro wench named Phobe, during her life, 10 pounds Sterling. Sarah and Susannah Papot, all residue and remainder of my furniture. Exors.: son, James; friends, James Galashe, Philip Allman. Wit: N. W. Jones, John Goldwire, H. Cuyler.

D: 24 Jan. 1776. P: 18 Feb. 1777. R: 14 Mar. 1777. Codicil (28 Jan. 1777, Wits: George B. Spencer; Ann Goldwire, her

106

mark; Henry Cuyler): Susannah Papot, Negro woman named Juliet. My old clothes to Negro women, Julie and Phebe. Son: Peter Papot, 20 pounds Sterling. Anything remaining to be divided equally among my children.

Document attached in which William Stephens, Esq., is empowered to administer the oath of exor. to James Papot, James Galashe, and Philip Allman. Dated 18 Feb. 1777.

Oath of exor. sworn to James Papot and Philip Allman (14 Mar. 1777) and James Galashe (4 April, 1777).

pp. 302-306 WBAA.

Henry Parker, Christ Church Parish, planter. Wife: Elizabeth, household goods and furniture, 10 Negroes to be held for the maintenance and education of my children William, Henry, Ann and Elizabeth, until they are of age of twenty-one. If wife marrys, she shall have two Negroes, the other eight going to my brother, James, and my brother-in-law, Samuel Farley, both of Savannah, on the condition that they shall apply the profits from the labor of these slaves to maintenance of my children. If wife remainds a widow, when she dies, these slaves to James Parker and Samuel Farley. Son: William, 250 acres called Brewton, granted me by the late Trustees of the Providence of Georgia; 250-acre tract called Brewham. Second son: Henry, half of tract called Brewton, containing 250 acres, which tract descended to me, as heir of my brother, Edward Parker, Decd.; a half of tract of 250 acres at Brewham. Exors.: wife, James Parker, Samuel Farley. Wit.: Richard Williamson, John Spencer, Susannah Hover, her mark.

D: 16 Nov. 1771. P: 14 Aug. 1772. R: n.d. pp. 1-3 WBAA.

Joseph Parker, Savannah, silversmith. Mother: Ann Parker, and Brother: William Henry Parker, all real estate, to hold for use of my three sisters, Grace, Mary, and Susannah, to be equally divided among them as tenants in common, when they are twenty-one. Remainder of estate equally divided among my three Sisters. Exors.: brothers, William Henry; James Parker,

The Honorable John Graham, Esq. Wit.: Minis Minis, James Anderson, William Young.

D: 15 Dec. 1766. P: 18 May 1770. R: 21 May 1770. pp. 347-349 WBA.

Thomas Parker, Gent. Leaves Charles Watson, Francis Harris and William Russell of Savannah, Esqs., town lot in Savannah, now occupied by James Muter; tract of land on island of 300 acres called Chelmsford; all other lands, to be sold. Profits to pay legacy to children or child of my deceased sister, Prudence, late wife of John Fitch of Chelmsford in Essex County in England, leather cutter. To the Church Wardens of Christ Church Parish, Savannah, 5 pounds Sterling, to be distributed among the distressed widows of the Parish. Ann, wife of Charles Watson; Elizabeth, wife of Charles Pryce, Esq.; Leah Minis of Savannah, spinster; a mourning ring each, of value of one guinea. Exors: Charles Watson, Francis Harris, William Russell. Wit.: Robert Baillie, William Abbott, John Fox.

D: 16 April 1759. P: 11 Dec. 1759. R: 20 June 1761. pp. 55-56 WBA.

John Parkinson, Gent., late of the island of Jamaica but now of Christ Church Parish. Nephew: John & Niece: Eleanor (son & dau. of my brother, Thomas Parkinson in Lincolnshire in Great Britain), 100 pounds Sterling each. Negro woman: Maria, now in Jamaica, her freedom & manumission. Remainder of estate to be equally divided among my brother, Thomas Parkinson; sister, Agness Parkinson; & Elizabeth Atkinson. Exors: brother (now in Great Britain); his son, Edmund (now in Jamaica); & his son John (now in Great Britain); Joseph Woodruff of Savannah, merchant. Wit: Jonathan Peat, Thomas Pope, George Vallance.

D: 8 Nov. 1769. P: 2 Oct. 1771. R: 4 Oct. 1771. pp. 417-418 WBA.

Thomas Peacock, St. John's Parish, planter. Brother: William Peacock, 30 pounds Sterling. Congregation Church in St. John's Parish (under the charge of the Revd. Mr. Osgood), 10 pounds Sterling. Wife: Elizabeth, annuity of 15 pounds Sterling as long as she remains my widow. Slaves to be kept together on my plantation until my youngest child shall be twenty years old, for the benefit of my children. At that time all my personal estate to be divided by my children. Son: John, tract of land, containing 500 acres, on the lower part of Turtle River. Son: Thomas, three tracts of land in St. John's Parish where I live, containing 378 acres; tract of 200 acres of pine barren near John Stewart's land. Son: William, tract of land on Bultown Swamp in St. Andrew's Parish, containing 150 acres; my lot on the Bay in Sunbury. Son: James, tract of 350 acres at the public landing on the Boin Swamp in St. John's Parish; another tract of 200 acres near Turtle River. Exors. to sell lot in Savannah, profits to personal estate & divided. Exors.: Parmenas Way, Esq.; John Wynn, Jr.; Josiah Osgood, Jr.; sons, John & Thomas (when they come of age). Wit.: John Osgood, Jr., Richard Shave, Thomas Osgood.

D: ___ Nov. 1769. P: 3 Jan. 1772. R: 4 Jan. 1772. pp. 428-430 WBA.

John Penrose, Savannah. Wife: Margaret, for the support of herself & two children, Mary & John, my town lot on the bay in _____, remainder of my property after debts are paid. Boat, tract of 300 acres on Whit marsh Island to be sold, profits to wife. Catherine Cammeron, lot, late James Turner's, if she pays 10 pounds Sterling. Exors.: Henry Hamilton, Benjamin Goldwire, Richard Milledge. Wit.: John Pye, Joseph Stanly, David Snook.

D: 6 Nov. 1754. P: 4 Nov. 1754.(?) R: n.d. pp. 3-4 WBA.

John Perkins, now commanding at Fort George on Cockspur Island in Georgia. Wife: Christian, entire estate, real and personal, extrix. Wit: John Simpson, Thomas Hasney, William Cray(s).

D: 2 July 1766. P: 16 Dec. 1766. R: 16 Dec. 1766. P. 179 WBA.

John Pettigrew, Sunbury, St. John's Parish. "I have no exception to any person in town being at my Funeral, but John Hardy, carpenter who I despise on account of his bad character,

& as I hate all villains as I do snakes, I desire that my Executors shall turn that Scoundrell from my funeral should he have the impudence to attend it." Exors. to take upon themselves the management of the copartnership under the firm Pettygrew & Paterson, during the absence of Simons Paterson, Sr. of Glasgow or Simon Paterson, Jr., his son. If both are absent, the exors. are to sell the firm. Exors. also to collect debts of the firm & send them to Britain. Mother: Janet Pettigrew, my gold sleeve buttons, gold seal, silver shoe buckle, stone knee buckles, my seal with a white stone, my Bibles, silver watch. If mother is dead at my decease, the above articles to my eldest sister, Janet Pettygrew. Robert Baillie of St. Andrew's Parish, Esq., 5 pounds, current money. Roderick Macintosh, Esq., of St. Andrew's Parish, my broad sword. Walter Wilson in Glasgow, my brass barrel pistols. David Fleming, 5 pounds, Georgia currency. Donald Fraser, collector of the country duties for this district, three copies of my books. Simon Paterson, Sr., at Glasgow, five pounds, current money. Simon Paterson, Jr. of Glasgow, a mourning ring. James Beverly, school master in Sunbury, two copies of my books. William Wallace, my clerk, my beaver hat, linen apparel. Sisters: Janet, Grizzel, Elizabeth, Mary, Margaret, & Agnes Pettygrew, my real estate in Parish of Barony of Glasgow and County of Lamerk (Lanark), known by the name Green in Scotland, which my mother at present life rents, remainder of personal estate. Exors.: Robert Baillie of St. Andrew's Parish, Esq.; David Fleming; Donald Fraser of Sunbury; Simon Paterson, Sr., and Simon Paterson, Jr.; both of Glasgow. Wit: Samuel Miller, David Laing, William Bosomworth.

D: 11 Sept. 1775. P: 8 Dec.(?) 1775. R: 8 Oct. 1775. pp. 208-212 WBAA.

John Pettycrow (Pettygrow), Augusta, Indian trader & victualler. Nephew: Robert Pettycrow, 150 pounds, South Carolina currency. My reputed natural son: John Pettycrow, two horses of his choice from my stock. Remainder of estate divided between my wife, Catharine and my dau., Jane Pettycrow. Sister: Mary Egan of Lisbane, Ireland, estate if wife dies or marries, and if dau. dies. Exors.: John Rea, Martyn Campbell, & Francis McCartan, Esqs. Wit: William Day, James McHenrey, N. Casbell.

D: 15 Feb. 1758. P: 15 April 1761. R: 24 June 1761.

Codicil (same date, same wit.) : William Clements, 200 pounds, South Carolina currency.

pp. 65-66 WBA.

(Will in French)   IN THE NAME OF GOD—AMEN

Testament and last will of me, **Daniel Phifer (Phifner)**, inhabitant of Hampstead in the province of Georgia.............

I emphatically declare that I am indisposed and sick of body but sound of mind and in good judgment and that this is my last will—NAMELY.............

I give my soul to God my Creator and my body to the earth, thinking I have some hope of mercy through the merits of Jesus Christ my Saviour and Redeemer.

As for my three children: Isabau (Isabelle), Ulric, Jean (John), my personal estate and real estate—I return it (all) to the hand of Michel Bourhalter, citizen of Hampstead, who has been so kind to, without charge, take care of and to help their father.

As for all my debts I declare that I owe a year and six months of provisions to my landlords The Honourable Trustees.

Besides I declare that I owe to Michel Bourhalter twelve pounds eleven shillings sterling to relieve my debts for aiding me in my passage from London to Georgia and for my needs from Calais to Savanna.

Besides I owe to Michel Bourhalter one (?) pound 10 shillings sterling for the transport of my old clothes from Berne in Switzerland to Calais.

Besides I declare that I owe to Peter Cobler (Coble) five pounds sterling for aiding me in my passage from London to Savannah in Georgia in America. I gave him a note of obligation, written in English (England) signed at London.

Witnesses   [Daniel Phifner]
   Louis Stamen
   Peter Thester, his mark
   Pierre Morel
   D: ___ _____ 1737. P: n.d. R: n.d.

Colonial Loose Will Collection.

HAMPSTEAD, a German village situated between four and five miles of Savannah upon the head of the Vernon River, laid out in 1733 for twelve families engaged in vegetable gardening, one mile from the French village at Highgate. Settlers of both these towns were engaged in gardening, and supplying the inhabitants of Savannah with vegetables. Now Dead Towns.
Collections of the Georgia Historical Society, Savannah, Volumes 1, 2, 3, 4.

Edmond Pierse, Savannah. Exors. to sell entire estate, to pay debts. Remainder of money to my brother, John; my sisters, Ellinore and Margarette; all in Ireland. Exors:. The Honourable Grey Elliott, Esq.; Matthew Roche. Wit: Thomas Tripp, James Caldou, John Harvey.

D: 16 Mar. 1757. P: 17 May 1769. R: 22 May 1769. pp. 307-308 WBA.

Seth Place, Tybee. Son: Hubbard Place, house and lands in the Island of Bermuda. Remainder of estate divided among my wife, Jeane (one-third), and my daus: Miriam, Jenny, and Mary (two-thirds, equally divided). Exors: wife; James Habersham and David Montaigut, Esqs.; Hubbard Outerbridge of the Island of Bermuda. Wit: A. DeMay, Daniel Nunes Rivers, Peter Laffitte.

D: 24 Sept. 1757. P: 11 May 1758. R: 11 May 1758. p. 42 WBA.

John Pletter, Ebenezer. Mother: Elizabeth Kesler & sister: Mary Kesler, 50-acre tract of land in Ebenezer. Wit: John Flerl, Sr.; John Ulrick Neidlinger; Samuel Kraus, planter.

D: 6 Mar. 1767. P: 4 Dec. 1773. R: n.d. pp. 66-67 WBAA.

Nathaniel Polhill, Berkley County, South Carolina. Wife: Hannah, entire estate, real & personal; sole extrix. Wit: Thomas Barksdale, John Fullerton, John Wingood.

D: 9 Nov. 1756. P: n.d. R: 3 Sept. 1761. pp. 69-70 WBA.

Mary Powell, wife of James Edward Powell of Savannah, Esq. Dau-in-law: Alicia Powell (wife of my son, Robert Williams Powell of Charlestown, Gent.), tract of 1000 acres in St. Philip's Parish on Great Ogeechee. Husband: James Edward Powell, 147 acres of land, adjoining Beaufort, called the Pidgeon House of Watson's Point in South Carolina; tract of 500 acres of land about 13 miles from Augusta; two lots of land near Savannah, Negro slaves. After his death these bequeaths to daus, Elizabeth Moore and Mary Yonge (wives of Philip Moore & Henry Yonge, Jr., Gent). By will of my late father Robert Williams,

Esq., I am entitled to distribute 2000 pounds, South Carolina currency. I bequeath it to my son, Robert Williams Powell, and my dau., Elizabeth Moore, equally divided. Exors: James Edward Powell, Esq.; Robert Williams Powell; Philip Moore. Wit.: Claudia Mullryne, Mary Wright, Elizabeth Morgan.

D: 8 Sept. 1776. P: 22 Nov. 1776. R: 22 Nov. 1776. pp. 261-263 WBAA.

William Priest, Province of Georgia. Statement of exoneration of my master, John Brown, who in his passion fired at me. Wit: Edward Pylon (?); James Landree, his mark; Mary Anne Landree, her mark.

D: 28 Feb. 1737. P: n.d. R: n.d.

Colonial Loose Will Collection.

Joseph Prenieres (Pruniere), Savannah, merchant. Entire estate, real and personal to James Mossman and Joseph Clay of Savannah, merchants to act as exors. Thomas, son of my slave, Maria, whom I have lately manumitted, his maintenance until he is twenty-one, remainder of estate to him, Thomas, commonly called Thomas Prunieres. If he dies before twenty-one, estate for the benefit of the poor of Christ Church Parish. Slave: Mary, her freedom. Wit: Francis Arven, Matthew Roche, William MacKenzie.

D: 23 April 1768. P: 19 May 1768. R: 30 May 1768. pp. 268-269 WBA.

Solomon Prothero, St. Matthew's Parish. Exors. to sell three Negroes, Peter, Harry, and Tom, 50 acres of land on which I now live (part of 100-acre tract), to pay debts. Remainder of estate to my wife, Elizabeth and children, equally divided. Exors: wife, John Wertsch, John Goldwire. Wit: Edward Boykin, John Boykin, Edward Vanzant.

D: 27 April 1775. P: 25 July 1775. R: 25 July 1775. pp. 176-178 WBAA.

Amie Pruniere, wife of Joseph Pruniere of Savannah, Gent. (and widow of David Jones, planter, deceased; and before that widow of Peter Mallet of Savannah, shopkeeper, deceased). (By virtue of a Deed of Settlement with Joseph Pruniere, bearing date of about 17 Jan. 1753.) Son: Thomas Jones, lot in Savannah containing five acres, another lot of 44 7/8 acres in Savannah. Dau: Priscilla Jones, 100 pounds (as mentioned due on Bond from Gideon Mallet, my father.) Son, Thomas and dau: Priscilla, personal estate, equally divided. Exors: James Campbell of Savannah, merchant, and William Ewen of Savannah, potter. Wit: Catherine Mallet, William Johnson, Charles Watson.

D: 19 Sept. 1755. P: 31 Oct. 1755. R: n.d. pp. 12-13 WBA.

Elizabeth Pryce, wife of Charles Pryce, Gent. (late widow of Samuel Mercer, deceased, and also widow of John Tisdale, deceased). Marriage settlement dated about 7 December 1757. Husband: Charles Pryce, entire estate, real and personal, exor. Wit: Will Knox, William Clifton, Charles Watson.

D: 9 Nov. 1759. P: 23 Feb. 1768. R: 27 Feb. 1768. pp. 251-253 WBA.

John Rodolph Pury, Fairhill. Exors. to sell entire estate to pay debts. Remaining money to the exors. Exors: The Revd. Mr. Bartholomew Zouberbuhler, and David Montaigut. Wit: Matthew Mauve, Jacob Waldburger, Benjamin Farley.

D: 15 Jan. 1756. P: 28 Jan. 1756. R: n.d. p. 15 WBA.

John Pye, his mark, Savannah. Wife: Deborah, entire estate real and personal, particularly tract of 200 acres near Highgate, 100 acres, two town lots, three Negroes, debts to following: Mr. Powell, dutch Butcher, Mr. Sheftal, Mr. Rasberry, Mr. Graham. Wife to provide for the maintenance of children, Mary Elizabeth and Elizabeth. Exors: wife, David Fox, Benjamin Goldwire. Wit: John Fox, Peter Nephew, Thomas Mathers, James Miller.

D: 6 April 1755. P: 8 Oct. 1755. R: n.d. pp. 10-11 WBA.

John Quarterman, St. John's Parish, planter. Wife: Hannah, one-third of my personal estate, use of one-third of my plantation (In lieu of her Dower). Son: John, 30 pounds Sterling (in lieu of land), one-sixth of my personal estate. Son: Thomas, one fifth of my personal estate. Son: Robert, one-third of my tract of 700 acres. Son: William, one-third of above tract, including the plantation on which I now live, one-third of my personal estate. Dau: Jemima, 40 pounds Sterling, 6 blue china cups and saucers, six silver teaspoons, one-half the remainder of my personal estate. Son: Richard, remaining one-third of my land, lot in Sunbury, remainder of personal estate. Exors: wife, sons: John and Thomas; John Elliott. Wit: James Maxwell, John Sacheverell, John Elliott, Jr.

D: 25 June 1763. P: 20 Feb. 1765. R: 5 Mar. 1765. pp. 129-131 WBA.

John Quarterman, St. John's Parish. Wife: Sarah, Negro wench named Daphne, six silver table spoons, my riding chair and chair horse, one-sixth of my personal estate (in lieu of her Dowery), also use of house and household goods and one-fourth of my land as long as she remains my widow. (My father-in-law, John Osgood). Dau: Sarah, 40 pounds Sterling, gold sleeve buttons. Son: John, one-half of my tract of land whereon I now live including the settlement and my lot and storehouse at Jericho Landing. Son: William, other half of tract of land I live on. Son: Elijah, tract of 300 acres near Sunbury, lot in Sunbury. My right to seats in the Meeting house pertain equally to all my sons. Remainder of estate equally divided among my five children (when they are of age or married.) Exors: wife, brothers, Thomas, Robert, William; John Stewart; John Elliott. Wit: John Evins, Josiah Osgood, Jr., John Sacheverell.

D: 11 July 1767 (?). P: 10 Nov. 1769. R: 21 Dec. 1769.

Document attached in which Parmenas Way, Audley Maxwell, and James Forrester are empowered to administer the oath of exors to the exors. Dated 10 Nov. 1769.

Oath of exor signed by Sarah, Thomas, Robert, William Quarterman. Dated 14 Dec. 1769.

pp. 332-336 WBA.

Conrad Rahn, St. Matthew's Parish, planter. Wife: Ann Barbara, use of land where I live during her widowhood. Eldest son: Matthew, tract of land containing 150 acres on which I now live, after his mother's death. Sons: Jonathan and Joseph, tract of land on the long swamp, containing 200 acres, equally divided. Son: Jacob, 100 acres of land in St. George's Parish. Daus: Lydia and Hannah Margareth, 30 head of my horn cattle. Remainder of estate equally divided among my wife and children. Exors: John Hangleiter and John Wertsch. Wit: John Martin Paulitsch, Urban Buntz, Timothy Lemke.

D: 21 Oct. 1773. P: 16 Jan. 1777. R: 31 Jan. 1777.

Document attached in which John Adam Treutlen and Jacob Casper Waldhauer, Esqrs., are empowered to administer the oath of exor. to John Hangleiter and John Wertsch, merchant. Dated 16 Jan. 1771. Oath of exor. signed by John Wertsch. Dated 16 Jan. 1771.

pp. 288-291 WBAA.

Thomas Red, St. George's Parish, planter. Entire temporal estate divided among my wife and all my children, except my son John who already has his share. Exors: John and Ruben Red. Wit: John Adam Treutlen, Jacob Cronberger, Anna Unsald.

D: 11 Feb. 177___. P: 22 Feb. 1772. R: 24 Feb. 1772. pp. 431-432 WBA.

John Francis Reinier, St. Matthew Parish. Wife: Mary, 400 pounds Sterling, use of Negro wench named Sukey, featherbed. Nephew: Alexander Reinier, land on Basserts Cowpen Branch. Rest of estate divided into three parts; one part to nephew: Alexander Reinier; one part to my niece, Jane Reinier; one part to niece: Silvia Reinier. Exor.: John Wertsch. 30 pounds Sterling to exor. Wit: Charles McKay, John Rentz, Emanuel Kieffer.

D: 8 Mar. 1775. P: 13 June 1775. R: 14 June 1775. pp. 163-164 WBAA.

Mary Reinier, St. Matthew's Parish, widow. For the use and support of the Revd. Mr. Fredrich Christopher Triebner's Church

116

and School in Ebenezer, half of my money out at interest. Sibella Glaner, widow, four pounds Sterling, part of the other half of my money out at interest. Eva Haberer, feather bed, Negro girl Susanna. Barbara Deiniger, widow, feather bed, bolsters, one-third remaining money. Morgan Finck, feather bed, one-third remaining money. Peter Fry, one-third remaining money. Exor: John Wertsch in Ebenezer, merchant. Remaining moveables divided among Barbara Huberer, Barbara Deiniger, Marged Finck, Peter Fry. Wit: Jacob Mulygar, Emanuel Kieffer.

D: 16 Aug. 1776. P: 16 Jan. 1777. R: 31 Jan. 1777.

Document attached in which John Adam Treutlen and Jacob Casper Waldhauer, Esqs., are empowered to administer the oath of exor. to John Wertsch. Dated 16 Jan. 1777.

Oath of exor signed by John Wertsch. Dated 16 Jan. 1777. pp. 292-294 WBAA.

John Matthias Reinstetler, his mark, Vernonburgh, planter. Benjamin Goldwire (by Deed of Gift dated 12 Nov. 1764) to hold in trust plantation in Vernonburgh, containing 100 acres, Negro man named Prince, my stock of horses and cattle, household goods, all personal estate; all above in trust for Susannah Tubear, wife of David Tubear of Savannah, gunsmith and for Mary and Elizabeth Tubear, her daus. To be held as tenants in common. Exor: brother-in-law, David Tubear. Wit: Charles Hamilton, Robert Hamilton, Thomas Morgan, Robert McDonald.

D: 11 Dec. 1776. P: n.d. R: n.d.

Colonial Loose Will Collection.

Badasar Rieser, St. Matthew's Parish, planter. Debts to be settled out of my horses, chattels, and hogs. Wife: Mary, 50-acre tract of land on which I now live, houses and household furniture, during her widowhood. Eldest son: Benjamin, tract of land on which I now live, after widowhood of my wife. Second son: John Godhelp, 50-acre tract. Third son: Michael, 100 acres pine barren, called the two pans. Moveable effects to be divided among my wife and children: Exor: eldest son, Benjamin. Wit: Timothy Lemke, John Adam Frayermuth, Jacob Buhler.

D: 13 May 1775. P: 9 Jan. 1776. R: 9 Jan. 1776. pp. 222-224 WBAA.

Michael Rieser, his mark, St. Matthew's Parish, planter. Wife: Appolonia, use of 50 acre tract on which I now live during her life. Eldest son: Israel, the above tract, after my wife's death; 50 acres of swamp land joining Bear Creek, Savannah River, and Charles Flerl's land. Children: Nathaniel, Hanna, Mary, and Christina, 200 acres of land over Savannah River, joyning Colmon's Lagoon and Savannah River, equally divided. Son: David, town lot in Ebenezer, joining Christian Ridelsperger; two-acre garden lot joyning John Smith. Moveable effects divided among wife (one-third) and children (two-thirds). Exors: David Steiner and John Wertsch. Wit: Saloman Zands; _____Rufner (?); Georg Zitterauer, his mark.

D: 5 Feb. 1775. P: ___ May 1775. R: n.d. pp. 155-156 WBAA.

Nicholas Rigby, Savannah, Gent. Wife: Sarah, house in Savannah and its garden and farm lots. Remainder of real estate, in England or elsewhere, to be held by my two daus. Elizabeth and Sarah, and held as tenants in common. Personal estate equally divided among wife and daus. Exors; wife and Newdigate Stephens, Gent. Wit: David Montaigut, Peter Laffitte, Charles Watson.

D: 19 Aug. 1754. P: 5 April 1756. R: n.d. pp. 16-17 WBA.

Charles John Fredrick Ritter, Acton, planter. Wife: Elizabeth, entire estate, real and personal, including land I now live on at Black Creek, cattle, household goods. Exors: wife and son-in-law, John Shick. Wit: J. J. Zubley, John George Maurer, John Pfisll (Flerl?).

D: 28 Aug. 1766. P: 4 Mar. 1767 (?). R: 12 Feb. 1767. pp. 195-196 WBA.

Israel Robe(r)son, (W)rightsburough Township. Jonathan Roberson, son of Silvinus Roberson, horses & mares. Sarah Roberson, dau. of David Roberson, two cows & calves. To Jonathan, David, Andrew, and William Roberson, children of David Roberson, profits from sale of remainder of my cattle, and hogs, equally divided. David Roberson, Jr., plantation I now live on, including 100 acres. David Roberson, Sr., 100 acres of land on the head of the Beaver Dam in South Caroline, "where it is thought there is an iron mine." Mentions: Elener, wife of David Roberson. Exor: David Roberson, Sr. Wit: Benjamin Cooper, Isaac Cooper, Mary Brown.

D: 10 Feb. 1773. P: 24 July 1773. R: n.d. pp. 105-108 WBAA.

John Robinson, Savannah, mariner, 'imeadtly going on a cruize against His Majesties Enemies." Hester Minis, dau. of Abigal Minis of Savannah, entire estate, real and personal. Wit: Thomas Lord, Jonathan Remington.

D: 12 July 1758. P: 9 Oct. 1758. R: 19 Oct. 1758. p. 41 WBA.

Alexander Rose, his mark, St. John's Parish, planter. Thomas Young of St. John's Parish, entire estate, real and personal, sole exor. Wit: John Irvine, Hugh Mathewson, William Bosomworth.

D: 18 June 1767. P: 1 Mar. 1771. R: 2 Mar. 1771. pp. 391-392 WBA.

Hugh Rose, St. Peter's Parish, Granville County, South Carolina, planter. Exors. to sell whatever part of estate including plantation whereon I now live, Negroes, tools, cattle, to pay debts. Remainder of estate to wife: Jane and dau.: Ellen (both now residing in Great Britain). Exors.: Patrick Mackay of Melville in St. Peter's Parish, South Carolina, and James Houstoun of Savannah, Gent. Wit: Joseph Prunieres, Andrew Johnston, Peter Laffitte.

D: 26 Sept. 1761. P: 24 Nov. 1761. R: 25 Nov. 1761. pp. 72-73 WBA.

Daniel Ross, Christ Church Parish, overseer. Mulatto girl named Sally, dau. to my Negro woman Phillis, her freedom, but she shall live with my friend Mr. Thomas Ross of Christ Church

Parish, vendue master, until she is fifteen, to be educated. Friend: Thomas Ross, Negro man named Sandy, Negro woman named Phillis, remainder of estate, real and personal, sole exor. Wit: Jonathan Remington, John Allane, John Ross.

D: 2 Mar. 1770. P: 15 Mar. 1770. R: 16 Mar. 1770. pp. 338-340 WBA.

Hugh Ross, Savannah, shopkeeper. Wife: Ann Stewart, dau. of the late Daniel Steuart, shipmaster from Inverness, Scotland, household goods, one-third my personal estate in trust for my children, management of my town lot in Savannah, (to my son, John, after death of my wife), sole extrix. Wit: Peter Blyth, David Brydie, Michael Swiser.

D: 1 Nov. 1762. P: 27 April 1775. R: n.d. pp. 156-158 WBAA.

John Ross (power to administer his effects in case of death.) "I am in a short time to depart from this place for the Upper Creek Country . . . . considering the dangers I am daily exposed to" grant all my estate to Lachlan McGilvray, "the only friend that I have got in this part of the world." One tract of land near Savannah, to John Ross, eldest son of Hugh Ross of Savannah. Handwriting sworn to by William Struthers, John McGillivray, William Trewin.

D: 6 Sept. 1759. Attested: 25 Aug. 1760. R: 22 June 1761. pp. 59-60 WBA.

Thomas Ross, Augusta, Indian trader. Katron Douglass, Negro fellow called Rainbow. John Douglass, Negro fellow called Cork. Exor: David Douglas to pay debts. Wit: Lacklan Mackintosh, Joseph Oaks, David Douglass.

D: 3 Jan. 1759. P: 16 Oct. 1766. R: 16 Oct. 1766. p. 175 WBA.

Simon Rouvier, Christ Church Parish, tanner and shoemaker. Wife: Rosannah and Dau: Mary, entire estate, equally divided. Extrix: wife. Wit: James Muter, Paynter Dickinson, John Rouvier.

D: 17 Aug. 1766. P: 28 Oct. 1771. R: 29 Oct. 1771. pp. 421-422 WBA.

John Roviere, Savannah, cordwainer. Brother: Simon Roviere of Highgate, lot, containing 50 acres at Highgate, adjoining lands of his own. Sister: Anne Guindre, wife of David Guindre, lot at Yamacraw. Negroes: Tom and Judith, their manumission. Remainder of estate, real and personal, equally divided between aforesaid brother and sister. Exors: David Montaigut, Joseph Prunieres of Savannah. Wit: John Smith, Nicholas Lawrence, Wilhaim Trenfield.

D: 3 Feb. 1767. P: 30 July 1767. R: 4 Aug. 1767. pp. 223-224 WBA.

(copy of will)

William Russell, formerly of Savannah, but lately of St. Mary's Parish, White Chapel, County of Middlesex. Exors: wife, Jane; Francis Harris, Fleury Yonge, John Smith, Noble Wimberly Jones, Joseph Clay, Esqrs. Wife: Jane (now residing with me in England), all my real estate in Georgia (town lot number six, Jekyl Tything Derby Ward in Savannah; five-acre lot near Savannah; tract of 14 farm lots east of Savannah, containing 700 acres): Anna Hunter, dau. of Dr. Joseph Hunter, "who now lives with me," dowery of 300 pounds Sterling (on day of her marriage or when she is of age). Wife's brother: James Gallache of Savannah, carpenter, 10 pounds Georgia currency. Three Negro children at Savannah, to my wife. Exors., ten pounds each for a mourning ring. Remainder of my personal estate to wife. Wit: Thomas Lawrence, Thomas Mason, John Talley. Mentions: William Gallache, son of John Gallache, late of Savannah, gunsmith, deceased; Henry Stevens, John Stevens, J. Gosling (Deputy Registers); Henry Farrant.

D: 21 Feb. 1768. P: 13 June 1769. R: 15 June 1769. pp. 308-313 WBA.

Morgan Sabb, South Carolina, planter. Wife: Mary and children, entire estate, real and personal, equally divided. Exors.: wife, John Maxwell, Francis Arthur. Wit: Sarah Scott, Mary Hall, Richard Proctor.

D: 1 Jan. 1760. P: 22 Jan. 1762. R: 26 Jan. 1762. pp. 78-79 WBA.

Anna Salter, widow of Thomas Salter, deceased of Frederica. Grandson: William Thomas Harris (following in care of my dau., Ann Demetree until grandson is twenty-one), eight Negroes, cattle, stallion. Dau: Pennellope Cassell (her maiden name), one large silver tablespoon. Dau: Ann Demetree, wearing apparel, lands in Great Britain or elsewhere. Son-in-law: Daniel Demetre, one-half the sawed lumber to buy two Negroes for William Thomas Harris and to pay twelve pounds Sterling to put William Thomas Harris out to a trade. If grandson dies, his bequest to dau, Ann. Exors: dau, Ann Demetree, Samuel Marier. Wit: Mary Young, Richard Milledge, John Pye.

D: 19 Dec. 1753. P: n.d. R: n.d.

Colonial Loose Will Collection.

Thomas Salter (will is partially missing), Savannah, sadler. Godson: John Anderson (?), debts owed me on lot number 9 in Wilmington Tything Derby Ward, cow & Heiffer (as now in the yard of Stephen Parry). Wife: Ann and dau: Ann, house and lot number 8 in Torvers Tything Deckers Ward (now occupied by William Spencer, Esq.), personal effects. William Harris, the son of Ann, Salter's Island, about three miles from Savannah. Exors.: Henry Parker, Esq, and William Russell, Gent. of Savannah. To exors: my breeding mares and horses. Wife and dau. shall discharge the mortgage due on lot number 8 in Torvers Tything, Deckers Ward.

D: 28 Oct. 1751. P: n.d. R: n.d.

Colonial Loose Will Collection.

Thomas Schweighofer, Ebenezer, (translation of will). Son: Abiel, 100 acres of land where the barn is build upon. Second son: Thomas, 50 acres of land where my dwelling house stands. Third son: Elisa, 50 acres of land adjoining Strings Road. Fourth son: Obadja, six pound Sterling. Dau: Elizabeth, five pounds Sterling. Children: all cattle, horses, house furniture, equally divided. Exors: John Flerl, Samuel Krauss. Wit: Ulrich Neidlinger, John Reimshardt, David Steiner.

D: 26 Nov. 1772. P: 18 Dec. 1772. R: n. d. pp. 19-21 WBAA.

Agnesia Seckinger, her mark, Ebenezer. Son: Luke Ziegler and dau: Agnesia, entire estate, real and personal, equally divided. Exor: Jacob Casper Waldhauer. Wit: Jacob Bushler, Daniel Burgsteiner, Jacob Gnann.

D: 20 Sept. 1776. R. 15 Jan. 1777. R: 30 Jan. 1777.

Document attached in which John Adam Treutlen, Esq., is empowered to administer the oath of exor. to Jacob Casper Waldhauer. Dated 15 Jan. 1777.

Oath of exor. signed by Jacob Casper Waldhauer. Dated 30 Jan. 1777.

pp. 282-284 WBAA.

Andrew Seckinger, his mark, St. Matthew's Parish. Wife: Agnesia, entire estate, after debts are paid. Exor: John Casper Wertsch. Wit: Jacob Casper Walthour, Henry Ludwig Buntz, Lucas Ziegler, Daniel Zettler.

D: 10 Oct. 1772. P: 10 Oct. 1776. R: 22 Nov. 1776. pp. 257-258 WBAA.

Solomon Shad, his mark, Savannah. Wife: Catherine, to keep land slaves, all my belongings together until children shall come of age or marry. Land to my three sons. Remainder of estate equally divided among my wife and the rest of my children. Exors: wife, Frederick Herb, Frederick Fahm. Wit: J. J. Zubly, George Ditter, John Eppinger.

D: 2 Jan. 1768. P: 19 Feb. 1768. R: 20 Feb. 1768. pp. 247-248 WBA.

Benjamin Sheftall, Savannah, merchant. Wife: Hannah, my dwelling house, lot, and household furniture, Negro wench and her two children; after her death, the above bequest (except two Negro children) to my son, Levi (one-half) and my two grandchildren, Sheftall Sheftall and Perla Sheftall (one-half, equally divided). Any money due me, and the proceeds of the sale of 200 acres I bought from John Snooke, to be put at interest for my wife during the rest of her life. On her death, amount to be divided between my son, Levi, (one-half), and my above two grandchildren (one-half, equally divided). Son: Mordecai, discharge from 12 pounds Sterling debt he owes me; 18 pounds Sterling. Exors: wife; sons, Mordecai and Levi. Wit: Peter Tondee, Thomas Club, Adrian Loyer.

D: 4 Aug. 1765. P: 4 May 1772. R: 5 May 1772. pp. 434-436 WBA.

George Scheveiger (Schweiger), Ebenezer, St. Matthew's Parish, planter. Wife: Anne Margareth, stock of cattle and income brought to me; my stock of cattle, use of my plantation during her life, household goods, all moveable effects; sole extrix. Stepson, Ernst Christian Zittrauer, 250 acres of land by the Cypresses (to his wife, Hannah, on his death). Youngest stepdaughter: Gratiosa Zittrauer, rest of all my lands including 350 acres, provided that after my wife's death Gratiosa pay her sister Christiana Elizabeth Zittrauer, 35 pounds Georgia currency. All remaining estate, after my wife's death to be divided equally among my three step children. Wit: Robert (Ruprecht) Zimmerrebner, Christian Stainer, David Steiner.

D: 7 July 1772. P: 22 Nov. 1776. R: 22 Nov. 1776. pp. 259-260 WBAA.

Thomas Shruder, Christ Church Parish, Esq. Exors to sell any part of estate to pay debts in Georgia and elsewhere, "since my arrival in America." All remaining estate, real and personal to wife, Elizabeth, for her lifetime and thence to her heirs. Exors: Wife; James Edward Powell, Esq.; Henry Yonge, Sr., Esq. Wit: George Fraser, William Yonge, David Brydie.

D: 1 Feb. 1775. P: 14 Mar. 1775. R: n.d. pp. 141-142 WBAA.

George Sigfritz, Savannah, carter. Just debts and funeral expenses to be paid by exor. Friend: Abraham Gable, Savannah, house carpenter, and his heirs forever, all estate, real and personal, sole exor. Wit: Thomas Ross, Thomas Burns, James Nelson.

D: 9 May 1775. P: 19 Nov. 1777. R: 19 Nov. 1777.

Colonial Loose Will Collection.

William Simpson, St. John's Parish, planter. Wife: Elizabeth use of entire estate, real and personal, during her life, including 350 acres on Conoochee in St. John's Parish, lot number 233 in Sunbury, eight Negroes, lot in George Town on Sassafrass River in Kent County in Maryland (first the property of my grandfather, Thomas Simpson), Negro woman named Venus. Mentions William Woodland of Maryland, Esq.; Thomas Burnley, son of my wife, Elizabeth Simpson; William Carson in Craven County, South Carolina. Exors: wife; William Carson of South Carolina, Roger Kelsall of Sunbury, merchant; Wit: Simon Munro, John Mcleod, Thomas Bilney.

D: 21 Mar. 1772. P: 25 Mar. 1774. R: n.d.

Document attached in which Parmenas Way and James Screven, Esqs. are empowered to administer the oath of extrix to Elizabeth Simpson. Dated 25 Mar. 1774.

Oath of extrix signed by Elizabeth Simpson. Dated 4 April 1774.

pp. 90-92 WBAA.

William Simpson, Chief Justice of His Majesty's Province of Georgia. Wife: Elizabeth (in England for near two years because of her bad health), because of the great wealth which is her own already, Negro girl named Kate, which I bought of Charles Stevenson, late of Charlestown. Eldest son: James, one-fourth of my real and personal estate. Son: John, one-half of my real and personal estate. Other one-fourth of estate to my wife if she renounces her Dower; if she fails to do so, her one-fourth to my two sons, equally divided. Exors. authorized any part of estate to pay debts. Mentions: Lownder Rawlins, Esq., and John Burn, Esq., both of South Carolina. Exors: son, James and John. Wit: Charles Pryce, Henry Preston, Charles Pryce, Jr.

D: 4 Nov. 1766. P: 21 Dec. 1768. R: 22 Dec. 1768. pp. 284-286 WBA.

William Sludders (Struthers), Augusta, Indian trader. Brother: John Struthers, living in the Parish of Alva in Scotland, one-third of my estate. Sister: Helen Struthers, living in Scotland, and Nephew: William Struthers, and Niece: Jean Struthers son and dau. of my deceased brother, Thomas, one-third of my estate, equally divided. Remaining one-third to be divided among: my partner, Patrick Brown of Augusta; my partner, Lacklan McGillivray of Augusta; my partner, Daniel Clark of Augusta; my hireling, Albert Frederick. A mourning ring to be given each of my partners. John Rae, my partner, and his wife, a mourning ring. Samuel Eveleigh of Charlestown, merchant, a mourning ring. Alexander Petrie, Charlestown, goldsmith, a mourning ring. Nicholas Swarts, my best riding horse, saddle, and furniture, my pistols and gun. Nicholas Chinnery, Indian trader, a mourning ring. Exors: Patrick Brown, Lachlan McGillivray, Daniel Clark. Wit: James Germany, John Kitt, John Ross.

D: 1 Dec. 1751. P: 5 Mar. 1761. R: 25 June 1761. pp. 66-68 WBA.

Matthew Smallwood, St. John's Parish, Planter. Mother: Mary Bateman, use of one room in my dwelling house. Wife: Rebecca, use of one-half my dwelling house, all the rest of my estate, real and personal. On death of my wife, the estate to my dau, Mary Smallwood, at the age of sixteen or marriage. If she dies before sixteen or marriage, estate to children of my brother, Robert, equally divided. Exors: John Baker and Josiah Bacon. Wit: George Beaird, Jesse Tennison, Matthew Beaird.

D: 8 April 1772. P: 8 July 1773. R:

Document attached in which Roger Kelsall, Simon Munro, John Mitchell, and Parmenas Way, Esqs., are empowered to administer the oath of exor. to John Baker and Josiah Bacon. Dated 30 April 1773.

Oath of exor. signed by Josiah Bacon.

pp. 38-41 WBAA.

Robert Smallwood, St. John's Parish, planter. Personal estate to be sold to pay debts. Son: Isaac, 250 acres of land on the Altamaha. Son: Francis, 150 acres, being one-half of a 300-acre tract in St. John's Parish. Dau: Martha, 150 acres, being other one-half of a 300-acre tract in St. John's Parish. Dau: Sarah, 280 acres, two tracts, in St. John's Parish. Wife: Nancy, use of my plantation for her widowhood. All remaining real and personal estate equally divided among my wife and children. Exors: wife, John Mittchell, John Baker. Wit: Sarah Mittchell, her mark; John Hopkins; Matthew Beaird.

D: 31 May 1774. P: 24 Aug. 1775. R: 25 Aug. 1775. pp. 178-180 WBAA.

David Smith, his mark, Sunbury, Gent. Children of my late brother, Thomas, of Belfast, Ireland, and of my sister, Elizabeth, wife of James McGee of Belfast, Ireland, entire estate, after debts, divided into two parts, one each to each family. Exors: William Maxwell of Belfast, Georgia. Wit: R. Kelsall, John Stout, James Crosswell.

D: 23 Oct. 1772. P: 7 Jan. 1774. R: n.d. pp. 79-80 WBAA.

Ebenezer Smith, St. Paul's Parish, planter. Wife: Jean, one-third of all my lands during her life. Son: John, and daus: Sarah and Mary, 5 shillings each. Son: Elierer, bay horse, five pounds. Sons: Samuel and James, one-third each of my lands. Dau: Jamimi, feather bed and bedding, three pounds Sterling. Remaining monies of my estate, after above bequests to daus: Jamima, Jean, and Abigail. Son: Ebenezer, tract of land held by me in right of Samuel Morton. Extrix: wife. Wit: Abram Ayres, Jediah Smith, Joshua Bradley.

D: 30 Sept. 1774. P: 15 Mar. 1775.

Codicil to will (same date, same wit): Son: Ebenezer, ten pounds, when he is twenty-one.

Document attached in which Joseph Maddox (Maddock), Jonathan Sall (Sell), and John Oliver, Esqs., are empowered to administer the oath of extrix. to Jean Smith. Dated 1 Mar. 1775.

Oath of extrix. signed by Jane Smith, her mark. Dated: 15 Mar. 1775.

pp. 159-162 WBAA.

John Smith, Savannah, block maker. Exors. to pay debts, selling 250-acre tract in St. Thomas' Parish, if necessary. Remaining money to my wife and child, equally divided. Wife: Ann, lot at Yamacraw which I lately purchased of Mr. Zubly; after her death, this bequest to my son, John. Exor: Charles Watson of Savannah, Esq., and James Huston of Whitemarsh Island, planter. Wit: Clotworthy Robson, William Gregory, Ettsel Lawrance.

D: 8 May 1770. P: 1 June 1770. R: 2 June 1770. pp. 349-350 WBA.

Joseph Smith, New York City, mariner, "now on a voyage to sea." Wife: Elizabeth, all my estate, real and personal, after my debts are paid, extrix. Wit: Theunes Thew, Joseph Montanga, Cornelius Cooper.

D: 15 Mar. 1764. P: 5 Dec. 1771. R: 21 Dec. 1771. pp. 426-427 WBA.

Mary Smith, Savannah. William Holzendorff, son of the late Fredrick Holzendorff, doctor of physick, deceased, tract of 100 acres in Christ Church Parish. Captain Nicholas Nielson, wharf lot in Savannah, number three. Thomas Goldsmith, son of Captain Thomas Goldsmith, silver plate. Sarah Palmer, dau. of Thomas Palmer, horses, mares and colts, 10 pounds, Georgia currency. Lucretia Triboudet, wife of John Francis Triboudet, 10 pounds. Elizabeth Ellis, widow, a bedstead and furniture, five pounds. John Mercier, Negro boy named Prince. Church Wardens of Christ Church Parish, 10 pounds for the poor. Thomas Lloyd of Savannah, merchant, town lot in Savannah, number 3 in Digby's Tything Deckers Ward (left me by last will and testament of William Francis). Lloyd to have land upon payment of 70 pounds to Sarah Holzendorff, dau. of Frederick Holzendorff of Sunbury, sadler. Estate, real and personal remaining to be sold, profits to Nicholas Nielson and Mary O'Neal, equally divided. Exors: Nicholas Nielson, Mary O'Neal. Wit: Frederick Holzendorff (Jr.?), Charles Pryce, Charles Pryce, Jr.

D: 29 Dec. 1763. P: 19 Sept. 1766. R: 27 Sept. 1766. pp. 171-173 WBA.

Edward Somerville, Savannah, merchant. Miss Jane Rae, 100 pounds Sterling. Sister: Judith Cammeron, 100 pounds Sterling. Remainder of estate equally divided among my brothers and sisters. Exors: John Rae Esq., Thomas Eaton. Wit: William Honey, Abraham Croft.

D: 10 Sept. 1762. P: 20 Sept. 1762. R: 20 Sept. 1762. pp. 85-86 WBA.

Jane Somerville, widow. Uncle: Robert Rae of Augusta, plantation on Savannah River, near Savannah, Little Island in Savannah River, my large silver tankard, tract of land on the north side of Hutchinson's Island. Niece: Ann Somerville, lot in Savannah, Negro girl named Sapho, 40 of my Negroes, remainder of my silver plate, watch, phaeton, pair of horses. Goddau: Ann Johnston, town lot in Augusta, three Negroes. Elizabeth Church, dau. of the wife of the aforesaid Colonel Rae, 500 pounds, Georgia currency. Negroes: Nancy, Tom, Bob, their freedom. Remainder of estate equally divided among my uncle, Robert Rae, cousin James Rae of Augusta, Elizabeth Elbert and her children, Isabella Habersham, Sarah Gwinn. Exors: Colonel Robert Rae, James Rae, Colonel James Elbert. Wit: James Grierson, Andrew Johnston, Robert Howe.

D: 10 Sept. 1779. P: n.d. R: n.d. pp. 327-329 WBAA.

John Somerville, Savannah, merchant. Wife: Jane:, use of my estate during her life; after her death to my brother, Thomas Somerville of Ireland. Sisters: Elizabeth Limerick, 500 pounds Sterling; Judith Cameron, 300 pounds Sterling. William Telfair, merchant, 250 pounds Sterling. All my stock in trade to be sold to pay my debts. Slaves: Tamar and Statire, their freedom. Exors: Edward Telfair; brother, Thomas Somerville. Wit: William Young, Jacob Oates, Thomas Tallemack.

D: 8 Oct. 1773. P: 24 Nov. 1773. R: n.d.

pp. 62-64 WBAA.

Richard Spencer, St. John's Parish, planter. Exors to sell tract of land in St. Andrew's Parish to pay debts, if necessary, and also my stock of cattle, and land I live on. When either dau.

is eighteen or married, entire estate to be divided among my wife and all my children. Exors: wife, Sarah; John Stewart; Richard Baker. Wit: James Andrew, Thomas Bacon, William Bacon.

D: 16 Feb. 1767. P: 30 June 1767. R: 14 July 1767.

Document attached in which Parmenas Way and John Martin, Esqs., are empowered to administer the oath of exor. to Sarah Spencer and Richard Baker. Dated 30 June 1767.

Oath of exor. signed by Sarah Spencer and Richard Baker.

Dated 9 July 1767.

pp. 218-221 WBA.

William Spencer, Christ Church Parish, Gent. Sons: John Spencer and George Basil Spencer, town lot in Savannah, with 45 acres belonging to it. (To my son, William Henry Spencer, on death of other sons.) Lot in Hardwick, number 50; 500 acres at Little Ogechee; 600 acres in St. Andrew's Parish; town lot in Brunswick, number 223; 100 acres in St. Philip's Parish; 400 acres in St. Philip's Parish, all above to be sold and profits divided equally among my children: Elizabeth Parker, Jane Bowen, Mary Thomson, Joseph William Spencer, Susannah, Sarah, and William Henry Spencer. Dau: Sarah, 40 pounds. Son: Joseph William, 40 pounds. Dau: Susannah, Negro woman named Pallas. Son: William Henry Spencer, Negro boy named Hereford, town lot number 224 in Brunswick. Exors: John Spencer, George Basil Spencer, son-in-law, Alexander Thomson. Wit: James Galache, Benjamin Mevis, James Flint. Mentions: Francis Harris, Henry William Parker, William Barns, Isaac Pacoton, Shem Butler, James Bolock.

D: 27 Jan. 1776. P: 22 Aug. 1776. R: 22 Aug. 1776.

pp. 224-227 WBAA.

Edward Splatt, St. John's Parish. Mother: Hannah Splatt, 500 pounds, South Carolina currency, Negro girl named Hannah.

Wife: Esther, all remaining estate, real and personal, sole extrix. Wit: Lyman Hall, Edward Ball, Josiah Bacon.

D: 31 Dec. 1773. P: 2 Mar. 1774. R: n.d.

pp. 81-82 WBAA.

Mary Spry, St. John's Parish, widow. Son: Samuel, Negro boy named Sandy. Son: Royal, Negro named Cain. Son: Josiah, Negro boy named Lymas. Dau: Elizabeth, Negroes named Nan and Feliss. Nephew: Daniel Dunham (a minor), forty pounds Sterling when he comes of age. Remaining money in my estate to be used to buy land for my sons, Samuel and Royal. Remainder of my estate equally divided among my four children. Exors: sons; Gideon Dowse; Samuel Spry; and Parmenas Way, Sr. Wit: John Winn, Senior; Thomas Way; Thomas Baker.

D: 27 Dec. 1771. P: 30 Dec. 1772. R: n.d.

pp. 24-26 WBAA.

Joseph Stanly (Stanley), Savannah. Friend: Samuel Elbert of Savannah, merchant, town lot number 7 in Savannah; all my real and personal estate; sole exor. Wit: Samuel Farley, Button Gwinnett, William Greene.

D: 29 May 1770. P: 24 Dec. 1771. R: 28 Dec. 1771.

pp. 427-428 WBA.

Peter Stedeler, Hallifax, St. George's Parish, planter. Wife: Lythey, house where I now dwell, furniture, horse, bridle, saddle. Son: John, tract of land at Hallifax, where I now live, containing 300 acres; one-half of my stock of horses, mares, gelding, cattle, and hogs; Negro man named Godfrey. Son: David, 200-acre tract of land, other one-half of my stock; Negro man named Bristow. Exors: John Rae of Savannah. Wit: William Harding, John Grayson, Clotworthy Robson.

D: 23 Oct. 1769. P: 15 Aug. 1771. R: 18 Aug. 1771.

pp. 408-409 WBA.

Henrich Steerman, Savannah, tailer. William Rheny of Savannah, tailor, my roan gelding, saddle, bridle. Barbara Wilson of Savannah, widow, my silver watch. Dau: Catherine, all remaining estate. Exors: William Rheny, Frederick Roseberg, Frederick Herb. Wit: James Gregory, Mathias Ash, Godfried Rodh.

D: 8 Dec. 1769. P: 21 Dec. 1769. R: 28 Dec. 1769.

pp. 336-337 WBA.

John Stevens, St. John's Parish, planter. One hundred and thirty pounds Sterling to be put at interest. Interest to support my dau, Mary Stevens (100 pounds) and my church (30 pounds). Dau: Martha Mitchell, 300 acres of my 500-acre tract called Rice Hope, at the joining of the north and middle branch of Newport Swamp. Son: John, other 200 acres of tract above; 300 acres of my tract called May Apple Swamp. Dau: Mary, 200 acres, part of tract called May Apple Swamp; one tract of 200 acres; one tract of 233 acres. Wife: Mary, her residence in my mansion house. After debts are paid, remaining estate divided among my wife and three children. Exors: wife; son, John; nephews, Samuel and Thomas Stevens. Wit: Thomas Way; John Osgood; Sarah Mitchell, her mark.

D: 7 Jan. 1759. P: 19 July 1759. R: 19 July 1759.

Memorandum attached (1759, wit: John Osgood, John Edwards): 200 acres bought of Moses Way and 300 acres bought of Joseph Winn, which I bought for the sons of my brother, Joseph, deceased. Therefore, these lands to Joseph and Thomas Stevens, (my nephews).

pp. 43-45 WBA.

Anna Yyels Christian Steinbibs (German spelling; the English spelling is Steinhavols), widow. Sister's children: David and Frederick Kyffer (Kiefer), entire estate, real and personal. Anna Elizabeth Kellers, cow and calf, bed. Wit: (?)

D: 17 May 1748. P:n.d. R: n.d.

Colonial Loose Will Collection.

John Stewart, St. John's Parish, planter. Dau: Sarah, wife of William Quarterman, four Negroes, bed and furniture, both bequests already in her possession, valued at 182 pounds Sterling. (An estate of equal value to each of my children.) Dau: Susanna, Negro girl named Leah. Son: Daniel, about 530 acres of land, my wearing apparel. Daus: Sarah, Susanna, Elizabeth, my tract of 700 acres in the Mortar Swamp in St. Andrew's Parish, equally divided; three lots of land in Sunbury, numbered 114, 115, 116. Dau: Elizabeth, tract of land given by last will and testament of Captain Robert Nichols to my late wife Sarah (his sister); three Negroes. Relation: James Girrardeau, mared branded "3S." Exors: William Graves; John Bacon; son-in-law, William Quarterman; brother, Daniel Stewart; son, Daniel. Wit: Samuel Miller, John Baker, George Law.

D: 29 Mar. 1776. P: 22 Nov. 1776. R: 22 Nov. 1776.

pp. 249-252 WBAA.

John Stewart, St. John's Parish, planter. Wife: Hannah, her riding horse, saddle, horse chair, half of my horses and household goods, one-third of my Negroes, rest of my personal estate; use of my house and plantation (567 acres) during her life. Son: James, rest of my real estate, and my plantation after my wife's death. Exors: wife, her brother, John Stewart; my son, James. Wit: John Winn, John Quarterman, Benjamin Baker.

D: 4 Sept. 1765. P: 30 Oct. 1765. R: 30 (?) Oct. 1765.

pp. 140-142 WBA.

Charles Story, Savannah, carpenter. Wife: Ann, four Negroes. Niece: Agnes Bryan, four Negroes, my plantation in St. John's Parish at Great Ogechee. Exors: wife; Jonathan Bryan, Esq. Wit: Gabriel Cooley, John Cooley, William Young.

D: 25 Feb. 1763. R: 29 Aug. 1766. R: 29 Aug. 1766.

pp. 166-167 WBA.

John Street, Savannah, carpenter. Catherine Clark of Guilford in Surry, 5 pounds Sterling. Brother: Henry, of Savannah, now living with me, my carpenter tools and wearing apparel, 10

133

pounds Sterling. Mother-in-law: Ann Cunningham, all my late wife's wearing apparel, 5 pounds Sterling. Son: John, all rest of estate, real and personal. Exors: Grey Elliott of Savannah, Esq., Peter Tondee of Savannah, carpenter. Wit: Joseph Wood, Jr., Martin Lyon, Benjamin Goldwire.

D: 6 Dec. 1768. P: 9 May 1771. R: 10 May 1771.

pp. 403-404 WBA.

George Stregle, his mark, Hallifax, blacksmith. Wife: Catrine, one-third of my real and personal estate. Son: Nicholas, my real estate. Remaining personal estate divided between my son, Nicholas, and dau., Barbara. Wife's dau: Elisabeth, one cow and calf. Exors: Nicholas Fisher, Michael Bener. Wit: Joseph Bell, Michael Bihner.

D: 18 Jan. 1767. P: 23 Mar. 1768. R: 23 Mar. 1768.

pp. 258-259 WBA.

George Strobhar, his mark, Christ Church Parish, planter. Wife: Jenny, two Negroes; one-third of my real and personal estate, including 250 acres, where I now live. Dau: Catherine, 250 acres of land, bequest granted above to my wife, after her death. Dau: Mary, three tracts of land in St. Matthew's Parish. Dau: Susannah Margaret Jones, 150 pounds Sterling. Brother: Nicholas, and Sister: Mary McKenzie, 20 pounds Sterling each. Exors: wife; John Gasper Wertsch, Esq.; Mathias Ash; Frederick Rossberg. Wit: Andrew Greiner; John Gasper Greiner; Rudolph Strohager, his mark.

D: 5 June 1771. P: 26 July 1771. R: 3 Aug. 1771.

pp. 414-415 WBA.

Michael Stutz, Christ Church Parish. Wife: Jane, use of entire estate, real and personal, during her widowhood. On her death, the estate to be equally divided between my two children, Jane and Ann. Exors: wife, James Gallash; Stephen Britton. Wit: David Truan, Powell Griggs, Peter Gandy.

D: 9 Feb. 1770. P: 2 Jan. 1775. R: n.d.

p. 115 WBAA.

Joseph Summers, Little Ogechee, planter. Wife: Mary, tract of land on which I live containing about 500 acres; tract at Little Ogechee containing 370 acres; both of these to her during her life. Son: William, the above tract of 500 acres, after my wife's death. Daus: Mary and Susan Summers, spinsters, other tract above given wife, after her death, to be held as joint tenants. To wife, use of all my personal estate, during her life; after her death, the same to be divided among my surviving children. Exors: wife; James Habersham; Francis Harris. Mentions: heirs of Samuel Summers (my father), who are in England, by Joan, his first wife. Wit: Thomas Tripp, John Milledge, Charles Watson.

D: 30 May 1759. P: 8 May 1767. R: 12 May 1767.

pp. 213-214 WBA.

Edmund Tannatt (Savannah). Wife, use during her life of any three of my Negro slaves; use of plate, china, and household furniture during her widowhood. Son: Edmund, 120 pounds for his education. Remainder of estate to Heriot Crooke, Charles Caines (my wife's brother-in-law), and Robert Crooke, her brother, to hold in trust for my wife, my dau. Mary, my son, Edmund, my daus: Elizabeth Crooke and Heriot Cunningham. Exors: Heriot Crooke, Charles Caines, Robert Crooke. Wit: Hugh Ross, Stephen Mellen, James Gee.

D: 5 Sept. 1761. P: 26 Jan. 1763. R: n.d.

pp. 89-90 WBA.

Stephen Tarrian, his mark, Christ Church Parish, cooper. Godson: Stephen Landry, all real and personal estate, after debts are paid, sole exor. Wit: Thomas Tripp, James Houstoun, Joseph Camuse, Jeremie Hallotton (?), Peter Gandy.

D: 2 Jan. 1762. P: 14 Jan. 1762. R: n.d.

pp. 114-115 WBA.

Michael Tattersell. Wife: Elizabeth, entire estate, real and personal. Wit: William Kirk, Jr.; John Floyd, Sarah Kirk.

D: 19 Sept. 1775. P: ___ Oct. 1775. R: 6 Oct. 1775.

p. 187 WBAA.

John Teasdale (copy of will). Son, town lot in Savannah, 50 pounds Sterling, my stock of horses, except one mare. Wife, mare. Granddau, town lot in Savannah, Negro girl. Granddau, Negro girl named Peg. James, son of James Dean, and Dinah, his wife, Negro man named Will. Wife, house and lot whereon I now live; to my son at her death. Remainder of estate to wife. Extrix: wife. Wit: (?)

D: 24 June 1752. P: n.d. R: n.d.

Colonial Loose Will Collection.

Jacob Telfair (Talfare). Wife, Mary, one Negro during her life; to dau, Sarah, after her death. Dau: Sarah, two Negroes. Exors: wife, Isaac Yonge. Wit: Jonathan Cochran, Thomas Ready.

D: 19 Dec. 1769. P: 5 April 1770. R: 17 May 1770.

pp. 345-346 WBA.

George Thomas, Parish of St. John Wapping in County of Middlesex in Great Britain, mariner, now being in Savannah. Debts to be paid. One-third remaining estate to wife, Hannah, of St. John's Parish aforesaid; other two-thirds of estate equally divided among my children: George, Frederick, Mary, and Margeret (when they are of age). Exors: wife; Thomas Eatton of Savannah, merchant. Wit: Joseph Wood, Jr.; William Herbert; James Furse.

D: 26 Sept. 1766. P: 16 Feb. 1767. R: 17 Feb. 1767.

pp. 200-201 WBA.

Richard Thompson, St. Matthew's Parish, planter. Friend: John Patton, my lands and slaves; sole Exor. Wit: Peter Brookes, Elener Jones.

D: 22 Aug. 1767. P: 30 Sept. 1767. R: 19 Oct. 1769.

pp. 325-326 WBA.

John Tinley, Augusta. Wife: Elizabeth, entire estate, real and personal, after debts are paid; sole extrix. Wit: James Dean, William Clark, James Jarvis.

D: 26 Jan. 1760. P: 2 July 1760. R: 22 June 1761.

p. 58 WBA.

John Todd, district of Midway, planter. Wife: Sarah, use of entire estate, real and personal, during her life, Negro named Cudgo. Son: Giles, plantation I now live on, after my wife's death or marriage; Negro boy named Ben; his horses and mares; hogs; my land in Virginia. Exors: William Ballowe of Midway, victular; John Mimmack of Midway, Gent. Wit: Robert Godfrey, Roger Hollan, Barton Rogett.

D: 2 July 1756. P: 11 April 1758. R: 20 June 1761.

p. 52 WBA.

Peter Tondee, Savannah, carpenter. Wife: Lucy, entire estate, real and personal. On her death, estate to my children, equally divided. Extrix: wife. Wit: (sworn 21 Aug. 1776 by William Pickering and Peter Gandy).

D: 21 Oct. 1775. P: 29 Aug. 1776. R: 29 Aug. 1776.

pp. 227-232 WBAA.

David Truan, Christ Church Parish, planter. Estate to Isaac Baillou of Savannah, Gent., and John Foulis of Savannah, merchant, to hold in trust for my dau., Mary (16 years old) until twenty-one or married. Exors: Isaac Baillou and John Foulis. Wit: Charles Yonge; Martha Coleman, her mark; Sarah Shaw, her mark.

D: 5 Oct. 1775. P: 6 Nov. 1775. R: 6 Nov. 1775.

pp. 197-200 WBAA.

David Unseld, St. Matthew's Parish, planter. Wife: Anne, entire estate, real and personal. Exor: John Adam Treutlen, Esq. Wit: John Paulus, George Gnann, John Niess.

D: 17 Sept. 1770. P: 23 Oct. 1771. R: 23 Oct. 1771.

p. 421 WBA.

Mary Vanderplank, Savannah, widow. The Revd. Mr. Zubly, household goods, books, claims, my right of property, my pretensions against the estate of John Vanderplank, my late husband, deceased. James Miller, my set of tea cups, two silver teaspoons. Daniel Demetry, my silver milk pot, one black heifer. John Farley, my second best bed. Goddaus: Anne Whitefield, Rebecca Lee, and Grace Polhill, all my wearing apparel, equally divided. Mrs. Wright, a red cow and calf, a black heifer. Mary Habersham, my gold ring. Elizabeth Wright, my worked gown. Remainder of estate to the Revd. Mr. John Joachim Zubly. Exor: John Joachim Zubly. Wit: Robert Bolton, Thomas Rasberry.

D: 8 April 1758. P: 10 Feb. 1762. R: n.d.

pp. 81-82 WBA.

Thomas Vincent, Savannah, merchant. Cousin: John Lawrance in London, five pounds Sterling for mourning. Wife: Hannah, all estate, real and personal, in England or America. Exors: wife; and John Morel, planter. Wit: Edmund Gray, Thomas Dowle, Jeremiah Campher.

D: 18 Mar. 1766. P: 13 Oct. 1767. R: 14 Oct. 1767.

pp. 230-231 WBA.

(fragment of will, in French)

Samuel Wagner, Hampstead. Wit: Patrick Graham, Michael Burghalter.

D: 12 Feb. 1736. P: 5 Mar. 17 (38?) R: n.d.

Colonial Loose Will Collection.

Nevile Wainwright, Savannah, merchant. Georgia Society, 5 pounds Sterling. Alexander Wylly, my wearing apparel, 10 pounds Sterling. Jonathan Bryan, 5 pounds Sterling for a mourning ring. Captain Seth Place, 5 pounds Sterling for a mourning ring. Matthew Roche, my watch. Remainder of estate to my mother, Margaret Wainwright of Ireland, and my brother, James Wainwright of Ireland. Exors: Jonathan Bryan, Alexander Wylly. Wit: Joseph Phillips, Lewis Johnson, Willett Taylor.

D: 25 July 1754. P: 10 April 1755. R: n.d.

pp. 5-6 WBA.

Thomas Walker, Granville County, South Carolina, carpenter. Wife: Mary, use of all my lands and lots in South Carolina, Georgia, or elsewhere, use of my personal estate, for her lifetime. At her death, the estate to be divided among my four children: Samuel, Levy, Humphrey, and Sarah. Exors: Dr. James Thomson of Beaufort, South Carolina; and my wife. Wit: Andrew Aggnew, John Stone, Will Gough.

D: 1 Nov. 1753. P: n.d. R: 23 June 1761.

pp. 63-64 WBA.

Charles Watson, Savannah, Gent. Daniel Tebeau (infant nephew of my late wife), two Negroes. Charles Tebeau, two Negroes. Ann Tebeau, four Negroes. Samuel Tebeau, three Negroes. John Tebeau (now at full age), two Negroes. Norris James Tebeau, a Negro. Dau-in-law: Sarah Dudley, Jr., two Negroes. Wife: Sarah, Negro boy; plantation in Christ Church Parish, three miles from Savannah, containing about 500 acres; after her death this bequest to Norris James Tebeau. To Samuel Farley, lawyer in Savannah, and Clotworthy Robson, my lot in Savannah, Negro girl, to be held in trust for my niece Sepha Watson. Ann Tebeau, half town lot in Savannah. Remainder of estate to Samuel Farley and Clotworthy Robson to pay my debts. Exors: wife, Samuel Farley, and Clotworthy Robson. Wit: Samuel Bowen, Jane Bowen, Richard Eaton.

D: 8 Nov. 1770. P: 7 Jan. 1771. R: 8 Jan. 1771.

Codicil (18 Dec. 1770, Wit: Samuel Frink; Stephen Miller; James Gender, his mark): William Stephens to replace Clotworthy Robson as Exor. to will. Plantation to John Tebeau **and** Norris Tebeau on my wife's death. Niece: Sepha Watson, one more Negro girl.

pp. 371-375 WBA.

Joseph Watson, Savannah. Nephews: Joseph Dacker and Edward Dacker, all my lands in Nova Scotia. Lands in County of Lincoln in England (if I outlive my wife, Sarah), equally divided between my three sisters, Martha Dacker, Christia Bateman, Esther Holsey. Lands in place formerly called Yamacraw, but

now called Watsonburgh, two lots to Hugh Ross. Mrs. Ottolenghe, Negro wench called Nanny. Remainder of estate in
Georgia to William Read. Exor: William Read. Gives details on
his funeral desire. Wit: Peter Blyth, James Wemyss, Susannah
Wemyss.

D: 28 Sept. 1757. P: 1 June 1758. R: 19 Oct. 1758.

Codicil (16 Jan. 1758, Wit: William Clifton, William Handley,
Thomas Gegg): Captain William Francis, my dwelling house in
Elliott Square. Further instructions to Exor.

pp. 37-40 WBA.

Sarah Watson, Christ Church Parish, widow of late Charles
Watson. Bequeaths to Samuel Farley and William Stephens, of
Savannah, attorneys, all estate, wherever found. To be exors
and administrators to hold in trust for use of dau, Sarah Dudley,
until age twenty-one or marriage, at which time to deliver up to
her. Exors: Samuel Farley, William Stephens. Wit: Margaret
Churchwell, John Tebeau, Frederick Churchwell.

D: 5 Mar. 1771. P: n.d. R: 21 Mar. 1771. p. 397 WBA.

Edward Way, St. John's Parish, planter. Wife: Ann, one-third
of my personal estate, use of my dwelling house, use of one-third
of my plantation during her widowhood. Dau: Ann, Negro girl,
two town lots in Sunbury, one-fifth of the remainder of my personal estate. Son: Edward, one-half my tract of 450 acres on
Newport, one-fourth remaining personal estate. Son: William,
one-half of tract of land I now live on, one-third remaining personal estate. Son: Joseph, remaining half of lands at Newport,
one-half the remaining personal estate. Son: John, remaining
half of land I now live on, remainder of personal estate. Exors:
John Elliott, John Stuart, Joseph Way, my wife. Wit: John
Winn, Edward Sumner, Thomas Quarterman.

D: 2 July 1762. P: 25 Feb. 1763. R: 25 Feb. 1763.

pp. 93-94 WBA.

Joseph Way, St. John's Parish, planter. Wife: Mary, tract of
250 acres of land, use of 500-acre plantation I now live on during

her widowhood; one-half my household goods and furniture, one-third of other estate, including two Negroes, chair and chair horses, spoons. Son: Joseph, plantation (500 acres) I now live on; 5 volumes of Mr. Henry's Exposition upon the Bible. Remainder of estate divided equally between my son, Joseph, and my dau., Mary. Mentions: my sister, Elizabeth Elliott. Exors: wife, Thomas Quarterman; Samuel Jones; John Elliott. Wit: James Andrew, Benjamin Andrew, John Irvine.

D: 5 Mar. 1766. P: 2 July 1766. R: 7 July 1766.

pp. 163-166 WBA.

Samuel Way, Midway, planter. Wife: Rebecca, 300 acres of a tract in Midway, all movable estate. Sister: Elizabeth Way, 100 acres of tract in Midway. Brother: William Way, 100 acres of tract in Midway. Exors: wife, and my brother-in-law, John Lupton. Wit: John Shave; Thomas Quarterman; William McGregory, his mark.

D: 14 Nov. 1757. P: 15 June 1758. R: 16 July 1758.

pp. 32-33 WBA.

Wentworth Webb, his mark, St. Philip's Parish, planter. Sons: Henry and Wentworth, all my lands, equally divided. Henry, Negro boy named Samson. Wentworth, Negro boy Peter. Wife: Rachel, Negro wench named Sarah, riding mare, all my personal estate during her widowhood; after her death or marriage, this bequest to my children, equally divided. Dau: Susanna. Exors: wife, and son Henry. Guardians: my brother-in-law, William Jones and Joseph Johnston. Wit: James Cook, William Jones, Joseph Cole.

D: 19 Aug. 1771. P: 6 May 1772. R: 9 May 1772.

pp. 437-438 WBA.

Ludwig Weidman, Ebenezer, St. Matthew's Parish, shoemaker. Wife: Anna Eva, 10 pounds Sterling, all the cleared grounds, and building where I now live for her lifetime. Eldest son: Daniel, tract of 100 acres on which I now live. Son: Mattheis, town lot in Ebenezer, lately purchased of William Sandersheir of Casper Granwetter, deceased; 50-acre tract of land. Sons: Jedethia and Solomon, tract of 250 acres on Tounsend's Pen Branch, equally divided. Remainder of estate divided among my wife and children. Exors: wife, John Casper Wertsch of Ebenezer, merchant. Wit: Christopher Rottenberger, his mark; Jacob Myer, his mark; Asa Emanuel.

D: 18 Oct. 1769. P: 31 May 1771. R: 3 June 1771.

pp. 404-406 WBA.

Absolam Wells, St. George's Parish, planter. Wife: Mary, entire estate, real and personal, during her widowhood. Daus: Elizabeth, 5 shillings, Mary, 5 shillings, Serah, 5 shillings. Sons: John, 5 shillings, Absolam, 5 shillings. After death of my wife, rest of estate to be divided equally between, Jane, Winny, Rice, Rachel, Nany, and Patty. Wit: David Emanuel, Jr.; Wrice Wells; Rachel Wells, her mark.

D: 4 June 1768. P: 8 Mar. 1769. R: n.d.

pp. 331-332 WBA.

Andrew Elton Wells, Savannah. Entire estate to be divided among wife, Jane, and all my children. "In the disposal of the lands (though left to the discretion of my executors), I would recommend to them to dispose of the Distillery first." Exors: James Maxwell, John Sandiford, (my brothers-in-law), my wife. Wit: Anthony Norroway, Thomas Hamilton, Thomas Burns.

D: 4 Jan. 1776. P: 31 Mar. 1778. R: n.d.

Colonial Loose Will Collection.

Thomas Wesbury, St. John's Parish, planter. Exors to sell all estate; profits divided between my wife, Mary, and my dau., Susana. Exors: wife, John Jurdine, William Rich Jurdine. Wit: Samuel Morecock, Thomas Powell, Edward Jones.

D: 15 Mar. 1773. P: 23 July 1773. R: 27 July 1773.

pp. 43-44 WBAA.

Charles West, St. John's Parish, planter. Exors to administer the estate for the benefit of my children. Land to be divided into three lots for my sons: Charles, Samuel, and William; to receive at the age of twenty-one, or when the exors think them fit. Wife: Esther, her maintenance during her widowhood out of the produce of my plantation. Remainder of personal estate to be divided into four parts for my four children: Elizabeth, Charles, Samuel, and William. Exors: Stephen Williams, Richard Baker, John Stewart. Wit: William Jones, Robert Jones, James Andrews.

D: 24 Dec. 1766. P: 23 Feb. 1768. R: 14 Dec. 1768.

pp. 278-280 WBA.

Thomas White, his mark, "late of the province of Georgia, planter." Father: David White, Sisters: Mary, Judith, and Catherine White, in Ireland, 70 pounds Sterling, equally divided. Wife: Mary, and dau: Mary, remainder of estate, equally divided. Exors: wife, Archibald Bulloch, Henry Lewis Bourquin, John Fox, John McClean. Wit: William Deveaux, James Papot, William Dunkin.

D: 13 Feb. 1770. P: 19 Dec. 1770. R: 20 Dec. 1770.

pp. 370-371 WBA.

George Whitefield, "clerk at present residing at the Orphan House Academy" at Bethesda in Georgia. Orphanage and all that goes with it to Selina, Countess Dowager of Huntingdon. If she dies before I do, I leave the orphanage to James Habersham, Esq. Building called Tabernacle, in London, England, with adjacent house, and all that goes with them, "and the building commonly called Tottenham Court Chapel with all the buildings, etc., I possess in that part of London," to Daniel West, Esq., in Church Street, Spittlefields, and Robert Keen, woolen-draper in the Minories. Countess Dowager of Huntingdon, 100 pounds Sterling. Friends: James Habersham, my late wife's gold watch, ten pounds for morning. Gabriel Harris, Esq., in Gloucester, 50 pounds. Ambrose Wright, 500 pounds. Brothers: Richard Whitefield, 50 pounds; Thomas Whitefield, 50 pounds. Bro-in-law: James Smith, hosier in Bristol, 50 pounds, and 30 pounds for family mourning. Niece: Mrs. Francis Hartford of Bath, 50 pounds, and 20 pounds for family mourning. "John Crane, now a faithful steward at the Orphan-House Academy, 40 pounds." Benjamin Stirk, 10 pounds for mourning. Peter Edwards, now at Orphan-House Academy, 50 pounds. William Trigg, now at Orphan-House Academy, 50 pounds. Thomas Adams of Rodborough in Gloucester, 50 pounds. The Revd. Mr. Howell Davis of Pembrokeshire in South Wales, "to Mr. Torial Toss, Cornelius Winter and all other present stated assistant preachers at the Tabernacle and Tottenham Court Chapel, 10 pounds each for mourning." To the three brothers of Ambrose Wright and the wife of his brother Robert Wright at the Orphan-House Academy, 10 pounds each for mourning. Richard Smith, 50 pounds, all my wearing apparel. 100 pounds to be distributed at discretion of executors for mourning among my London servants, the poor widows at Tottenham Court Chapel and the Tabernacle poor, especially to Mrs. Elizabeth Wood. All other monies, goods, chattels, "or whatever profits may arise from the sale of my books or any manuscripts that I may leave behind" to the Countess of Huntingdon or James Habersham, if she is deceased, to pay any arrears on Orphan-House Academy or for annual prizes for the best three orations that shall be made in English on the subjects mentioned in a Paper annexed to this will. Exors: James Habersham, Esq., Charles Hardy, Esq., Daniel West, Esq., Robert Keen. Wit: Robert Bolton, Thomas Dixon, Cornelius Winter.

D: 22 Mar. 1770. P: 10 Dec. 1770. R: 13 Dec. 1770. N. B. mourning rings to my friends, The Revd. Messrs. John and Charles Wesley. pp. 363-368 WBA.

Official copy in *Georgia Historical Society*, Hodgson Hall, 501 Whitaker Street, Savannah.

Jasper Shargold Whitehart, Savannah, joiner. Benjamin Goldwire of Savannah, carpenter, all my working tools, and all other real and personal estate; sole exor. Wit: James Campbell, John Feaster.

D: 15 Jan. 1757. P: 20 Sept. 1768. R: 23 Sept. 1768.

pp. 276-277 WBA.

Charles Whitehead, St. George's Parish. Wife: Susanna, 6 Negroes, 2 horses, one black cow. Son: Richard, my land and plantation, one bay horse, cow, 16 pounds. Exors: wife, Reason Whitehead, John Smith. Wit: Reason Whitehead, John Smith, Charles Burch, John Gambet.

D: 7 July 1776. P: n.d. R: n.d.

Colonial Loose Will Collection.

Thomas Whitehead, St. George's Parish, planter. Sons: Reason, 5 shillings Sterling; Thomas, 5 shillings Sterling. Dau: Sarah, wife of James Buoy, 5 shillings Sterling. Sons: Jacob, one cow and calf; Amos, one cow and calf; Charles, 100 acres of land including the plantation I now live on; Caleb, remainder of my land (100 acres). John, Negro boy named Punch. Wife: Alice, remaining personal estate for her lifetime, on her death, equally divided among my sons: Jacob, Charles, Caleb, John. Exors: wife, and son, Charles. Wit: David Emanuel, Sr.; David Emanuel, Jr.; Levi Emanuel.

D: 18 July 1765. P: 16 June 1768. R: 17 June 1768.

pp. 273-274 WBA.

George Williams, Christ Church Parish, bricklayer. Wife: Mary, household goods and movable effects. Sons: John and Henry Wilson William, remaining estate, equally divided when they come of age. Exors: wife, and Phillip Allman. Wit: William Trenfield, John Wilson.

D: ___ June 1773. P: 10 Sept. 1773. R: n.d.

pp. 59-60 WBAA.

John Francis Williams, St. Paul's Parish, planter. Exors: Colonel James Grierson, William Goodgion of Augusta, merchants; Zachariah Fenn of New Savannah, planter. Exors to sell my estate, including: 2000 acres of land, household furniture, carriages and horses, four Negroes. Wife: Catherine, 50 pounds Sterling. Dau: Elizabeth of the Island of Barbados (whom I never saw or heard of — she being born since I left that island), 1000 pounds Sterling. Samuel Perry, 50 pounds Sterling. Thomas Eady, Henry Perry, McLany Grant, Winifred Grant, Hugh Williams (son of Dr. John Williams), all formerly of the Island of

Barbados, 150 pounds Sterling to each in lieu of any demands they might have on my estate. Charlotte, Agnes, and Elizabeth Grant, 55 pounds each. Elizabeth Grant, widow, 54 pounds Sterling. John Walcott, also formerly of Barbados, 160 pounds Sterling. Edward Sayris, 65 pounds Sterling. Sarah Prescott and Susannah Clark, 26 pounds Sterling. Jane Hamilton of Barbados, 11 pounds Sterling. All of above bequests in lieu of any claim they might have against me or my estate. To exors: 5 pounds Sterling each to buy a ring. Remainder of estate to children of my brother, Hugh, in Jamaica. Wit: Sherwood Bugg, William Jackson, Titus Hollanger.

D: 7 Jan. 1774. P: 15 Mar. 1775. R: n.d.

Document attached in which Edward Barnard and John Daniel Hammerer, Esqs., are empowered to administer the oath of exor to James Grierson, William Goodgion and Zachariah Fenn. Dated: 19 Jan. 1775. Oath of exor signed by James Grierson and William Goodgion. No date.

pp. 142-146 WBAA.

Stephen Williams, St. George's Parish, planter. Wife: Elizabeth, all movable estate. At her death, Sarah Sheperson to have one feather bed. Wife also to have use of plantation during her life; after her death, to son, James Williams, paying my son, John, ten pounds and son, William, 5 pounds, and dau, Mary Web, 5 shillings, and dau, Elizabeth Godfree, 5 shillings. Exors: wife and A. Graham Lewis. Wit: Thittrell Mundine, Joseph Mundine.

D: 22 Jan. 1770. P: 18 May 1770. R: 21 May 1770.

pp. 346-347 WBA.

Benjamin Williamson, St. George's Parish. Eldest son: Robert, tract of 660 acres, including 150 acres that Asa Williamson is to make me a title, known by the name Millers Place; one Negro. Son: George, 660 acres of land; one Negro. Youngest son: Ben, plantation I now live on, including 660 acres; two Negroes. Wife: Lucy, 5 Negroes during her widowhood. Daus: Sarah Miller, Negro wench; Emily, Negro child; Betty, one Negro. Grandson: Nathaniel Miller, three two-year-old heifers. Exors: wife; sons, Robert and George. Wit: John Patrick Dillon, William Ashford, James Dannelley.

D: 8 Sept. 1774. P: 14 Mar. 1775. R: n.d.

pp. 138-140 WBAA.

(unsigned, probably a copy)

Richard Williamson, Christ Church Parish, planter. All lands to exors to be sold. Wife: Susannah, 7 Negroes now in the possession of Ann Parker, her mother; 500 pounds Sterling; household furniture. Lydia Eaton, spinster, 150 pounds Sterling; a Negro. Exors to purchase land or Negroes for my son, William. 43 Negroes to exors with remaining estate to administer my plantation during my son, William's, minority. William to have his estate at the age of twenty-one. If William dies before twenty-one, his estate to the children of Francis Rose of Collaton County, South Carolina, planter. Exors: William Williamson of Charlestoun, and Benjamin Williamson of St. Paul's Parish, South Carolina, Esqs.

D: (about) 25 Dec. 1772. P: n.d. R: n.d.

Colonial Loose Will Collection.

Barbara Wilson, her mark, Christ Church Parish, widow. Daus: Ann, Margaret, Jean, all my wearing apparel, equally divided. Remainder of estate to be sold; profits to be equally divided among all my children. Exor: The Rev. Mr. Zubly. Wit: Frederick Rossberg, Mathias Ash, George Williams.

D: 18 Jan. 1770. P: 26 Jan. 1770. R: n.d.

Colonial Loose Will Collection.

Christopher Wisenbaker, his mark, Savannah, laborer. Wife: Constance, entire estate, real and personal, sole extrix. Wit: Frederick Fahm, Rudolph Buckholder, Casper Garbut.

D: 20 July 1767. P: 19 Nov. 1767. R: 30 Nov. 1767.

pp. 232-233 WBA.

John Norton Wright, his mark, Savannah, freeholder. Mother: Penelope Fitzwalter, entire estate, real and personal, sole extrix. Wit: Mary Vanderplank, Charles Watson, Adrian Loyer.

D: 29 Jan. 1749. P: n.d. R: n.d.

Colonial Loose Will Collection.

Joseph Wright, Christ Church Parish, planter. Son: Joseph, town lot in Savannah, number two in Tyrronnel Tything Derby Ward; plantation of 500 acres called Litchfield in Christ Church Parish, bounded on land of Pickering Robinson, Esq., Great Ogechee River, land of William McKenzie; 20 Negroes. Dau: Mary Jane Wright, town lot in Savannah, number seven in LaRoche Tything Heathcote Ward, two tracts of land (total of 500 acres) in St. Mary's Parish; 20 Negroes. Friend: William Young, and exors each a suit of clothes and mourning ring. Wife: Mary, 500 acres of land in St. Mary's Parish; remaining Negroes; on her death, land to son, Joseph and Negroes divided between son, and dau: Mary Jane. Remainder of estate, real and personal, divided among my wife and children. Exors: wife (during her widowhood), Joseph Clay. Wit: William Young, Henry Lewis Bourquin, William Brabant.

D: 13 April 1771. P: 11 Aug. 1773. R: 14 Aug. 1773.

Codicil (dated 19 June, 1773, Wit: John Houstoun, Thomas Ross, Philip Allman): Plots of land granted my dau. and wife have lapsed in the Surveyor General's office and been given some other person. Therefore: to wife, annuity of twenty pounds, Georgia currency. Dau: 500 pounds, Georgia currency, as a dowery. Additional exors: Noble Wimberly Jones and James Habersham, Esqs.

pp. 48-53 WBAA.

Robert Wright, Savannah, carpenter. Exors to sell all estate, real and personal; profits, after debts are paid, to be equally divided between my brother, Ambrose Wright, and my sister, Susannah Hammond, both of Savannah. Sons of my late brother, Jacob Wright: William, Jacob, and Ambrose Wright, Jr., 30 pounds Georgia currency, when they come of age. Brother: Am-

148

brose, my silver tankard. Sister: Susannah, my desk, my late wife's gold ring, twelve silver spoons and tea tongs. John Crane, my horse called Buck. Edward Langworthy, one mourning ring. Exors: brother, Ambrose Wright and John Crane. Wit: James Habersham, Jr.; Leonard Cecil; Joseph Reynolds.

D: 3 Sept. 1773. P: 8 Oct. 1773. R: ___ _____ 1773

pp. 60-62 WBAA.

William Wright, late of the City of New York, but now of Savannah, innholder. Wife: Mary, now living in City of New York, all estate, real and personal, in City of New York or Savanah. Exors: wife, friends: Hugh Ross, Michael Germain, and Francis Robinson. Wit: George Tew (Few?), James Wemyss, Stephen Carren (?).

D: 28 Sept. 1756. P: n.d. R: n.d.

Colonial Loose Will Collection.

Peter Wynne, Sr., St. George's Parish, planter. Son: Thomas, tract of land I now live on, best feather bed, riding horse, crop of corn now on my plantation, Negro woman named Toney. Dau: Mary Whitehead, 5 pounds Sterling worth of cattle. Sons: Peter and Thomas, and dau: Patty Breazeal, remainder of estate, real and personal. Exors: son, Peter; son-in-law, Elijah Breazeal. Wit: Jesse Wiggons, his mark; Robert Morgan, his mark; Daniel Lott.

D: 18 Dec. 1770. P: 1 Mar. 1771. R: 5 Mar. 1771.

Document attached in which David Lewis and John Thomas, Esqs., are empowered to administer the oath of exor to Elijah Breazeal. Dated: 12 Feb. 1771.

Oath of exor signed by Elijah Breazeal. Dated: 1 Mar. 1771. pp. 392-395 WBA.

Isaac Young, Christ Church Parish. Son: William, 300 pounds Sterling, when twenty-one years of age. Son: Isaac, 300 pounds Sterling, when twenty-one years of age. Son: Thomas, 300 pounds Sterling, when twenty-one years of age. Dau: Mary, 300 pounds Sterling, at marriage or age of twenty-one. Mentions: Elizabeth Weddell, James Weddell. Wife: Martha, remaining real and personal estate, sole extrix. Wit: John Patton, John Brenson, Fredrick Churchwell.

D: 11 Oct. 1766. P: n.d. R: n.d.

Colonial Loose Will Collection.

(will is partially missing)

Robert Young, South Carolina. Wife: Hipse Baw, 5 Negroes, two mares and two horses. Bro-in-law: Henry Wood, my wearing apparel, my linen. Remainder of estate to my wife. Exors: Joseph Wraag; my bro-in-law, Henry Wood, my wife. Wit: John Christie, John Casmal (?), Martha Johnston.

D: ____ _____ 1734 (?). P: (?) 4 June 1734. R: n.d.

Colonial Loose Will Collection.

William Young, Savannah, Esq. Wife: Sophia, house and lot whereon I now live, number 6, Frederick Tything, Derby Ward; use of my house Negroes, during her widowhood; Negro man named Frank for her lifetime. Son: James Box Young, lot of land above, after my wife's marriage or death; seven farm lots, containing about 400 acres; Negro boy named Dick. Son to receive above at the age of twenty-one, or on my wife's marriage. Dau: Mary, house and lot near the meeting house, purchased of William Sanders; lot at Yamacraw; 500 acres in Christ Church Parish; Negro girl named Bess. Mrs. Christiana Dillon, Negro girl named Amaritta, now in her possession, during her lifetime. Mentions: children of my brothers, Philip Box and James Box; nephew, James Whitefield (son of James Whitefield of Savannah, Gent.). Exors: wife; brother, Philip Box and Amadeus Chiffele; Joseph Clay; William Stephens. Wit: Lewis Johnston, John Irvine, David Brydie.

D: 13 Jan. 1776. P: 15 April 1777. R: 16 April 1777.

Codicil (same date, same wit): Money remaining from any part of the estate which the exors sell to my two children equally divided.

pp. 322-327 WBAA.

Mathias Zettler, St. Matthew's Parish, planter. Son: Daniel, Negro wench named Jude, 100 acres of land. Son: Mathias, Negro man named Jack, 100 acres of land. Son: Nathaniel, Negro man named Samson, 100 acres of land. The above 300 acres of land near Ogechee River. Son-in-law: Lucas Zeglar, 100 acres at Turkey Branch. Debts to be paid out of my stock; remainder of stock to my son-in-law, Lamberth Lain and my two youngest sons, Mathias and Nathaniel. Exors: Daniel Zettler, Christopher Cremer, Hugh Kennedy. Wit: Frederick Schrompf; Hugh Kennedy; Mary Ottelia Kennedy.

D: 26 Dec. 1768. P: 15 Feb. 1769. R: 16 Feb. 1769.

pp. 299-300 WBA.

Bartholomew Zouberbuhler, rector of Christ Church Parish at Savannah. House and lot on bay in Savannah to be sold to pay debts and funeral expenses. Poor of Christ Church Parish, 50 pounds Sterling. Nephew: Jacob Waldburger of Purrysburg, South Carolina, my books and manuscripts, 1100 acres of land on an island in St. Matthew's Parish opposite Purrysburg, 8 Negroes; to have this bequest if he pays his mother, Catherina Barbara Listensburger, 20 pounds Sterling yearly. Mrs. Amelia Alther who has been afflicted with the palsey while in my service, by means of which she is helpless, residence on my plantation and Negro woman called Pegg. To Trustees, tract of 1000 acres on the main branch of Turtle River in trust for the Orphan House when it is founded, and if it is founded on the principles of the Church of England. Remainder of estate including 1237 acres of land (three tracts) in Christ Church Parish on which is located my plantation called Beth Abram; 43 Negroes, in trust to exors. Exors. to hire a person to instruct Negroes on my plantation in Christianity according to the Church of England. Negroes who are converted as a result of this and express a desire to convert other Negroes, they shall be manumitted and employed by the exors. for the purpose. Exors. empowered to sell and make title for tract of 1000 acres on Turtle River; profits toward the support of a college. Mentions: my uncle, Joannes Zouberbuhler of Faiss and Canton in Switzerland; Revd. Mr. Jacobs Wettes of Trogen, dean of Canton. Exors: James Habersham, Francis Harris, Grey Elliott, James Read, Joseph Clay, John Smith, and

Noble Wimberly Jones, Esqs. Wit: Noble Jones, Lewis Johnson, Nathaniel Hall.

D: 25 Nov 1766. P: 19 Dec. 1766. R: 19 Dec. 1766.

Codicil (dated: 30 Nov. 1766, same wit.) : If my nephew, Jacob Waldburger defaults in his payment to his mother, exors. to pay his mother, Catherine Barbara Listensburger, the twenty pounds Sterling annually.

pp. 184-188 WBA.

John Bowles, Savannah, vintner. Wife: Philippa Bowles, her heirs and assigns; the eastern undivided half, or half of all that lot of land, number 7 in the second Tything Reynolds ward, Savannah, sixty feet wide and ninety feet long; two Negro slaves named Jack and Sally; remainder of personal estate, goods, slaves, monies, and debts, of whatever kind in Georgia; sole extrix. Wit: William Stewart; Thomas Mills, storekeeper; Peter Papat.

D: 30 Aug. 1776. P: 25 Nov. 1777. R: 26 Nov. 1777.

Original in **Cuyler Collection,** University of Georgia Libraries, Special Collections, Athens, Georgia.

James Dormer, Savannah, mariner. Brother: Richard Dormer of Cowndon near Coventry in Warwickshire in England, his heirs; town lot in Savannah, number 4 in Wilmington Tything Derby ward; five-acre lot, number 61; farm lot, number 6 of 45 acres southeast of Savannah; and all buildings, etc., upon said lots; also all of my personal estate, goods, chattels, debts. If brother, Richard Dormer dies before I do, all aforesaid real and personal estate shall go to brother: Joseph Dormer of Cowndon. Exors.: James Habersham of Savannah, merchant; William Russell of Savannah, Trustees' Storekeeper. Wit: John Teasdale; John Teasdale, Jr.; Thomas Rasberry.

D: 5 Jan. 1747. P: n.d. R: n.d.

Original in **Cuyler Collection,** University of Georgia Libraries, Special Collections, Athens, Georgia.

Robert Fox, Fort Argyle, Georgia. John Milledge: entire estate, real and personal, after paying debts out of said estate. Nicholas Rigby: my gun at Ft. Argyle. If John Milledge should die without lawful heirs, the entire estate, real and personal, goes to Nicholas Rigby. Exors: John Milledge, Nicholas Rigby. Wit: Hugh Ross, Abraham Minis.

D: 19 Nov. 1746. P: n.d. R: n.d.

Original in **Cuyler Collection,** University of Georgia Libraries, Special Collections, Athens, Georgia.

William Mackay (deposition in the case of Mackay vs. Morrison, touching the administration of William Mackay's estate.)

John McLeod, St. Andrew's Parish, Darien, planter, aged about 55 years. John McLeod declares that he knew the deceased William Mackay, late of Darien, for 27 years; and his wife, Margaret, also deceased, for 20 years; that he understood that their intentions concerning William Mackay's estate were that Barbara, dau of Capt. James Mackay, should be the sole heir. This intention was declared openly by both William Mackay and his wife, Margaret, on many occasions, together and apart. Wit: James Wright; sworn in Open Court before His Excellency the Governour, and Ordinary.

D: 27 Mar. 1762.

Original in **Cuyler Collection,** University of Georgia Libraries, Special Collections, Athens, Georgia.

John Musgrove, Savannah. Sons: Edward and James Musgrove, lot in Georgia called Cowpin and all cattle thereon, equally divided. Son: James Musgrove, Indian man called Justice. Son: Edward Musgrove, Indian girl called Nanny. Wife: Mary Musgrove, Indian boy called Won, all rest of estate, sole extrix: Wit: Michael Moor, John Cheevers, Bassele Nowell.

D: 29 April 1734. P: 28 July 1735. R: n.d.

Original in **Cuyler Collection,** University of Georgia Libraries, Special Collections, Athens, Georgia.

Francis Scott, Esq., Savannah. Sister: Elizabeth Gordon, one Silver Medale; if she die before receiving it, to her eldest daughter. Mistress Frances Cox, widow, all other estate, sole extrix. Wit: T. Causton, George Dunbar.

D: 28 Dec. 1733. P: n.d. R: n.d.

Original in **Keith Read Collection,** University of Georgia Libraries, Special Collections, Athens, Georgia.

Abstracts of 413 wills included in this publication.

"There was also a small settlement of English at the Musquito shore, on the Continent, over which a King's Agent presided, who was appointed by the Governor of Jamaica; and many British subjects were settled in the Bay of Honduras, where they were permitted to cut logwood and mahogany &c. in consequence of the treaty of Paris between Great Britain and Spain. They had a considerable town at St. George's Key in the Bay, where much trade was carried on, until the Spaniards drove away all the British settlers in the last war."

Anthony Stokes' A VIEW OF THE CONSTITUTION OF THE BRITISH COLONIES, IN NORTH-AMERICA AND THE WEST INDIES, AT THE TIME THE CIVIL WAR BROKE OUT ON THE CONTINENT OF AMERICA. Published in London, 1783. (Page 17.)

---

*Anthony Stokes was His Majesty's Chief Justice of the Colony of Georgia.

INDEX TO WILLS

INDEX TO WILLS—Continued

INDEX TO WILLS—Continued

INDEX TO

ABSTRACTS OF COLONIAL WILLS

OF THE STATE OF GEORGIA

1733-1777

All testators and heirs, all persons mentioned in the wills
and all witnesses and executors are included in this index.
They are listed as spelled in the printed volume *ABSTRACTS
OF COLONIAL WILLS OF THE STATE OF GEORGIA, 1733-1777*. The
names of those empowered to administer the oath to executors have not been included.

The user is reminded that a name may occur upon a page more
than once although there be only one citation of the page
in the index.

                                        Willard E. Wight

February 29, 1964

Thomas, 27, 48
Cartlidge, Edmund, 80
Cary: Jane, 51; John, 51
Casbell, N., 110
Cashell, Catherine, 73
Casmal, John, 150
Cassell, Pennellope, 122
Cassie: John, 88; Mary, 88
Caughran, Joseph, 67
Cater: Ann, 3; Thomas, 90
Causton, T., 154
Cecil, Leonard, 149
Chambers, Elizabeth, 67
Chansat, James, 39
Chapman: James, 34; John, 76
Chappell: Christopher, 28;
  Elizabeth, 28
Chasser: Isabell, 74; Thomas,
  74
Cheeswright, Paul, 76
Cheevers, John, 153
Cherry, John, 33
Chiffelle: Amadeus, 106, 150;
  Christina, 16; Sophia, 16
Chinnery, Nicholas, 126
Chisholm: John, 21; Thomas, 21
Chrichton, Pat, 56
Christie: Alexander, 36; John,
  150; Thomas, 28
Christy: Archible, 9; Thomas,
  9
Church: Betsey, 28; Elizabeth,
  129; Giles, 28; Rebecca, 28
Churchwell: Frederick, 140,
  150; Margaret, 140
Clarendon, Smith, 46
Clark: Alexander, 29; Angus, 29;
  Barbara, 29; Catherine, 133;
  Daniel, 28, 126; Edmond, 30;
  Elizabeth, 30, 95; Henry, 26;
  Hugh, 29; John, 30; Joshua,
  30; Lawrence, 30; Margaret, 29;
  Matthew, 30; Morris, 30; Nath-
  aniel, 30; Patrick, 30; Sarah,
  30; Stephen, 7, 30; Susannah,
  146; William, 29, 30, 136
Clarke: (John), 33; Samuel, 52
Clay: James, 65; Joseph, 16, 21,
  23, 47, 65, 66, 87, 113, 121,
  148, 150, 151

Clements, William, 111
Clifton, William, 54, 114, 140
Club, Thomas, 124
Clubb: John, 31; Mary, 31
Clunie, John, 35
Coble, Peter, 111
Cobler, Peter, 111
Cochran, James, 28, 37, 73
Cochran, Jonathan, 73, 84, 92,
  136
Coffee, John, 31
Cole, Joseph, 141
Coleman, Martha, 137
Colers, Stephen, 7
Collins, William, 33
Collyer, Charles, 76
Colson, Francis, 62
Conner, Elizabeth, 81
Cook, James, 52, 141
Cooley: Gabriel, 133; John,
  133
Cooper: Benjamin, 119; Cornel-
  ius, 128; Isaac, 119; Thomas,
  48
Cornal, George, 40
Corneck: James, 31; John, 31;
  Joseph, 31
Cosson, John, 98
Couper, John, 88
Cowper, Basil, 19, 51
Cox: Ann, 27; Frances, 154;
  Richard, 59
Cramer, Christopher, 91, 94, 9?
Crane, John, 144, 148
Craw, Daniel, 18
Crawford, John, 55
Cray, William, 109
Crays, William, 109
Cremer, Christopher, 151
Creser, W., 16
Crespin, Elias, 82
Crighton: Alexander, 66, 86;
  Elizabeth, 86
Crocker, Margaret, 24, 25
Croft, Abraham, 10, 129
Cronberger, Jacob, 13, 68, 116
Crooke: Charles Cunningham,
  31; Clement, 31, 32; Elizabe
  135; Hariot, 32; Heriot, 31,
  33, 135; Richard Cunningham,

Finlay, William Atchison, 86
Fisher: David, 28; Mary, 28;
  Nicholas, 48, 134
Fitch: Ann, 73; Anne, 48;
  John, 48, 108; Prudence, 108;
  Tobias, 48
Fitzgerald: George, 30, John,
  38
Fitzsimmons: James, 49; Mary,
  49
Fitzwalter: Joseph, 49; Mary,
  49; Penelope, 49, 148;
  Pennellopy, 49
Fleming: Bartholomew, 28;
  David, 110; Thomas, 41
Flerl: Charles, 50, 118;
  Dorothea, 50; John, 14, 48,
  75, 94, 105, 118, 122; Israel,
  50; Mary, 50
Flint, James, 130
Floide, Richard, 79
Floyd: Abediah, 38; John, 135;
  Margaret, 79; Richard, 79, 94
Flyming, Thomas, 61, 63
Fonlayson, Mungo, 63
Forbes: Benjamin, 51; George,
  51; John, 33, 50
Ford, Thomas, 42
Forrester, James, 40
Foulis, John, 137
Fountain, Magdalene, 51
Fox: Ann, 51, 52; Benjamin, 51,
  52; Catherine, 51; David, 51,
  52, 62, 114; Elizabeth, 51;
  George, 51, 52, 58; James,
  51, 52; Jane, 58; John, 51,
  52, 66, 108, 114, 143;
  Jonathan, 52; Joseph, 51;
  Mary, 51, 52; Mary Ann, 52;
  Nancy, 52; Richard, 52, 65,
  90; Robert, 153; William, 51,
  52, 58, 76
Frail, John, 105
Francis: Benjamin, 53; Fred-
  erick, 53; John, 53, 54; Mary,
  53; Sterling, 53; William, 53,
  128, 140
Frank, Conrad, 21
Fraser: Donald, 74, 101, 110;
  George, 54, 124; James, 36;

  Margaret, 54; Sarah, 54; Sus-
  annah, 54; Thomas William, 54
Frayermuth, John Adam, 118
Frazer: Catherina, 55; Thomas,
  55
Frederick, Albert, 126
Frink, Samuel, 139
Fry, Peter, 117
Fullalove, Alice, 63
Fuller: Whitmarsh, 79; Wil-
  liam, 16
Fullerton, John, 112
Fulton: Christian, 55; John,
  55; Paul, 55; Samuel, 55;
  Sarah, 104
Furse, James, 136
Fyffe: Alexander, 56; Charles,
  56; Elizabeth, 56; James, 56;
  John, 56; Magdalen, 56; Wil-
  liam, 56

Gable: Abraham, 13, 124;
  Suzanna, 12
Galache, James, 130
Galashe, James, 106
Gallache: James, 17, 23, 56,
  121; John, 56, 121; William,
  121
Gallash, James, 134
Gallier, Charles, 39
Galphin, George, 40, 73, 86
Gambell, Richard, 57
Gambet, John, 145
Gandy, Peter, 134, 135, 137
Garbut, Casper, 147; Christiana,
  57; Gasper, 57; George, 57;
  Mary, 57
Garvey: Elinor, 57; James, 57
Gautier: Anthione, 56, 58; David,
  26, 58; Jean, 58
Gay, Abraham, 57
Gee, James, 135
Gegg, Thomas, 48, 140
Gegge, Thomas, 93
Gender, James, 139
Germain: Michael, 58, 77, 149;
  Priscilla, 58
Germany, James, 126
Gibbons: Ann, 59; Barrack, 90;
  Hannah, 59, 90; James Martin,

INDEX

Keen, Robert, 143, 144
Keesee, Thomas, 37, 97
Keiffer, Theobold, 14
Kell, John, 17
Kellers, Anna Elizabeth, 132
Kelley, Bryan, 73
Kelly: Ann, 74, 102; Bryan,
   48; John, 74; Sarah, 74;
   William, 74
Kelsall, Roger, 51, 101, 125,
   127
Kenedy, Darby, 74
Kennan: Elizabeth, 74, 75;
   Henry, 74, 75; James, 74, 75;
   John, 74; Marianne, 74, 75;
   Susannah, 74, 75
Kennedy: Hugh, 75, 151; John,
   74; Mary Ottelia, 151; Wil-
   liam, 75
Kent, Richard, 11
Kesler: Elizabeth, 112; Mary,
   112
Keys, Charles, 75
Kiefer: David, 132; Frederich,
   132
Kieffer: Christiana, 75;
   Dorothe, 75; Elizabeth, 75;
   Emmanuel, 75, 116, 117; Han-
   nah, 75; Israel, 75; Theobald,
   75
Killingsworth, Noel, 4
King: John, 62; Sarah, 62;
   William, 63
Kirk: Sarah, 135; William, 26,
   31, 71, 95, 135
Kirkwood, Robert, 63
Kitt: Ann, 76; John, 76, 126;
   Wade, 76
Knight, Edward, 82
Knott, Heremiah, 83
Knowles, Francis, 2, 86
Knox, Will, 114
Kraus, Samuel, 112
Krauss, Samuel, 122
Kremer, Christoffer, 13
Kubeler, Adam, 96
Kyffer: David, 132; Frederick,
   132
Kynnier, William, 64

Lackner: Fridrich, 94; Israel,
   94
Lacy: Grace, 76; James, 76;
   Mary, 76; Roger, 76; Theo-
   philus, 76
Ladson: Mary Ann, 19; Thomas,
   20
Lafitte, Peter, 112, 118, 119
Lain, Lamberth, 151
Laing, David, 110
Laird, Patrick, 28
Lambert, Mary, 71
Lamboth, John, 49
Landree: James, 113; Mary Anne,
   113
Landry, Stephen, 135
Lang, John, 95
Langworthy, Edward, 47, 148
Lanier, Benjamin, 73
Larking, Edward, 76
Laroch, Isaac, 31
Lavery, William, 76
Law: Andrew, 89; Charles, 17;
   George, 133; Joseph, 17; Mary,
   17
Lawler, Michael, 42
Lawrance: Ettsel, 128; John,
   138
Lawrence: Nicholas, 121;
   Thomas, 121
Le Conte: John, 43; Peter, 43;
   Valeria, 43; William, 43, 92
Lee: Ann, 76; Mary Ann, 76;
   Rebecca, 76, 138; Thomas, 42,
   76; William, 76
Leigh, Egeston, 5
Leman: Elizabeth, 84; James,
   84
Lemke: _____ (Rev. Mr.), 14;
   Timothy, 116, 118
Lesslie, William, 105
Lester: Henry, 77; John, 77
Lettimore, John, 15
Levenberg, Christian, 96
Lewis: A. Graham, 146; Abraham,
   77, 78; Ann, 77; Benjamin, 16,
   70; David, 16, 45, 72, 77;
   Demmes, 77, 78; Elijah, 77,
   78; Evan, 77; Isaac, 77, 78;
   Jacob, 45, 70, 77; John, 78;

Randell, John Bard, 89
Rasberry: Esther, 65; Thomas,
40, 99, 138, 152
Rawlins, Lownder, 125
Raynes, Joseph, 51, 52
Rea, John, 110
Read: James, 3, 87, 93, 151;
William, 140
Ready, Thomas, 136
Red: John, 116; Ruben, 116;
Thomas, 116
Reid, Thomas, 45, 49
Reimshardt, John, 122
Reinier: Alexander, 116; Jane,
116; John Francis, 116; Mary,
116; Silvia, 116
Reinstetler, John Matthias, 117
Remington, Jonathan, 119, 120
Rentz, John, 116
Reynolds, Joseph, 149
Rheny, William, 18, 132
Richards, John, 42, 57
Richardson: Elizabeth, 43;
Thomas, 43; William, 71, 72
Ridelsperger, Christian, 118
Rieser: Appolonia, 118; Badasar,
117; Benjamin, 117, 118;
Christina, 118; David, 118;
Hanna, 118; Israel, 118; John
Godhelp, 117; Mary, 117, 118;
Michael, 117, 118; Nathaniel,
118
Rigby: Elizabeth, 118; Nicholas,
118, 153; Sarah, 118
Ring: Chris. F., 70;
Christopher, 23, 47, 61
Ritch, William, 106
Ritter: Charles John Frederick,
118; Elizabeth, 118
Rivers, Daniel Nunes, 112
Robe: Frances, 6, 49; (John?),
49
Roberson: Andrew, 119; David,
119; Elener, 119; Israel, 118;
Jonathan, 118, 119; Sarah,
118; Silvinus, 118; William,
119
Roberts: Elizabeth, 48; James,
48, 71; Susannah, 75
Robertson, James, 5, 7, 20, 32,
91

Robeson, Israel, 118
Robinson: Francis, 149; John,
119; Pickering, 148; Sophero,
97; Townsend, 97
Roboson, Clotworthy, 131, 139,
182
Roche: James, 75; Matthew, 77,
112, 113, 138
Rock, Matthew, 7
Rodh, Godfried, 132
Rogers, William, 105
Rogett, Barton, 137
Rook, Elizabeth, 106
Rose: Alexander, 119; Ellen,
119; Francis, 147; Hugh, 119;
Jane, 119
Roseberg, Frederick, 132
Ross: Daniel, 119; Hugh, 18,
26, 54, 66, 70, 120, 135, 140,
149, 153; James, 24; John, 26,
44, 70, 120, 126; Thomas, 70,
119, 120, 124, 148; William,
70
Rossberg, Frederick, 134, 147
Rottenberger, Christopher, 142
Rouvier: James (or James
Gregory), 64; John, 96, 120;
Mary, 64, 120; Rosannah, 120;
Simon, 64, 96, 120
Roviere: John, 121; Simon, 121
Russell: Jane, 100, 121; Wil-
liam, 16, 23, 59, 99, 108,
121, 122, 152
Rutherford: Elizabeth, 27;
Robert, 28
Rutledge, John, 29
Ryn, James, 96

Sabb: Mary, 121; Morgan, 92,
100, 121
Sacheveral, John, 44
Sacheverell, John, 115
Sackes, Margaret, 28
Sallans, Peter, 43
Sallens, Peter, 55
Sallet, William, 84
Salter: Anna, 122; Thomas, 39,
122
Salters, Samuel, 104
Sanders: Herdy, 4; Lydia, 44;
William, 150

Wanton: John, 43; Lydia, 43
Warden, James, 28
Wardrope, Joseph, 27
Ware, Henry, 4
Warner, Lewis, 49
Warren, Richard, 52
Wason, John, 26
Waterlund, William, 76, 85
Waters: I., 11; Sinclair, 18
Watson: Ann, 108; Charles,
    11, 41, 47, 49, 65, 96, 108,
    114, 118, 128, 135, 139, 140,,
    148; John, 11; Joseph, 139,
    Sarah, 139, 140; Sepha, 139
Watt, William, 66, 100, 141
Watts, Robert, 98
Way: Andrew, 59, 78, 84;
    Ann, 140; Edward, 9, 140;
    Elizabeth, 141; John, 140;
    Joseph, 9, 79, 101, 103, 104,
    140, 141; Mary, 8, 103, 140,
    141; Moses, 132; Parmenas, 43,
    95, 104, 109, 131; Rebecca,
    141; Samuel, 141; Sarah, 103,
    104; Thomas, 24, 90, 104,
    131, 132; William, 140, 141
Weatherly, Joseph, 23
Weathers, Edward, 69
Web, Mary, 146
Webb: Henry, 141; John, 73;
    Rachel, 141; Susanna, 141;
    Wentworth, 141; William, 72
Weddale, John, 106
Weddall: Benjamin, 64; Isaac,
    76
Weddell: Elizabeth, 150; James,
    150
Weidmann: Anna Eva, 141; Daniel,
    141; Jedethia, 142; Ludwig,
    141; Mattheis, 141; Solomon,
    142
Wells: Absolam, 142; Andrew
    Elton, 28, 91, 92, 142;
    Elizabeth, 142; Jane, 142;
    John, 18, 142; Mary, 142;
    Nany, 142; Patty, 142; Rachel,
    142; Rice, 142; Robert, 18;
    Serah, 142; Winny, 142; Wrice,
    142
Welsh, Wakelin, 106

Wemyss: James, 5, 140, 149;
    Susannah, 140; Susannah
    O'Neal, 5
Wertsch, John, 1, 22, 48, 50,
    113, 116, 117, 118; John
    Casper, 123, 142; John Gasper,
    105, 134
Wertsh, John Casper, 14
Wesbury: Mary, 142; Thomas,
    142
Wesley: Charles, 144; John,
    144
West: Charles, 143; Daniel,
    143, 144; Elizabeth, 143;
    Esther, 143; John, 76; Samuel,
    143; William, 143
Western: Elizabeth, 106; Emanuel,
    106; Samuel, 106; Sarah, 106
Weston, Rachel, 97
Wettes, Jacobs, 151
White: Catherine, 143; David,
    143; Judith, 143; Mary, 143;
    Thomas, 143
Whitefield: Anne, 138; George,
    66, 67, 143; James, 54, 76,
    150; Richard, 143; Thomas,
    143
Whitehart: Jasper Shargold, 144;
    Jasper Shargots, 62
Whitehead: Alice, 145; Amos,
    145; Caleb, 145; Charles, 144,
    145; Jacob, 145; John, 145;
    Mary, 149; Reason, 145;
    Richard, 144; Susanna, 144;
    Thomas, 145
Wickes, Nehemiah, 76
Wiggons, Jesse, 149
Williams: Catherine, 145;
    Elizabeth, 145, 146; George,
    145, 147; Henry Wilson, 145;
    Hugh, 145, 146; Jacob, 83;
    James, 12, 146; John, 28, 67,
    74, 145, 146; John Francis,
    145; Mary, 145; Robert, 28,
    112; Stephen, 73, 143, 146;
    William, 146
Williamson: Asa, 146; Ben, 146;
    Benjamin, 63, 146, 147; Betty,
    146; Emily, 146; George, 146,
    147; John, 20, 21; Lucy, 146;